109

Press Critics Are the Fifth Estate

Recent Titles in
Democracy and the News

Press Critics Are the Fifth Estate

Media Watchdogs in America

Arthur S. Hayes

Democracy and the News

Jeffrey Scheuer, Series Editor

Westport, Connecticut
London

Library of Congress Cataloging-in-Publication Data

Hayes, Arthur S.
    Press critics are the fifth estate : media watchdogs in America / Arthur S. Hayes.
       p. cm. — (Democracy and the news, ISSN 1932–6947)
    Includes bibliographical references and index.
    ISBN-13: 978-0-275-99910-0 (alk. paper)
1. Press criticism—United States—History. I. Title.
PN4888.C83H39 2008
071'.3—dc22   2008007288

British Library Cataloguing in Publication Data is available.

Library of Congress Catalog Card Number: 2008007288
ISBN-13: 978–0–275–99910–0
ISSN: 1932–6947

First published in 2008

Praeger Publishers, 88 Post Road West, Westport, CT 06881
An imprint of Greenwood Publishing Group, Inc.
www.praeger.com

Printed in the United States of America

The paper used in this book complies with the
Permanent Paper Standard issued by the National
Information Standards Organization (Z39.48–1984).

10 9 8 7 6 5 4 3 2 1

Contents

Series Foreword

It might not occur to the average citizen that media critics are essential to our democracy. We tend to think of constitutions, laws, and elections as the main tools that get the job done. But journalism is essential to an open society (whatever one may think of the screaming headlines and sound bites of the day), and so is media criticism: news about the news. And not just any journalism or any media criticism; quality counts.

The reasoning is not complicated. Our system of self-government is based not just on laws but on informed and active citizens; and such citizens need timely, relevant, clear information—facts and their explanatory contexts—in order to reason, to debate, and to make intelligent decisions. (We also need watchdogs, investigators, the stimulus of informed opinions, and places in the media to argue and converse.) Democracy, therefore, does not simply demand journalism; it demands journalistic excellence. And that in turn demands—along with education, to sustain both the supply of and the demand for excellence—a culture of criticism.

Such criticism is a rare and undervalued civic commodity. And like journalism —like democracy itself—it requires continual reexamination and redefinition. That is what democracies do, after all: they continually redefine themselves, shaping their founding principles to the times. Like the peer-review process in the scholarly world, a critical news culture maintains standards for the brokering of information that ultimately secure democracy itself, as a system of government based on information rather than force.

Moreover, we need at least two kinds of criticism: professional critics, reviewing the work of their peers; and citizens with critical skills for consuming media intelligently, including reviewing the work of those professionals. Democracy demands, in short, widespread media literacy. It behooves us as citizens to be attentive to the media, and to how the media cover and criticize themselves: we should care how journalists (as much as our elected representatives) do their job and how they might do it better.

Addressing the state of media criticism in America, Arthur Hayes, a scholar with both a legal and a journalistic background, writes in a rich and important tradition, and one that fits squarely with this series on Democracy and the News. It is a tradition of social criticism aimed at—and often by—the press; external and internal critics are equally important. Hayes's broad-based approach will be useful to both journalists and ordinary citizens. Like any good book about the media, it is also, in its own way, a handbook of media literacy.

As democratic citizens we are by definition equal in our rights. But some of us are—in Orwell's words out of *Animal Farm*—"more equal than others," in terms of our level of information and engagement. We can only wish for and work toward a society of information elitists, in which every citizen is a member of that elite. Meanwhile, the true guardians of our democracy are not (just) the lawyers or politicians, but the teachers and journalists and critics, too. To discover how complex and important their function is, read on.

Jeffrey Scheuer
Series Editor
Democracy and the News

Preface

I joined academia in August 1998, about two months after the debut of *Brill's Content*. The timing of the two events is unrelated. Yet there is a connection—no matter how tenuous—and it relates to this book.

I teach journalism and mass communication courses. During my first year of teaching, I used Steven Brill's "Pressgate" exposé in an attempt to illustrate the ethics and practice of attribution. I say attempt because, sadly, the 25,000-word, 29-page cover story of the inaugural issue of *Brill's Content* was not the best teaching tool for today's aliterate generation.

But I found great value in "Pressgate." That is largely because I had been a newspaper and magazine writer and editor before I started teaching. To me, Brill's account of how top-level reporters breached core journalism principles of proper attribution, allowing special prosecutor Kenneth Starr to spin the news and put pressure on persons of interests and witnesses to testify, was disheartening and infuriating. How could they get to the top of the news business and conduct themselves as though they were neophytes? If this is how some of the nation's best journalists operate, had I been naïve all those years when dealing with sources?

I understand and appreciate Brill's motivation for writing "Pressgate." His legal publications relied a great deal on anonymous sourcing. But he had strict rules for granting anonymity and presenting anonymous quotes in a manner that bolstered their credibility and reliability. I know. I worked as a staff writer for two years at his *American Lawyer* magazine.

I was considering using "Pressgate" again as a teaching tool in early 2005 at Fordham University in New York where I now teach. While rereading it in an effort to extract excerpts, the following thoughts came to mind: *Brill's Content* was exceptional for its genre. Is there a connection between the press critics of the blogosphere and the magazine? Did *Brill's Content* close up shop three to four years too soon, missing the popularity of press criticism that bloggers were now mining? I addressed those questions in a paper I delivered at an American Journalism Historians Association–Association for Education in Journalism and Mass Communication History Division meeting in March 2006. The paper,

"The Nobility of Failure: The Rapid Rise and Fall of *Brill's Content* and the Futility of Press-Media Criticism as a Profit-Making Venture," became the inspiration and template for this book and a chapter in it, *"Brill's Content:* 'An Inside-the-Sausage-Factory Look at Media for People Who Eat Sausages, Not Those Who Make Them.'"

Here is what I learned from my reporting and research for the *Brill's Content* article that convinced me there was a larger work on press criticism that had not been written: (i) much of mainstream media is hostile or indifferent to individuals they disparage as "self-appointed" critics even as the number of press critics in the blogosphere increases; (ii) no one has established criteria for judging whether a press critic is effective, though it is widely believed that a handful have been merely influential, whatever that means; (iii) right-wing press critics, now quite prevalent in the blogosphere, have been ignored by scholars; (iv) self-appointed press critics such as Jon Stewart were having an impact on news performance that had eluded professional press critics and scholars; (v) most professional press critics talk *at,* but not *to* news consumers.

I believe this book offers a novel analysis: a defense of the self-appointed citizen press critic as well as press critics in general that offers objective criteria to judge such critics' effectiveness. I hope it talks *to* mostly citizen press critics, news consumers in general, and those concerned with the state of democracy and the free press. I also believe there is a message here for professional press critics and journalists, too.

Acknowledgments

Writing a book is a solitary endeavor. Nevertheless, one needs a support network. For me that network served mostly as a sounding board: Everette E. Dennis, the Felix E. Larkin Distinguished Professor at Fordham University's Graduate School of Business, and my colleagues Professor John M. Phelan, Professor Robin Andersen, and Assistant Professor Jonathan Gray. Finally, I thank my wife, Dorothy, for her encouragement, patience, and feedback.

CHAPTER 1

Introduction

Bloggers have claimed the attack on CBS News as their Boston Tea Party, a triumph of the democratic rabble over the lazy elites of the MSM (that's mainstream media to you). But on close examination the scene looks less like a victory for democracy than a case of mob rule.
　　　　　—*Columbia Journalism Review* assistant editor Corey Pein[1]

I don't get up in the morning trying to figure out how to destroy freedom of the press in America. Instead, I keep trying to persuade the folks at Newsweek, CBS, etc. not to flush free expression down the toilet through their irresponsibility and bias...I think that the survival of free expression depends on the responsible behavior of businesses in the media field.
　　　　　—Glenn Reynolds of *Instapundit.com*[2]

This book offers a defense for press critics in general, but mostly for the "democratic rabble" among them—the citizen press critic.[3] For much of the twentieth century, the mainstream press in the United States has swatted away its critics, even those it employed as ombudsmen and media reporters, as illegitimate interlopers in its relationship with its audience. Lee Brown observed in *The Reluctant Reformation: On Criticizing the Press in America*, "In terms of guardianship of its right to criticize itself, the press has generally dealt with criticism from outside its membership by discounting it, ignoring it, or by counterattacking with what has sometimes been described as paranoiac fervor."[4] In "Honor Without Influence," Marion Tuttle Marzolf summed up the typical libertarian response of many in the news industry: "The marketplace decides. People either buy our paper or watch our broadcast or they don't. When they stop buying or watching, it's time to worry. We don't need monitors on our performance—that's a violation of free speech."[5]

Today, as the above quotes from *Columbia Journalism Review* editor Pein's and blogger Reynolds's responses to *Reason* magazine media columnist Matt Welch attest, professional press critics seem to have adopted the arrogance of their managers and employers. They disparage other critics—citizen press critics—as ideologically driven or uncivil threats to press freedom and democracy. But where has it been set forth in stone that legitimate press critics must come to the discussion with a fixed set of credentials?

We have heard this complaint before about the dangers of the mob and the rabble, but in a different context. Pein's use of "mob rule" and "rabble" evokes notions of democratic elitism. In *The Theory of Democratic Elitism: A Critique*, Peter Bachrach argues that under such a form of democracy, the ordinary citizen plays a role in democracy but is expected to "remain relatively passive—in fact the health of the system depends upon it."[6] At the heart of the theory of democratic elitism is the belief that during political controversies and crises, the unsophisticated, irrational, and shortsighted ordinary citizen cannot be trusted to support democratic rights. Similarly, Pein's comments suggest that ordinary news consumers should refrain from the business of press criticism because they lack the expertise and sophistication to comport themselves responsibly in the public sphere and that their voices are interference, a threat to the stability of democracy, and the institution of the free press.

The defense of citizen press critics offered in this book argues to the contrary. Such critics are the embodiment of democracy, if one subscribes to the belief that a democratic system encourages participation of citizens in public decision-making forums. Generally, citizen press critics are merely exercising their right, if not duty, to debate the merits of an institution that plays a large role in shaping public opinion and influencing the actions of elected officials. By engaging in public debates about press performance or by organizing in media-monitoring groups, private individuals transform themselves into public citizens, this book argues. And under several theories of democratic discourse, democracy is enhanced when its private individuals engage in public debate, seeking accountability from powerful institutions. How is it then that vociferous, seemingly relentless news media-monitoring groups and individuals undermine the capability of citizens to be self-governing?

Though it may seem so to some editors and reporters, freedom of the press is not truly threatened when nongovernmental individuals and organizations seek to hold the news outlets accountable by bringing the weight of public opinion to bear upon their targets through the use of aggressive rhetorical tactics of public protest, or telephone, e-mail, and blog-swarming campaigns, or by the use of ridicule or vitriol. Such tactics carry no force of legal or extra-legal coercion. Striking a publisher, as John Ward Fenno did to Benjamin Franklin

Bache in 1797, is true intimidation.[7] This rabble that targets mainstream media (MSM)—though it may be angry, often ideological and partisan, contemptuous of the ethics of public discourse, railing in an uncivil and seemingly ceaseless shrill—adds an important voice to the dialogue of the public sphere in our democracy by holding the powerful institution of the MSM accountable to citizens. Some have argued that press criticism requires expertise: a knowledge of journalism ethics and practices.[8] Of course, such a criterion excludes most citizen press critics. Yet, under the overwhelming majority of democratic theories, economic and educational status provides no special privilege for participation. Why then would we demand expertise from a press critic? I contend that the most significant criterion for voicing criticism or praise for press performance in a democracy is consumption by the critic of specific news content or coverage of the critic's government and society by a news outlet.

History supports my position. For about four centuries, many of the nonjournalists who have critiqued the press were hardly Vulgarians, Philistines, or the great unwashed. A few were merely geniuses. In *The Invention of Journalism Ethics: The Path to Objectivity and Beyond*, Stephen J.A. Ward points out that citizen critics—"a chorus of criticism...from courtiers, offended factions, literary icons, and outraged parsons"—arose almost as soon as periodic journalism took hold in England: "Our culture's long debate over journalism was well underway by 1700. Ben Jonson's satirical play of 1626, *A Staple of News*, portrayed the 'newsmonger' as a person who sells lies to the credulous hoi polloi for credit."[9]

Today's citizen press critics are part of a long tradition, one almost as old as the Western press. They are important members of the Fifth Estate, monitoring the powerful watchdog news media that some have argued act more like lapdogs "submissive to status quo political and economic authority" or like guard dogs acting as "a sentry not for the community as a whole, but groups having sufficient power and influence to create and control their own security systems."[10] It would seem, then, that those requiring a high level of a specific type of expertise on the part of a press critic want to break from history and, it seems, from the future as well. In a world where many U.S.–based media organizations disseminate their printed, video, or digital images to international audiences via satellite and the Internet, literacy is not necessarily a prerequisite to voicing meaningful complaints about media performance.

This book's scope extends beyond citizen press critics. Included are profiles of journalists, scholars, and professional press critics: Ben Bagdikian, Steven Brill and his *Brill's Content*, the public journalism movement's scholars and journalists, and the Washington News Council, a mix of news professionals and nonjournalists. The nonjournalists/nonjournalism scholar critics included are the late Reed Irvine and his Accuracy in Media (AIM), the "pajamahadeen" bloggers who targeted CBS, CNN, and the Associated Press in 2004 and 2005, Jeff Cohen and his Fairness & Accuracy in Reporting (FAIR), satirists Jon Stewart and Stephen Colbert, and David Brock and his Media Matters for America (MMA). I have chosen these critics of news media performance and media watchdog groups because their critiques have proven effective, which is high praise because so few in 400 years have managed to prod the news media to reform. Where relevant, I have placed critics in their historical context, noting whether they are unique, rare, or part of a particular subgenre of journalism criticism.

What do I mean by effective? I looked at several well-known press critics, press review magazines, media reform efforts, and monitoring groups seeking to document impact. Were their critical reviews or commentary more than just eloquent verbiage? Did the critics help shape public opinion about the news industry? Did their critical reviews, commentary, or campaigns result either directly or indirectly in a tangible change in media practice or policy? And was there evidence that their targets were taking them seriously? Mostly, has the critic/watchdog made a news entity accountable to the public—and equally as important—has the entity publicly acknowledged its accountability? (One hears news executives and editors identify a well-known critic as being "influential," but they fail to specify the changes in practice and policy that resulted from that influence.) I ask the following:

1. Has the critique led to the dismissal, resignation, or reassignment of a reporter, broadcast public affairs personality, editor, or news executive?
2. Has the critique led to content or programming changes consistent with widely acknowledged journalism ethical standards?
3. Has the critique led to a reform of a news organization's standards and practices?
4. Has the critique spurred public debate in public forums and in the news media about news media performance or the business of mass media, helping to shape public opinion on the issue?
5. Do news media outlets quote the individual or organization as an authority on news media ethics and performance?
6. Does the individual or organization have a longtime and substantial following, measured in viewers, books sales, or Web-site hits?
7. Has the individual or organization inspired a movement?
8. Has the individual or organization established standards of inquiry, analysis, or proposals used by other critics?
9. Have the individual's critiques gained currency among other critics and scholars who point to the individual as a groundbreaking activist or thinker in news media criticism?

I place great weight on criteria Nos. 1–4. Generally, critics aspire to make their specific targets better and improve the genre that they review, at least as they see it, whether they review movies, literature, restaurants, consumer goods, or the news media. Sometimes, from a critic's eye, the object of his or her analysis is so egregiously bad that it deserves to be shunned. Implicit in all criticism is the notion of the public good: that the critic's assessment is offered to help the moviegoer, the lover of novels, and, for our discussion, the news consumer make informed choices.

I place less weight on Nos. 5–9. Up until the late 1990s, the ability of a press critic to stimulate a public response from MSM, to sell books about the problems of the media, and to gain recognition among scholars and peers was considered about the best results for which a press critic could hope. But Pyra Labs' 1999 innovation, the Weblog, or blogs, changed all that.[11] The interactivity and accessibility of the Internet allow just about any literate individual to disseminate a message worldwide. Now with blogs, discussion boards, e-mails, and electronic video postings, a news media watchdog's message is not limited to the discretion of a newspaper letters column or a broadcaster's switchboard operator. Consequently, citizen press critics' abilities to put pressure on their targets have increased substantially, to a level unprecedented in history, because they now can present their cases directly to the public.

Accordingly, the accomplishments of Irvine's AIM in the 1980s are quite impressive. In 1985, an AIM campaign compelled Public Broadcasting System (PBS) to air "Vietnam: Op/Ed," a conservative rebuttal to *Vietnam: A Television History*, a 13-part series aired by PBS during the fall of 1983. To this day, "Vietnam: Op/Ed" is a unique PBS program. Though the PBS decision to air the rebuttal was lamented by many, it was, however, a programming change consistent with PBS's own standards of balanced presentation of controversial programs. Thus, it meets criterion No. 2. Founded by Irvine in 1969, AIM assumed the point for the politically conservatives' assault on the so-called liberal media now so active in the blogosphere. Irvine also pioneered the concept, operation, and tactics of a citizen media watchdog group, a type of press criticism that spawned several imitators on the left and the right of the political spectrum. In so doing, Irvine's AIM also satisfies criteria Nos. 4–8 as presented in "Reed Irvine's Accuracy in Media: Barking at the 'Liberal Media'" (Chapter 2).

The pajamahadeen are AIM's progeny; they are Pein's rabble and mob. (A portmanteau word, "pajamahadeen" combines pajama, because bloggers, as the stereotype goes, blog in their pajamas while at home, with the last half of Mujahadeen, as in warriors committed to jihad.) Their campaign against CBS for airing the segment "For the Record" on *60 Minutes Wednesday* on September 8, 2004, ranks as one of the most effective efforts to hold a news organization accountable. In the end, CBS dismissed four journalists, Dan Rather resigned, and the news organization created a Senior Vice President of Standards and Special Projects to oversee a revised vetting process. That one accomplishment satisfies criteria Nos. 1–4. Soon after, the pajamahadeen toppled Eason Jordan from his post as CNN chief news executive. The right-wing bloggers, however, were not as successful against the Associated Press. Their exploits are examined in "Let a Thousand Bloggers Swarm" (Chapter 3).

Bagdikian used to be a full-time journalist, and a pretty good one. When he worked at the *Washington Post*, the legendary Ben Bradlee once told him, "I've got to hand it to you, buddy. You've really got big ones"—for spending six days in a maximum security prison solely to gain a first-hand perspective on prison life. But during most of his years in journalism he was moonlighting as a press critic. He was more than good at it; he was visionary and intellectual. He advocated for the creation of news ombudsmen in the 1950s and the 1960s. He served as the *Washington Post*'s second ombudsman from 1970 to 1972. Today, the Organization of News Ombudsmen reveres Bagdikian's March 1967 *Esquire* magazine article, which called for newspapers to hire ombudsmen, among other reforms, as a seminal text. In that article, he also called for the creation of news councils. And as president of the Mellett Fund for a Free and Responsible Press, Bagdikian oversaw the first systematic trial of local press councils, a one-year experiment (1966–1967) conducted in Bend, Oregon; Redwood City, California; and Sparta and Cairo, Illinois. But since 1983, many observers have thought of Bagdikian as an alarmist, a "Chicken Little" raising unfounded concerns about conglomerates taking over the mass media industry. Bagdikian has been writing about consolidation in the news business since the late 1960s, but his *The Media Monopoly* (1983) is the text that defines him in the eyes of many. After the media reform movement successfully opposed the Federal Communication Commission's attempt to have Congress adopt its relaxation of media ownership rules in 2003, few now call him an alarmist. His story and how he ranks as a highly effective critic under criteria Nos. 3–9 are covered in "Ben H. Bagdikian: Ahead of the Curve" (Chapter 4).

News councils offer citizens a public forum where an impartial tribunal hears their complaints against a news organization. Because councils require complainants to waive their rights to sue, many believe councils have played a significant role in reducing the number of libel suits brought against news organizations. Apparently, such complainants find comfort in moral vindication even when the target of their complaints ignores a news council's ruling. But the *Spokesman-Review* of Spokane did not ignore the findings of Seattle-based Washington News Council (WNC). Following some of the council's recommendations, the *Spokane Spokesman-Review* revised some of its editing and editorial-writing procedures and personnel and part of its ethics code in 2007. The accountability method the WNC used to accomplish this feat is unique among news councils in the United States, possibly the world. The *Spokane Spokesman-Review* hired it as an independent review panel, suggesting a new role for other press councils. The WNC's unique accomplishment meets criteria Nos. 3–5 and is presented in "The Washington News Council: Third-Party Intervention" (Chapter 5).

FAIR, founded by Jeff Cohen in 1986, is a leader in the media reform movement. Thus, it shares credit for the movement's 2003 success. Cohen is the only nonaffiliated MSM news media critic to have appeared regularly on national television, including as a co-host of CNN's *Crossfire,* as a weekly *Fox News Watch* panelist, and as a commentator on MSNBC. The organization is partly a think tank, publishing studies widely respected by corporate media because, for the most part, FAIR's staff conveys verifiable factual assertions and scientifically sound statistical findings, couching them in the careful language of think-tank experts. MSM quotes Cohen and FAIR's staffers as authorities on news media performance. Mostly, these studies have won FAIR press coverage in which the merits of their findings are debated, meetings with editors and recognition by news ombudsmen that their claims have merit, and recognition in academia. There also is evidence to support the conclusion that the findings of its studies have led to changes at ABC's *Nightline* and at Yahoo!News. Based on this evidence and more, a strong case is made that FAIR satisfies criteria Nos. 3–9 as presented in "FAIR: Press Criticism from a Progressive Think Tank" (Chapter 6).

Steven Brill's "Pressgate"—a 25,000-word, 29-page exposé—the cover story for the inaugural issue of *Brill's Content*, ranks as a historically significant piece of press criticism because only a handful of reports or essays have provoked a similar level of public discussion of press performance and public self-examination by the news media. Of course, the collaborative effort of bloggers—blog swarming—has produced a similar magnitude of complaints, discussion, and hand wringing, but by definition a blog swarm relies on an aggregation of postings to make its mark. "Pressgate," however, appeared in June 1998, just as blogging was blossoming, and it is a single article written by one journalist turned press critic. *Brill's Content* is the only press review magazine to reach 300,000 subscribers. It folded in October 2001. Nevertheless, Brill proved that the public was hungry for news about the information industry—its journalists and owners, and the way they went about gathering and packaging news. He just could not persuade enough high-end advertisers to come on board. For those accomplishments and others, Brill and his magazine rank as highly effective press critics, meeting criteria Nos. 4, 5, and 8 as documented in "*Brill's Content*: 'An Inside-the-Sausage-Factory Look at Media for People Who Eat Sausages, Not Those Who Make Them'" (Chapter 7).

Public journalism (sometimes referred to as civic journalism): today some journalists think of the movement as a fad that has faded. Indeed, the movement's heyday was from 1988 to 2003. And it has moved on. Today, many of its adherents operate under the banner of citizen journalism, seeking no longer to reform MSM, but to create a noncorporate news media as an alternative. Yet, never before has a press reform movement persuaded so many newsrooms to reexamine how they practice news gathering, reporting, and editorial decision making in so short a span of time.

Its advocates argue that it is not enough for journalists to provide information about the decisions and conduct of politicians, government officials, and powerful private citizens. Journalists must also provide ways to engage the public in a conversation about public affairs in an effort to resolve or solve civic controversies, public journalism argues. But by 2003 many of the movement's leaders grew disillusioned with MSM's public journalism efforts. At the same time, Internet technology's interactive capabilities allowed public journalism's proponents to experiment with efforts such as "crowdsourcing," creating a news story by aggregating reports from a large group of unaffiliated citizens. But as "Public Journalism: Press Criticism as an Ongoing Experiment" (Chapter 8) shows, there are still traditional news outlets pursuing public journalism. Without a doubt, public journalism has led to the reform of hundreds of news outlets' practices. For that reason and more, public journalism is a highly valuable news media critique, satisfying criteria Nos. 3–7 and 9.

"Press Criticism as a Laughing Matter" (Chapter 9) explores the critique offered by Comedy Central's *The Daily Show with Jon Stewart* and its spin-off *The Colbert Report*. Both shows are known for their political satire, but they also satirize the press by their actors' poses, tones, mannerisms, and words. Stewart, Colbert, their cast, and writers often act like clowns, but they are nobody's fools. And their laugh-out-loud cutting criticism of the news media seems to stem from a tacit belief that television news anchors, reporters, and pundits have breached a social contract with the public: that the news outlets have a responsibility in a democracy to exercise news judgment for more than high ratings and self-aggrandizement. They often cast themselves as the public's representatives, attempting to ridicule, implore, or shame the news media into living up to their obligation to give the public information it needs to be self-governing. Effective? CNN's *Crossfire* is gone, largely due to Stewart's funny, in part profane, trenchant comments on *Crossfire*'s October 15, 2004, broadcast. Meanwhile, some news media outlets are seriously considering how they can be as hip as Comedy Central's so-called "fake news." "Press Criticism as a Laughing Matter" (Chapter 9) shows how the news satire shows have met criteria Nos. 1, 2, 4, and 5.

Had Ryan Chiachiere, 26, not watched the nationally syndicated *Imus in the Morning* show on April 4, 2007, it is likely that Don Imus and his executive producer Bernard McGuirk might still be heard and seen five times weekly on CBS radio and MSNBC cable network. But he did watch because that was what he was paid to do as an employee at Media Matters for America. He also was paid to select what the leftist media watchdog group believes is egregious examples of racial or sexist language. He heard Imus use a slur to refer to the mostly African-American players of the Rutgers University women's basketball team. So Chiachiere posted a brief report and a transcript and video of Imus's offending remarks on MMA's Web site. The watchdog group e-mailed the package to its subscribers and others. Two days later, outraged viewers' complaints swamped MSNBC. Neither the MSM nor Rev. Al Sharpton were involved at that point. Soon after, the Internet, MSM, and the nation were abuzz with talk about Imus's remarks, race, hip-hop culture, and profane language on the airways. How Media Matters for America's critique meets criteria Nos. 1 and 4 is explored in "It Takes a Watchdog and a Village: News Media Accountability in Seven Days" (Chapter 10).

The absence in this book of some well-regarded press critics testifies to the appropriate and greater weight placed on criteria Nos. 1–4. For example, I found little documentation to support a conclusion that commentary from ombudsmen in general, the two leading journalism reviews—*Columbia Journalism Review* and *American Journalism Review*—or even A.J. Liebling, for that matter, changed industry practices and standards or led to changes in format or personnel in a substantial and apparent way. Liebling is held up as saint-like among the chattering class and literati. And, yes, he inspired other journalists to become press critics. But as *Slate.com* media critic Jack Shafer argues: "Liebling probably owes more of his reputation as a press critic to his skill at manufacturing quips and composing toothsome prose than his fans would like to admit."[12]

Lately, it has been the vogue among media accountability advocates in academia to reference the four requirements of media social responsibility identified by the Hutchins Commission on Freedom of the Press's *A Free and Responsible Press*.[13] But the Commission, and its report published in 1947, are textbook examples of how to be an ineffectual press critic as I explain in "A Prescription for Effective Press Criticism in a Democracy" (Chapter 11). Journalism scholar and lawyer Stephen Bates summed up the Commission's ineffectuality succinctly:

> The press proved unreceptive—in fact, indignant—producing yelps of umbrage that nearly drowned out the Commission's recommendations. Over the half-century since, the report has appreciably influenced academic thinking about journalism, but not journalism itself. A flawed success as an analysis, *A Free and Responsible Press* has proved, as a call to action, a magnificent failure. Consequently, the experience of the Hutchins Commission makes for a revealing, sometimes poignant case study of a reformist flop.[14]

Similarly, after interviewing 30 media reporters and critics—those employed by the news media—Susanne Fengler concluded, "Few interviewees were fully confident that they could help improve the news media's service to the public by holding the media accountable."[15] In 1995, the now defunct *Media Studies Journal* identified nine "critics who count" from interviews with MSM gatekeepers: Jonathan Alter, Ken Auletta, Jeff Greenfield, Jon Katz, Howard Kurtz, Rush Limbaugh, Howard Rosenberg, Tom Shales, and David Shaw.[16] None of these high-profile critics, however, played a pivotal role in the cancellation of a program as Stewart did, transformed newsroom practice and culture as Jay Rosen and the civic journalism movement have, or attracted more than 300,000 news consumers to subscribe to a monthly press criticism magazine as did Brill.

What insights about the role of the press critic and its value to democratic society can we draw from the critics examined here? First, citizen press critics with no direct financial ties to a news outlet tend to be the most effective in spurring press reforms and increasing public awareness about news media performance. They provide what James Carey argued was a necessity: "sustained critical attention from intellectuals, scholars, writers and ordinary citizens... outside the apparatus of the newspaper."[17]

Second, such critics galvanize the public that then pressures a news outlet through letters, phone calls, and, of course, blog discussions and e-mails. Galvanizing public opinion is critical. Most professional press critics are really talking to other journalists and the power elite. Citizen press critics, particularly media watchdog groups and bloggers, are foremost engaged in dialogues with their subscribers, other bloggers, and the public in general. Many of the press critics I have selected operate in a manner prescribed by Carey: "[T]he press should be analyzed for the audience which regularly consumes the press...and not merely for coteries of professionals and students."[18] Of course, citizen press critics go one step further. They not only analyze *for* the audience, they *are* the audience. And, as I argued earlier, that generally is a good thing and certainly is as valid as criticism from professionals.

Carey also contended that a "democratic tradition of criticism" required at least "a language relatively neutral in terms of affect and emotional coloring."[19] Here Carey echoes theories of the normative standard of civility, detachment, and distrust of rhetoric, a legacy of the Enlightenment: "[Civility] is a way of speaking politically that does not inflame passion or permit *ad hominem* attacks upon other speakers. It is not the same as detachment...but it dovetails nicely with detachment. Detachment focuses on one's emotional relationship to one's ideas while civility is about how one treats the ideas of those who disagree."[20] The language used by some of the effective critics here—Stewart told *Crossfire's* Tucker Carlson, "You know what's interesting, though? You're as big a dick on your show as you are on any show"[21]—does not meet such a standard. It is a sarcastic *ad hominem* attack. Yet Stewart's diatribe sparked a responsive chord among other viewers of the *Crossfire* program. Was Stewart acting as little more than a smart-ass demagogue stirring the *mobile vulgus*? Is such uncivil rhetoric an anathema to republican democracy? It would seem so by the norms of representative liberalism democracy as expressed in the *Federalist Papers* No. 55: "In all very numerous assemblies, of whatever character composed, passion never fails to wrest the sceptre from reason. Had every Athenian citizen been a Socrates, every Athenian assembly would still have been a mob."[22]

Publius—either James Madison or Alexander Hamilton—subscribed to only one theory of democracy, and no well articulated theory of democratic discourse. But four theories of public discourse and democracy discussed below—discursive, participatory liberal, constructionist, and responsive—embrace uncivil and passionate speech or acknowledge that it holds some value in public deliberation and, thus, provide a defense for the seemingly undemocratic tactics of passionate, ideologically, rancorous press critics as part of the U.S. democratic tradition. Among such democratic theorists, it is widely agreed that public discussion of civic issues is critical to the health of democracy, a political system in which sovereignty resides with its common citizens and is exercised by them typically by free elections of representatives and referenda. Deliberative or discursive democratic theorists, however, argue that voting is the end product of a process of public discussions in which citizens aim to persuade a majority to reach consensus on political, economic, and social issues and actions, though not all such theorists require consensus. In short, debate and discussion of public affairs are essential to ensure that citizens govern themselves. Political philosopher James F. Bohman argues that most proponents of deliberative democracy believe "political decision making is legitimate insofar as its policies are produced in a process of public discussion and debate in which citizens and their representatives, going beyond mere self-interest and limited points of view, reflect on the general interest or on their common good."[23]

Today, German political philosopher Jürgen Habermas's concept of the public sphere holds a central position in democratic discourse theory. Briefly, in his *The Structural Transformation of the Public Sphere: An Inquiry into a Category of Bourgeois Society* and *Moral Consciousness and Communicative Action,* Habermas argues that in public spheres—originally the coffeehouses and salons of eighteenth century Europe—members of the middle class "came together to engage in reasoned argument over key issues of mutual interest and concern, creating a space in which both new ideas and the practices and discipline of rational public debate were cultivated. Furthermore, the emergence of this new public space... shaped and was shaped by the emergence of a philosophical concept and consciousness of 'publics" and their importance."[24] According to Habermas, the modern industrialized welfare state and the commercial mass media have eclipsed the ability of individuals to deliberate publicly to reach consensus on public opinion. Today, a number of scholars are examining the possibility that the Internet holds promise for reviving the public sphere, because the Internet seems to have created a public space for egalitarian, civic-oriented debate.

Notions of the public sphere, media scholar Peter Dahlgren says, have always existed as an appendage to democratic theory.[25] But democratic theorists differ on the kinds of speech that are best in promoting a fully democratic public sphere. Or, put another way, what kinds of speech hinder an individual's ability to engage in effective political discourse and deliberation? As we will see, under the representative liberal model that values expertise and the elite, the prescribed form of communication is civil, detached, and reasoned.[26] The discursive (Habermas) and participatory liberal models of democratic discourse are somewhat more open to uncivil and passionate communication than the representative liberal model.

In contrast, the constructive and responsive (or constitutional) models allow for activism, rudeness, outrageousness and passionate discourse, and other forms of uncivil speech. I argue that the responsive model and its related constitutional concept of public discourse, a phrase coined by Yale law professor Robert C. Post, are the most appropriate to test the legitimacy of the words and tactics of citizen press critics because they stem from the U.S. democratic experience and Constitution tradition and are not idealized, untried conceptions such as the Habermasian-discursive theory, for example.

DISCURSIVE

Habermas is "the most commanding figure" in the discursive theory tradition.[27] He insists on rational discourse "that the structure of their communication, by virtue of features that can be described in purely formal terms, excludes all force—whether it arises from the process of reaching understanding itself or influences it from the outside—except the force of the better argument (and thus it also excludes, on their part, all motives except that of a cooperative search for the truth)."[28] And though dialogue and mutual respect are highly valued, "civility is not tantamount to emotional detachment."[29]

PARTICIPATORY LIBERAL

Many participatory liberal theorists believe that a democratic system should maximize citizens' participation in public decision making and are skeptical about or reject requirements of expertise, detachment, and civility on public discourse. According to Mayra Ferree et al., "[S]ome advocates of the participatory liberal tradition extend the criterion of empowerment to reject the norm of civility...Thus, while participatory liberal theorists cannot be said to endorse slogans and polemics as a means of discourse, they do not reject such styles of expression out of hand."[30]

> Style, in this view, is intertwined with empowerment. Speech that mobilizes people to participate places them in a position in which their awareness of the complexity of politics can grow through their participation in the political process itself. Thus even "emotional" slogans such as "abortion takes an innocent life" or "my belly belongs to me" should directly foster a more inclusive public sphere and indirectly lead, through greater participation, to a more politically competent and knowledgeable public.[31]

CONSTRUCTIONIST

According to construction or agnostic theorists, democratic life is a struggle of socially diverse participants in public debate in multiple public spheres. According to Iris Marion Young, the disadvantaged and excluded struggle "to engage others in debate about social problems and proposed solutions, engage them in a project of explaining and justifying their positions. Disorderly, disruptive, annoying, or distracting means of communication are often necessary or effective elements in such efforts to engage others in debate over issues and outcomes."[32] Additionally, constructionists see rules of civility—limits on rhetorical style—as antidemocratic, enforcing the powerful's norms on the less powerful.

> Civility in discourse is a matter of socially secured agreements to conform to the local culture, and such local culture and specific cultures are deeply imbued with power. What is normal in public discussion in some places is rude in others; and what is considered a normal way of showing respect in some venues seems mannered and arid in others. Constructionists remind us that in identifying normative criteria about deliberative discourse, we must be careful to attend to different dimensions of power, including those that act discursively to restrict content and participation through the limits they place on acceptable style.[33]

RESPONSIVE

Yale Law's Post is the leading proponent of a responsive conception of democracy, rooted in First Amendment jurisprudence. In *Constitutional Domains: Democracy, Community, Management,* Post argues that the U.S. Supreme Court has endorsed the "individualist premises of responsive democracy" by interpreting the First Amendment to require that "in public debate our own citizens must tolerate insulting, and even outrageous speech."[34] In an earlier work, Post called his First Amendment–based theory of public discourse the constitutional concept of public discourse.[35] Post noted that the Court's constitutional concept of public discourse is analogous to sociologists' conflict theory. (Conflict theory is influenced by the Marxist theory of class struggle. It maintains that society operates so that opposing forces—individuals and its groups—struggle to maximize their benefits, which inevitably contributes to social change.) Post writes that about the time the Court was fashioning its concept of public discourse, sociologist Carroll Clark in 1933 maintained that "social organization is widened and complicated by economic and cultural differentiation that entails incompatible schemes of group behavior."[36]

From a public discourse view, this means that public opinion in a free democratic society is reached through the oral and verbal clashing of opposing and dissimilar views voiced in public forums. Consequently, "individuals must be free within public discourse from the enforcement of all civility rules, so as to be able to advocate and to exemplify the creation of new forms of communal life in their speech."[37] Accordingly, *Hustler* magazine's hurtful, outrageous parody of Rev. Jerry Falwell—a cartoon suggesting that the Christian evangelist Falwell had sex with his mother in an outhouse—though not "the stuff of rational deliberation," is still a vital part of public discourse.[38] According to Harvard Law professor Frank I. Michelman, "Post understands that American responsive-democracy theory to posit...unprejudiced participatory access for all to a ceaseless communicative process of determining the social order—a process in which majoritarian resolutions are always unrestrainedly open to reexamination."[39]

According to Post, the constitutional concept of public discourse forbids the state from enforcing a standard whereby one community's idea of appropriate speech would be imposed upon another "because to do so would privilege a specific community and prejudice the ability of individuals to persuade others of the need to change it. Outrageous speech calls community identity into question, practically as well as cognitively, and thus it has unique power to focus attention, dislocate old assumptions, and shock its audience into the recognition of unfamiliar forms of life."[40] Consequently, restrictions on uncivil and ethically dubious words and peaceful activism should be imposed only by agreement of speakers involved in a public discussion because First Amendment doctrine rests on the possibility of using uncivil and unseemly speech to create new community norms.[41]

Thus, under a constitutional concept of public discourse, what some consider over-the-top criticism—bloggers slurring the Associated Press as "terrorist-sympathizing, anti-Bush press"[42] or Stewart calling Carlson a "dick"—is legitimate. Similarly, FAIR subscribers' e-mail barrages, Irvine and AIM's branding of journalists as un-American based on selective personal information, the pajamahadeen's or any other type of blogger's use of pseudonyms and anonyms are legitimate, largely because such words and tactics allow for individual self-expression and political speech in public forums and do not coerce the speaker's target into pursuing a course of action it would otherwise not have taken.

Post reminds us that under a number of theories of democratic discourse, including the constitutional concept, coercion "is precluded from public debate because the very purpose of that debate is the practice of self-determination."[43] In other words, generally a speaker may fear to engage in a vigorous debate when the first speaker has threatened direct physical or financial harm that prevents the second speaker from exercising his or her free speech and other rights and privileges.

What precisely is coercive speech? We know its outer boundaries. The U.S. Supreme Court has told us that generally public speech constituting a direct and imminent threat of harm is coercive and does not deserve constitutional protection.[44] (Private threats generally do not enjoy such protection.) Consequently, racist and sexist language without a direct and imminent threat of harm is not deemed coercive. Speech that simply embarrasses or persuades an individual to act out of fear of social ostracism is protected.[45] The Supreme Court also has told us that a threat of a boycott is protected speech.[46] Additionally, according to the Court, threats against political figures in the form of hyperbole are not necessarily coercive. In *Watts v. United States*, a speaker at a political debate at a small public gathering vowed: "If they ever make me carry a rifle the first man I want to get in my sights is L. B. J."[47] The Court found his words to be mere political hyperbole and protected under the First Amendment. Under those terms, press critics threatening or employing boycotts or spearheading mass phone call and e-mail campaigns that harass news outlets are engaging in valid democratic practices. Distilling the legal precedents, legal and communications scholar C. Edwin Baker offers a definition of coercive speech to distinguish it from legitimate offerings and warnings that may prove helpful: "In general, a person coercively influences another if (1) she restricts the other to options that are worse than the other had a moral or legitimate right to expect or (2) she employs means that she had no right to use for changing the threatened person's options."[48]

Where press critics are concerned, I add the direct and indirect threat of the coercive power of government action to the list of coercive speech. A press critic in a position to invoke the coercive power of the state against a media outlet poses a threat to a free exchange of ideas, and that is what we seek, an honest discourse among critics, the public, and the news media. But when a government official scolds the press there is almost always a tacit threat of censorship via criminal prosecution or regulatory sanctions or approvals. Thus, such a scolding can coercively intrude into the editorial integrity of a news organization, restrict-ing the options the organization has a right to expect. Under such circumstances, government has no right to use such an implicit threat to narrow the news media's options, according to Baker's standard of coercive speech.

Therefore, criticism of the press by an elected or government official is pre-sumptively inappropriate in a democracy because typically it is more than a mere exchange of opinions. Even when an elected or government official expresses no direct threat, the threat is often implied because government has the power to prosecute or regulate in ways that might disadvantage or advantage a news organization. For example, a media conglomerate waiting for Federal Communi-cations Commission (FCC) and Justice Department approval of a proposed merger may feel coerced into silence in the face of criticism from White House officials or Congress. Because they are government licensees, broadcasters are particularly susceptible to implied and direct threats from government.

Unregulated media is not immune. Elected and government officials from the U.S. president to the local police chief have the power and sometimes the authority to restrict journalists' access to important forums and documents. For example, the police chief complaining about media coverage of his or her private life has the power to make a police blotter "disappear" when a journalist makes his or her daily checks. Of course, such a restriction is illegal under state sunshine and public records statutes, requiring open meetings and access to public docu-ments. A news organization can file a complaint or pursue litigation against the police chief to regain access. Still, most local newspapers would prefer to avoid even a temporary loss of access to such information.

Almost always, a high government official comes to a discussion of news per-formance with the ability to coercively influence a news organization. President Richard M. Nixon, Vice President Spiro T. Agnew, and Nixon's speechwriter, Patrick J. Buchanan, mounted such an assault on the national television news media starting November 13, 1969, in Des Moines, Iowa.[49] Similarly, all those who value genuine democratic discourse should be troubled when a government official criticizes the press immediately before or soon after he or she steps into private life because the politician, judge, or administrator arguably still is in a position to use or order others to use state power to intimidate the news media. Tony Blair comes to mind. Fifteen days before he resigned his post as British prime minister, Blair assailed the British press that he said "hounded, badgered, blustered the nation's leaders since he came to power 10 years ago."[50]

Additionally, the claims ex-CBS anchor Dan Rather makes in his lawsuit filed in New York State Court in September 2007 against Viacom, the owner of CBS, illustrate the potential for coercion that some may overlook or elect not to acknowledge. Rather alleged a connection among bloggers, the Bush administration, and his boss's effort to "curry favor with the White House by demonstrating its intent to minimize CBS News' criticism of" Bush's Texas Air Force National Guard record.[51] To buttress claims that Viacom sought to stay on the White House's good side even to the point of interfering with the news division's editorial independence, the lawsuit claims CBS management tried to bury the Abu Ghraib prisoner abuse exposé that 60 *Minutes II* broke in April 2004.[52] Whether the claims have merit is not the issue here. These claims raised in *Dan Rather v. CBS Corporation* are offered merely to show the possibility of indirect and subtle government pressure that broadcasters may face.

It follows, then, that press critics should assiduously avoid relationships with elected and other government officials, and their goals, ideology, and funding sources should be explicit. There is an obvious conflict of interest there, of course. (See *"Brill's Content:* 'An Inside-the-Sausage-Factory Look at Media for People Who Eat Sausages, Not Those Who Make Them'" [Chapter 7].) Beyond that, there is the more troubling image of the ostensibly "little guy" press critic confronting a news outlet, when behind him stands the government giant wielding a huge club. The addition of government does not make the fight fair, even when the news organization is a conglomerate.

AIM's Irvine's campaign against PBS in 1984–1985 raised such concerns; he was famously close to the White House. Similarly, AIM's Cliff Kincaid flirted with invoking the coercive power of government when he called for the U.S. attorney general or the FBI to investigate CBS for criminal fraud for using what many said were "forged" documents in its 60 *Minutes Wednesday* report about President George W. Bush's Texas Air National Guard service during the Vietnam War. (See "Reed Irvine's Accuracy in Media: Barking at the 'Liberal Media'" [Chapter 2].) Similarly, bloggers' use of pseudonyms or anonyms raises the specter of coercion. (See "Let a Thousand Bloggers Swarm" [Chapter 3].)

In my estimation, even a press critique raising the mere hypothetical threat of government crackdown is coercive and counterproductive, one of the major shortcomings of the Hutchins Commission's *A Free and Responsible Press,* which warned in 1947: "Our society requires agencies of mass communication. They are great concentrations of private power. If they are irresponsible, not even the First Amendment will protect their freedom from governmental control. The amendment will be amended."[53] Ultimately, none of the critics examined here acted in undemocratic ways, though a case can be made that some of their words and tactics were ethically dubious.

As noted earlier, the constitutional concept of public discourse model is preferred for historical reasons, because it is uniquely American and because it is committed to maintaining a profound national commitment to the principle that debate on public issues should be "uninhibited, robust, and wide open."[54] Additionally, Post contends the concept "enables the formation of a genuine and uncoerced public opinion in a culturally heterogeneous society."[55] And Post's model is not an idealized construct such as the constructivist or discursive models; it is a reality. For example, the historical underpinnings for Habermas's concept of democratic dialogue in the public sphere—the European coffeehouses of the 1700s as "a paragon of Augustan politeness"—was a "myth," Brian Cowan tells us in *The Social Life of Coffee: The Emergence of the British Coffeehouse,* "finally ensconced in the historical record by Jürgen Habermas, who relied primarily on [Joseph Addison and Richard Steele's] accounts for his influential discussion of the rise of the coffeehouse as an example of the emergence of what he called the 'bourgeois public sphere.'"[56] This is a positivistic approach, an analysis stressing practice over the ideal. On such an analysis, those who marginalize sharp-tongue satirists, agenda-motivated activists, and caustic bloggers as undemocratic are at best misguided, ahistorical, or fearful of the rough-and-tumble nature of true democratic discourse.

Even so, for the sake of maintaining meaningful public discourse, we need ground rules. We should not expect a news organization to respond to any and all disparagements and condemnations. Where, then, is the basis for a news organization's obligation to respond to its critics? There is the belief that the First Amendment's grant of freedom to the press obligates the press to operate for the public good. But that extremely vague concept of the public good does little more than obligate an organization to let the marketplace decide: "People either buy our paper or watch our broadcast or they don't"[57]

Nor can a news organization's obligation to respond to its critics be rooted in the social obligation rationale posited by the Hutchins Commission's *A Free and Responsible Press*.[58] The Commission rooted its expansive idea of the press's obligation to society on the premise that the "press is not free if those who operate it behave as though their position conferred on them the privilege of being deaf to ideas which the processes of free speech have brought to public attention."[59] It argued that the press was obligated to provide "a truthful, comprehensive, and intelligent account of the day's events in a context which gives them meaning...[provide] a forum for the exchange of comment and criticism ...a means of projecting the opinions and attitudes of the groups in the society to one another...a method of presenting and clarifying the goals and values of society...a way of reaching every member of the society by the currents of information, thought, and feeling which the press supplies."[60]

The Commission's theory was predicated on its perception of the mass communication market of the 1940s, which it contrasted to the newspaper industry that existed in the late 1700s. The social obligation of a newspaper owner in the 1780s was quite narrow because "[i]t was not supposed that any one newspaper would represent all, or nearly all, of the conflicting viewpoints regarding public issues. Together they could be expected to do so, and, if they did not, the man whose opinions were not represented could start a publication of his own."[61] Now, in the early twenty-first century, blogs allow such an individual the ability to share his or her own opinions with the world at a low cost. Hence, the justifications for compelling all owners of news outlets to abide by one set of externally opposed obligations to the public are not as compelling today as they arguably were in the late 1940s.

I contend that the appropriate theory of journalism's social responsibility is one that recognizes the editorial freedom of each individual or owner to shape its mission and scope of social responsibility as it sees fit. In other words, the individual journalist or news organization should be judged by the critic on the basis of the terms of the social contract the news organization has struck with its public.

Journalism historian and ethicist Stephen J. A. Ward explains that a "social contract in journalism is an agreement that a journalist makes with the public to balance the freedoms and responsibilities of their profession. The interpretation of the social contract may vary according to society, but in all contracts journalists promise to act responsibly in return for some measure of freedom and independence."[62] Moreover, each outlet's contract is unique. In two sentences of its report, the Commission appeared to acknowledge the right of each news outlet or journalist to fashion its own standards of reporting, editing, coverage, and tone and terms of accountability with its audience: "The press must be free for the development of its own conceptions of service and achievement. It must be free for making its contribution to the maintenance and development of a free society."[63] Yet, in the following paragraph it contradicts itself by establishing what it deems as a universal term for news entities' social contracts: "[The press] must be accountable to society for meeting the public need and for maintaining the rights of citizens and the almost forgotten rights of speakers who have no press."[64] The news organization or journalist is free to develop its own terms of its social contract, provided that it includes the Commission's requirement of a right of access. Apparently, the Commission had a narrow view of free choice and editorial integrity. Did the Commission mean that the then-flourishing black press be required to give the Ku Klux Klan space on its op-ed pages?

Where do we find the terms of a news organization's contract? Sometimes, the terms are explicit, set forth in the industry's or an outlet's code of ethics or standards of practice, or detailed in mission statements, or inferred from mottos. (The *New York Times*' "All the news that's fit to print" is one such example. The phrase expressed Adolph S. Ochs's promise to the public in 1896: a promise that it would not engage in the sensationalism of yellow journalism. Marzolf observes that by 1901, "It was the *Times* that critics singled out for praise and emulation."[65]) Additionally, terms can be drawn from a news entity's pattern, tone, and scope of coverage. Often the public's expectations of press performance are drawn from a combination of all such sources. In the case of government-regulated broadcast, the concept of public interest as defined by the FCC also provides terms of the social contracts radio and television outlets are obligated to follow.

Under a social contract theory, each media outlet's social obligation varies. This means that NBC's television stations' social contract may be different from that of 24-hour cable news service MSNBC, though General Electric owns both. That is because the FCC directly regulates television outlets, but only indirectly regulates cable TV and the Internet. Under the Communications Act of 1934, radio and television outlets are required to serve "the public interest, convenience, and necessity," a standard that has been interpreted broadly and narrowly during the last 60 years or so.[66] The FCC licensee's public interest obligations do not apply to cable TV or the Internet.

The *New York Times' Ethical Journalism: A Handbook of Values and Practices for the News and Editorial Departments*, for example, places restrictions on its news employees' non-work-related political activities and community service that exceed similar restrictions at most news outlets.[67] The media giant Time Warner Inc. published its Corporate Social Responsibility Report in 2006, imposing the same ethical obligations on all its properties, cable television, magazines, the Internet, and movies.[68]

Predicating a press critique on a news outlet's professed standards and long-time practices serves all parties in the public dialogue—the public, the critic, and the press. A debate cannot progress to compromise or resolution unless all parties involved in it, or affected by it, agree on core concepts and terms. And agreement on the ground rules allows the critic and the news outlet to present assertions and arguments that the jury—the public—can rationally assess. This examination of effective press critics also shows that the most successful critics held news organizations such as PBS ("Reed Irvine's Accuracy in Media: Barking at the 'Liberal Media'" [Chapter 2] and "FAIR: Press Criticism from a Progressive Think Tank" [Chapter 6]), CBS ("Press Criticism as a Laughing Matter" [Chapter 9] and ("Let a Thousand Bloggers Swarm" [Chapter 3]), and CNN ("Press Criticism as a Laughing Matter" [Chapter 9]) accountable to the terms of their own or industry-recognized social contracts.

The chapters that follow will also show how the *New York Times* rejected public journalism in the mid-1990s as discussed in "Public Journalism: Press Criticism as an Ongoing Experiment" (Chapter 8), based on its longtime adherence to objectivity, and how the *Wall Street Journal*'s editorial page publicly dismissed criticism from right-wing bloggers by appealing to the bond it believed it had established with its readers: "We hope readers buy our newspaper because we make grown-up decisions about what is newsworthy, and what isn't"[69] ("Let a Thousand Bloggers Swarm" [Chapter 3]).

The examination of press critics that follows is not an endorsement of any critic's philosophy, ideology, or concept of an ideal press. I have, however, pointed out where I believe the critics profiled here have conducted themselves in less than ethical ways. Whether such conduct undermines the persuasiveness of their critiques is a judgment I leave to the court of public opinion.

CHAPTER 2

Reed Irvine's Accuracy in Media: Barking at the "Liberal Media"

Even to its moderator, the television program was a bit odd, a matryoshka of sorts, a set of wooden dolls of diminishing sizes placed one inside another. The moderator, Harvard Law School professor Arthur Miller, dubbed "Vietnam: Op/Ed" "a program about a program about a program."[1] It aired in late June 1985 on Public Broadcasting System (PBS) stations.[2]

The original program was a documentary, *Vietnam: A Television History*, a 13-part series aired by PBS during the fall of 1983. Writing for *Time* magazine, Richard Zoglin called it "scrupulously researched," and the series was praised as "a comprehensive and balanced piece of work."[3] Historian Patrick J. Furlong called it "the most ambitious and the most controversial historical documentary ever broadcast on American television."[4] The document won a Peabody Award,[5] six Emmys for news and documentary excellence, and six for outstanding informational, cultural, or historical programs.[6] According to the Museum of Broadcast Communications, it was "the most successful documentary produced by public television at the time...Nearly 9% of all U.S. households tuned in to watch the first episode, and an average of 9.7 million Americans watched each of the 13 episodes. A second showing of the documentary in the summer of 1984 garnered roughly a 4% share in the five largest television markets."[7]

The second program was another documentary about Vietnam, *Television's Vietnam: The Real Story*, which aired June 26 and 27, 1985. Hollywood screen star Charlton Heston narrated it. Then–Oklahoma State University professor Peter C. Rollins wrote and directed it. Reed Irvine's Accuracy in Media (AIM) raised the money for it.

Irvine had formed AIM in 1969, a "grassroots citizens watchdog of the news media that critiques botched and bungled news stories and sets the record straight on important issues that have received slanted coverage."[8] Almost always, AIM targets centrist and so-called liberal media outlets, contending that their perceived slant disfavors the political conservative view and presents an inaccurate take on events and history. The film was Irvine's idea, a rebuttal to *Vietnam: A Television History*. He said the award-winning program was filled with "inaccuracies, a lot of errors."[9] Irvine was a former economist in the Far East Section of the Federal Reserve's Division of International Finance.[10] He had friends in high Republican Party circles, such as Ronald Reagan's White House. Irvine also had a friend in fellow Republican William J. Bennett, then-chairman of the National Endowment for the Humanities, soon after Reagan's secretary of education. For his friend, Bennett dipped into an "emergency fund he controlled without going through the endowment's council."[11] Before Bennett headed the endowment, its council had given the makers of *Vietnam: A Television History* $1.2 million.[12]

Before AIM's *Television's Vietnam: The Real Story* was produced, the organization waged a public campaign to drive home its claims, among others, that the PBS series had wrongly portrayed Ho Chi Minh as a Vietnamese nationalist and patriot who led the fight for independence. On July 27–28, 1984, for example, C-SPAN aired part of that campaign, a panel discussion by Vietnam experts about the documentary's alleged flaws.[13] If Irvine did not pioneer this type of press criticism activism—banging a steady drumbeat to galvanize public opinion, rather than restricting criticism to commentary in publication and broadcast— he certainly made more effective use of it than previous press critics, establishing a tactic that would be mimicked by subsequent media watchdog organizations. He won endorsement from the White House for his rebuttal documentary. The film premiered there on December 13, 1984, with "Heston, Assistant Secretary of Defense James Webb, and John Agresto," National Endowment for the Humanities Chairman William Bennett's special assistant.[14] PBS executives had declined an invitation to attend the special screening.[15] According to Michael Massing, a *Columbia Journalism Review* contributing editor, Reagan saw the film and wrote a note to Heston praising the film as "just great and is something all Americans should see."[16]

"Vietnam: Op/Ed," a special edition of *Inside Story*, was the largest of the matryoshka-like containers. *Inside Story* was Hodding Carter III's award-winning media criticism series. Now this largest of the containers, which aired in prime time on June 26 and 27, 1985, offered four segments: "a 20-minute introduction, AIM's 57-minute *Television's Vietnam: The Real Story*, an interview with *Inside Story* producer Joseph M. Russin, and a panel discussion that" included "representatives of PBS, *Inside Story* and AIM, as well as news executives, scholars and consultants from military and news organizations."[17] It was a two-hour program.

Earlier that June, Irvine sought to rally the troops—AIM subscribers—to make his rebuttal documentary a cause célèbre, a tactic adopted by media-monitoring groups launched years after AIM.

> You can help generate interest in the program by writing a letter to your local paper praising PBS (Public Broadcasting Service) for showing the program on June 26. (Be sure to mention the date and the fact that the program will be shown in prime time—9:00 to 11:00 P.M. in most places, but the time may vary). Point out that this should serve as an example to the private television networks, encouraging them to provide greater access to critics of their programs. Suggest that this is a function that public broadcasting, which is paid for out of tax dollars, should perform, since it has been especially tasked by Congress to give both sides of controversial issues. Urge people to watch the program.[18]

Irvine also told the AIM subscribers to "expect to see our film attacked and PBS criticized for airing it."[19] Steve Daley of the *Chicago Tribune,* among others, fulfilled Irvine's expectation: "There is little to AIM's so-called analysis beyond the sort of jingoistic tub-thumping that got America mired in Vietnam in the first place. But there is panic loose at PBS, and watching two hours of it on a Wednesday night is disheartening stuff indeed."[20]

Those involved in the original *Vietnam: A Television History* took great umbrage at the June 26 airing. Peter McGhee was program manager for national productions at Boston's WGBH-TV, the outlet that had produced the award-winning documentary. According to McGhee, the AIM-produced film was "an obvious smear; it was a bad idea to put it on the air in any form, and it sets a terrible precedent for PBS, because it means we now no longer have a standard to appeal to."[21]

Yet, in the estimation of *Time*'s Zoglin, *Television's Vietnam*

> cannot be completely dismissed. It has marshaled its own cadre of authorities to help make a case that the Vietnam series, among other things, inaccurately portrayed North Vietnamese Leader Ho Chi Minh as a benign nationalist rather than a ruthless Communist; denigrated the South Vietnamese government and people; overstated the extent of drug abuse and morale problems among U.S. soldiers in Viet Nam; and underplayed the brutality of the Communist regimes that took over in Southeast Asia after the U.S. departure. *The Inside Story* analysis lends credence to some of these complaints, though it also points out several factual errors and oversimplifications in the AIM program.[22]

"Vietnam: Op/Ed" was a highly unusual two hours of PBS programming. Before the June 1985 airings, there had not been a program quite like it, a program that allowed such a lengthy rebuttal to another PBS program. In his book *War and Television,* University of Chicago history professor Bruce Cumings echoed the complaint of one faction of critics who interpreted "Vietnam: Op/Ed" as a dangerous capitulation by PBS executives to political pressure.

> PBS apparently did so in deference to "balanced" programming. This is an odd, interior, auto-induced damage, because implicitly PBS equated itself and its own laboriously produced film with AIM and its ludicrous conception of "the real story." But what this remarkable departure from independent, self-assured programming really did was certify the prison-house of our politics: it stretches from a WGBH which can give us Vietnam in wonderful footage, a commendable range of interviews and liberal pablum by way of interpretation, to an AIM interested above all in polemics and censorship, giving us a "Vietnam" that no honest person can countenance.[23]

Another way of interpreting PBS's "rare, if unprecedented"[24] concession to AIM is to score it as a victory for a citizen's media watchdog organization. Here, AIM's campaign led to a programming change consistent with PBS's own standards of balanced presentation of controversial programs. Thus, by that measure alone, AIM is an effective press critic. Riding the crest of the Reagan revolution, AIM was at the height of its efficacy in the mid-1980s. By that period, its founder Irvine met regularly with mainstream media news executives, penned a syndicated news column, appeared as an authority on talk shows, and mobilized AIM's subscribers to flood media organizations with complaints, infuriating many editors and reporters. He was dogged. For instance, PBS vice president for news and public affairs programming Barry Chase refused to air a sequel to *Television's Vietnam: The Real Story*, called *Television's Vietnam: The Impact of Media*, in late 1985. "Accuracy in Media, which holds strong, philosophically partisan views concerning the performance of the press is, frankly, suspect as a regular producer of informational programs on PBS," Chase wrote Rollins, the film's writer and director.[25] Undaunted, Irvine offered PBS stations free copies of the second rebuttal, secured another preview at the White House, and eventually "more than 150 PBS affiliates agreed to air it."[26]

Irvine pioneered the concept, the operation, and the tactics of a citizen media watchdog group, a type of press criticism that spawned several imitators on the left and the right of the political spectrum. Such influence is another measure of a press critic's effectiveness: Irvine was a groundbreaking activist who laid down a major support beam for today's thriving right-wing press critics, spurred public debate about news media performance, and helped shape public opinion on the assertion that a great deal of the mainstream media presents news with a liberal bias.

A profile of Irvine in the *National Journal* in May 1986 took note of his organizational and marketing skills: "From only a handful of allies a few years ago, he has attracted thousands of mostly conservative supporters and contributors. If not wholly respected and admired within the journalistic community, he is nonetheless a recognizable presence, though he is identified less as the media's conscience than as a thorn in its backside."[27] Irvine, who died in 2004, often claimed he merely sought a fair shake for the politically conservative view; he was only trying to ferret out "left-wing, pro-communist and anti-anticommunist bias in the nation's newsrooms that nurtured history-making errors."[28]

The record, however, shows that sometimes his activism verged on coercion. Coercion, under the constitutional concept of public discourse, is inimical to public debate in democracy "because the very purpose of that debate is the practice of self-determination."[29] Generally, coercive speech is a threat that limits an individual's choice to a range of actions imposed by someone else, and not as varied as an individual would otherwise have.

As I argued in the "Introduction" (Chapter 1), a press critic who enjoys close ties with the state is in a position to invoke the coercive power of state censorship. Such censorship does not have to take the form of a court-ordered prior restraint. Rather, the improper threat of state censorship stems from government's authority to grant or withhold privileges to a media business on matters unrelated to the press critic's complaints. It can be a form of indirect blackmail. Let us say, for example, the federal government does not want a news organization to run a story about its possible illegal surveillance activities. The government could take the news organization to court, arguing for a restraining order, or prior restraint. That would not constitute coercive speech because the government employed means it had "a right to use for changing the threatened person's options."[30] If instead, government officials intimated that the media organization's parent company was unlikely to win approval for a proposed acquisition if it failed to suppress the story, such a statement would constitute coercive speech because it restricts the media business to "options that are worse than the other had a moral or legitimate right to expect."[31]

Consequently, Irvine's close association with the Reagan White House, gaining its imprimatur for his rebuttal film to the original PBS *Vietnam: A Television History,* raised the specter of coercion—government pressure—since Congress may authorize as much as 40 percent of the Corporation for Public Broadcasting's revenues. But Irvine had no authority to cast a vote in Congress, and thus he had no direct power to pressure PBS executives. Similarly, he made no direct threat that he would call upon the White House and other Republicans to cut off PBS funding. Consequently, his campaign against PBS was not coercive.

Though the quality of his rebuttal films is questionable, the corporation was mandated under the Public Broadcasting Act of 1967 to obtain content "with the strict adherence to objectivity and balance in all programs or series of programs of a controversial nature."[32] Additionally, the Act declares that the corporation's mission includes airing programming that "addresses the needs of unserved and underserved audiences."[33] From the view of political and cultural conservatives, the commercial networks at the time—ABC, CBS, and NBC— did not meet their needs. Irvine was not alone in his criticism of the original series, which should not come as a surprise given the highly controversial nature of U.S. involvement in the Vietnam War. The original series drew objections from veterans and Vietnamese refugees. But PBS's Chase denied that he felt

pressure from the White House to air AIM's documentary. He told *Time* magazine, "I think a response mechanism of some sort is badly needed on TV. And
there's no reason in the world why a producer ought not to respond to attacks."[34]

In a 2004 tribute to Irvine, Republican U.S. Senator Jeff Sessions of Alabama
said, "Some day, I hope that the mainstream media will lose its leftwing bias...
I hope that the work of Reed Irvine and the movement he helped launch, Americans have now accepted media bias as a fact of life. The American Society of
Newspapers published a study in 1999 that showed 78 percent of Americans
believe there is a bias in the media."[35] The findings of that study, *Examining
Our Credibility: Perspectives on the Public and the Press*,[36] do not support Sessions's
assertion that nearly 80 percent of Americans believe the news media has a
liberal bias. It is true that study found that "78 percent of U.S. adults agreed with
the assessment that there is bias in the news media,"[37] but the 78 percent of the
respondents did not attribute the bias to ideology. The respondents identified
commercialism as the key bias: 49 percent said, "They just want to sell newspaper," and 71 percent said about television, "They just want higher ratings."[38]
Nevertheless, among Irvine's ideological kin, he is perceived to have made a
major impact as a press critic.

Over the years, Irvine repeated the tale of the origins of AIM. The idea of such
a media watchdog organization, he said, grew from discussions by members of the
Washington, D.C., luncheon groups in the 1960s—including the International
Economists Club and the Arthur G. McDowell Luncheon Group, named in
honor of an anti-Communist union official—led to the creation of AIM.[39] The
members were unhappy with television news coverage of urban riots and the
1968 Democratic Convention. There were "charges of staging, and activities
on the part of the TV cameras intended to stimulate the disturbances,"[40] and
concerns that an "anti-Vietnam War message was being delivered to the public
on the nightly news."[41] When, according to Irvine, the national media were cool
to the group's request to police itself, "it seemed we would have more clout if we
had an organization behind us."[42]

About the same time, President Richard M. Nixon, Vice President Spiro
T. Agnew, and Nixon's speechwriter, Patrick J. Buchanan, launched an assault
against the national television news media. On November 13, 1969, in Des
Moines, Iowa, Agnew attacked the "instant analysis and querulous criticism" of
the national television news media, labeling them "a tiny and closed fraternity of
privileged men, elected by no one and enjoying a monopoly sanctioned and
licensed by government."[43] Buchanan recalls, "Broadcast on all three networks,
the speech was a sensation...By Monday, *Newsweek* and *Time* had the network
anchors on their covers. The issue of liberal bias cohabiting with immense media
power was on the table."[44] Later, Irvine offered, "In a sense, AIM and Agnew's
speech were on the same track; there was a lot of discontent with the way the media
was behaving."[45]

Throughout most of the 1970s, Irvine busied himself with gadflying, writing
letters to mainstream media, buying advertisements to publicize his claims, and

buying stock in media companies, such as the *New York Times*, the *Washington Post*, ABC, and NBC, allowing him and other AIM representatives to attend annual meetings. Once inside, they proposed shareholder resolutions to advance their causes.[46] In one such campaign in 1976, Irvine asked the three television networks, ABC, CBS, and NBC, to present their shareholders with a resolution recommending that management consider appointing ombudsmen for each network news department.[47] Nothing came of it. For instance, shareholders at RCA, owner of NBC in 1975, rejected AIM's motion to install an ombudsman.[48]

The *Washington Post* was a favorite and frequent target of such forays. Starting in the 1970s and continuing into the 1990s, phrases such as "Most of the session was devoted to questions or criticism of management....by Reed Irving" became almost boilerplate in the paper's news accounts of its shareholders' meeting. The paper reported that its 1977 annual shareholders' meeting "lasted more than two hours and was dominated by questioning and complaints from three sources—representatives of Accuracy in Media, Inc. (AIM), a Washington-based media watchdog organization; professional stockholder Evelyn Y. Davis, and Lester Kinsolving, an Episcopal minister, columnist and local radio commentator."[49]

The *Post* described the annual shareholders' meeting on May 10, 1978, as "a two-hour session dominated by questions and criticism about *Washington Post* reporting by half a dozen representatives of Accuracy in Media, Inc."[50] It was pretty much the same in 1981: "Most of the meeting was dominated by objection to editorial or advertising policies of *The Post* newspaper by three persons who have attended and dominated the company's annual meetings in recent years—professional stockholder Evelyn Y. Davis; Accuracy in Media Chairman Reed Irvine, whose group monitors press performance from a conservative point of view; and Lester Kinsolving, a minister and editor of his own publication."[51]

For most of the 1970s, running AIM was only a part-time job for Irving who retired from the Federal Reserve in 1977.[52] In 1975 his moonlighting as a media watchdog drew fire. A congressman asked the Federal Reserve to investigate Irvine for allegedly using a Federal Reserve form to request information from federal agencies for the purposes of gathering information for AIM, an allegation first made by the news columnist Jack Anderson.[53] The Federal Reserve, however, concluded that Irvine "did not abuse his official position."[54]

Washington Post ombudsman Charles Seib praised him in 1977: "The same logic that says the institutions of government require a vigilant and critical press must also say that the press needs vigorous criticism, including the Irvine Brand."[55] *Washington Post* editor Ben Bradlee, however, detested him, calling him in writing "a miserable, carping, retromingent vigilante,"[56] a quote Irvine displayed with pride in his office.

In 1984, AIM took on ABC over the airing of the television movie *The Day After*. The movie drama, broadcast on November 20, 1983, depicted the effects of a nuclear war involving the United States, Europe, and the Soviet Union on families and individuals in the United States. Irvine said it was "potent propaganda" for the Soviet Union and persuaded the network to include the following resolution in proxy materials sent to shareholders: "We ask the board of directors to take note of the danger that ABC's facilities may be used to disseminate Soviet propaganda and to undertake an investigation to determine whether or not this has been done in the past and to devise measures to insure that it is not done in the future."[57] ABC shareholders rejected the proposal emphatically: 23.3 million shares to 751,000.[58]

Only one minor, concrete revision of a media organization practice or policy can be traced to complaints AIM and Irvine raised at a shareholders' meeting: Donald Graham conceded that the *Washington Post* was wrong to have run an advertisement in 1999 that accused the Serbs and the Russians of practicing genocide.[59] An AIM spokeswoman adds that she is "not aware of any shareholder resolutions introduced by AIM representatives that have actually been adopted but AIM's attendance at the meetings has certainly resulted in publicity and awareness of the problems with the companies' reporting."[60] AIM, however, continues to pursue shareholder activism, though it appears to be a high-cost, low-yield tactic.

Another AIM tactic—argument *ad hominem*, illogical and though arguably unethical—yielded some success. Irvine made a habit of impugning specific reporter's patriotism or fairness by selectively reciting a reporter's personal or professional background, or making unfounded accusations of complicity with communists. An AIM Report in 2000 iterates one such accusation:

> One prominent journalist, I.F. Stone was both an intelligence collector and a disinformation agent working for the KGB. In 1992, Romerstein, Reed Irvine and Joseph Goulden, who was then with AIM, charged that Stone, an icon of the Left, was a paid Soviet agent. This was based on information obtained from Oleg Kalugin, a former KGB general who re-recruited Stone after he had broken with the Soviets in the late 1950s. *The Washington Post* and *The New York Times* denounced Romerstein, Irvine and Goulden for using information from an unreliable source, the KGB. The Venona intercepts confirmed that Stone was a paid agent, but the *Times* and the *Post* haven't reported that, nor have they apologized.[61]

But Cassandra Tate, in a 1992 *Columbia Journalism Review* article, "Who's Out to Lunch Here?" revealed, "In early September, Kalugin told several journalists attending a *Nation*-sponsored conference held in Moscow that, while he had indeed been referring to Stone in his Exeter speech, he had not meant that Stone had been a paid KGB agent—only that he had sometimes lunched on the Soviet tab. He went on to say that by 'agent' he had simply meant a useful contact, not an intelligence tool. After 1968, he said, Stone refused to let the Russians buy him any more lunches."[62]

Irvine reportedly called the ex-CBS anchorman Walter Cronkite a "Communist dupe,"[63] in 1982. Later, he denied having used those exact words, but still charged that Cronkite "'has consistently, over the years, done a number of peculiar things. After the Tet offensive he came on the air and said it was a defeat for our side even though he'd been over there and knew that not to be true.' Irvine also recalled having said of Cronkite that, 'Anyone who'd served in Moscow as a correspondent and not come back making anti-communist statements had to be under some suspicion.'"[64]

A similar personal attack against *New York Times* reporter Raymond Bonner proved successful. Within months of a campaign to discredit Bonner and his reports on the civil war in El Salvador, which AIM played a key role in stoking, management ordered him back to New York, a professional setback for Bonner.

On January 27, 1982, the *Times* ran a front-page story by Bonner about a massacre of villagers in El Mozote, El Salvador.[65] The Reagan administration and the Right supported the El Salvadorian government, and from their perspective the Leftist guerrilla forces opposing the regime were communists. Bonner's story appeared about two months before Reagan administration–backed elections were to take place in El Salvador and while the president urged Congress to vote for more money to finance U.S. military assistance there. Consequently, the Right lashed out at news media reports that cast the El Salvadorian government in a bad light. Bonner's account cited 13 peasants "who said that all these, their relatives and friends, had been killed by Government soldiers of the Atlacatl Battalion in a sweep in December."[66] The *Times* account, however, made it clear that the peasants' accusations could not be confirmed: "It is not possible for an observer who was not present at the time of the massacre to determine independently how many people died or who killed them."[67] (The *Washington Post* ran a similar account of the massacre by Alma Guillermoprieto.) Soon after, conservatives launched a campaign, denouncing the accounts of the massacre as false. It was all part of a liberal propaganda effort, they contended.

The *Wall Street Journal*'s February 19, 1982, editorial page launched the first salvo, but it did not accuse Bonner of having ulterior motives based on his past affiliations. He was "overly credulous," the *Journal*'s editorial writers argued, to accept the accounts given to him by the Leftist guerrillas engaged in a propaganda exercise. There was, however, no evidence to confirm conclusively that a massacre had occurred, the *Journal* said.[68] In contrast, the *Post*'s Guillermoprieto, the editorial said, noted that the guerillas had taken the reporters to the site with the "purpose of showing their control and providing evidence of the massacre."[69] Even the insinuations of then–*Wall Street* Deputy Editor of the Editorial Page George Melloan on the PBS *The MacNeil/Lehrer Report*—"I think some reporters tend to identify with guerrilla and revolutionary movements to some degree....this comes partly out of the tradition of American journalism to support the underdog and sometimes it goes somewhat beyond that into the genuine political orientation that is Marxist in nature, but that's in very few cases, I think"[70]—stopped short of attributing Bonner's alleged bias to his past affiliations.

In a February *AIM Report*, Irvine was not as measured in his words as the *Wall Street Journal* editorial writers. Without any evidence, he accused the reporters and their editors of, among other alleged transgressions, delaying publication "in order to try to influence President Reagan's thinking on El Salvador aid."[71] Irvine further argued,

> Reporters are supposed to be competitive, dashing to the nearest telephone or tele-
> type to get in their hot story. Here we have reporters from two rival papers who view
> the scene of what they take to be the massacre of hundreds of men, women and chil-
> dren in early January, and their stories are not run in their papers until January 27
> (*Post*) and January 28 (*Times*). If they weren't held up in Washington and New York,
> it would appear that the reporters themselves delayed the stories by mutual
> agreement.[72]

The *AIM Report*, July 1982, gives an account of a June 17 meeting "between the two top officials of *The New York Times*, Arthur Ochs Sulzberger and Sydney Gruson, and the two top officials of AIM, Reed Irvine and Murray Baron."[73] According to this account, Bonner's objectivity and the accuracy of the story were suspect because Bonner had worked with left-leaning organizations before the *New York Times* hired him.

> Mr. Irvine made the statement that Mr. Bonner had been worth a division to the
> communists in Central America. He pointed out that Bonner had a rather odd back-
> ground for a *New York Times* correspondent. He was a lawyer by training and had
> worked for Ralph Nader and Consumers Union for a time. Then Bonner showed
> up in Latin America. Unconfirmed information from two different sources indicated
> that during this period he had some connection with the Pacific News Service, a
> spin-off from the radical Institute for Policy Studies.[74]

Urging its subscribers to write Sulzberger and suggest "that he re-examine" Bonner's performance, the July 1982 *AIM Report* relies upon an unidentified "journalist who met Bonner in Bolivia" who said the Pacific News Service (PNS) had awarded a fellowship to Bonner and an unidentified State Department official who "said that he heard that Bonner had written stories for PNS under a pen name."[75] The report acknowledges that PNS denied "it employed Bonner, but if there were a connection they might what to conceal it. Before accepting that, I would prefer to learn what *The Times* knows about Bonner's means of support in the period after he left Consumers Union and before he went on the payroll of *The Times*."[76]

That August, *Times*' A.M. Rosenthal, then the executive editor, ordered Bonner transferred to New York.[77] His transfer did not seem to be the subject of news reports at that time, which might explain why the *AIM Report*'s first mention of what was later widely considered a demotion did not appear until its April 1984 issue. In that issue, AIM takes some of the credit for Bonner's transfer: "Ray Bonner, the former *New York Times* Correspondent in El Salvador who was rotated back to New York after coming under heavy criticism from AIM and the American embassy in San Salvador for his pro-guerilla reporting."[78] The report's item on Bonner resulted from AIM's dispatching backers to attend what it called a left-wing gathering in Westport, Connecticut, that March, in an effort to get Bonner to state publicly "the reasons he was recalled."[79] Rosenthal, who stepped down as the *Times* top editor in 1986, maintained that pressure from outside forces did not shape his decision to end Bonner's El Salvador coverage and Bonner, a recent hire, simply needed more training. Many saw a different motive. "He distrusted as partisan the reporting of Raymond Bonner and pulled him out of Central America," *Slate* press critic Jack Shafer wrote.[80] In his analysis of the journalism decision making involved in the El Mozote coverage, Stanley Meisler, a former *Los Angeles Times* foreign correspondent, noted, "The reassignment...was interpreted in some journalistic circles as a repudiation of Bonner and a surrender to pressures from the Reagan Administration."[81]

So what does one make of AIM's attacks and Rosenthal's reasoning now that we know Bonner's reporting was accurate, as confirmed by a Truth Commission Report in October 1992?[82] AIM's accusations—attributing the delay of the Bonner story to political motives and claiming that Bonner's reports were inaccurate because he had worked for Leftist organizations—were irresponsible, unfairly selective, and misleading. Meisler points out that editors at the *Times* and the *Post* delayed publication until they discussed the stories with their reporters. He commends such a delay because "a foreign editor, should he or she feel the slightest uneasiness about a story, has the right and, in fact, the obligation to hold up the story until satisfied that the evidence justifies the conclusions. This is especially true when the story contradicts U.S. policy and the editor knows that there are knives out there ready to carve up the story, the reporter and the newspaper."[83]

It was irresponsible at best for Irvine to publicize some of Bonner's past affiliations to make a case for the bias of his reporting while failing to note, for instance, "that he had been a Marine Corps officer in Vietnam, and all but calling him a communist agent, as *Columbia Journalism Review*'s Mike Hoyt pointed out."[84] Such an appeal to personal considerations rather than to logic or reason is little more than scurrilous Red-baiting. The fallacy of Irvine's *ad hominem* attack is that it is a non sequitur; it does not necessarily follow that a reporter given to one set of beliefs cannot fairly and accurately report on highly politically polarizing events. Since it is now known that the reporting on El Mozote was correct, apparently Bonner was capable of objectivity and fairness. Furthermore, at news outlets that adhere to objectivity, part of a news editor's obligation is to edit out editorializing in news coverage or label it so. According to Meisler, Bonner and Guillermoprieto "seemed to have amassed every available bit of information that a massacre had taken place. The reporters were also careful not to blame the government troops but to allow survivors to make such accusations. Both stories also featured denials from Salvadoran government sources."[85]

Nevertheless, under the constitutional concept of public discourse "many things done with motives that are less than admirable"[86] are nonetheless legitimate in debate about public affairs. That means, as First Amendment scholar Richard C. Post argues, "individuals must be free within public discourse from the enforcement of all civility rules."[87] And since Irvine's criticism of Bonner as a reporter for the *Times* writing about matters that are "substantively relevant to the processes of democratic self-governance,"[88] Irvine's erroneous and personal attack on Bonner is not undemocratic, however unethical and illogical it might be.

Here, the fault lies with Rosenthal, not Irvine. It was Rosenthal who undermined journalism editorial integrity at the *Times* when he took Bonner out of El Salvador in the midst of the unfounded attacks from the Right. The *Wall Street Journal* editorial page made a similar point when, in response to a *Times* columnist scolding it for its role in attacking the credibility of Bonner's report, it said, "We did not fire Mr. Bonner."[89] Neither did Irvine. Regardless of Rosenthal's disclaimers, many on both sides of the political aisle and among journalists read the transfer as an indictment against Bonner, a tacit acknowledgment that his critics' accusations had merit, and a message to other journalists to engage in self-censorship, as Meisler pointed out,

> The reassignment may have chilled El Salvador coverage. Reporters, according to Michael Massing of the *Columbia Journalism Review*, became "wary of provoking the embassy." "If they can kick out the *Times* correspondent," said one foreign correspondent in San Salvador, "you've got to be careful." A *New York Times* correspondent heading off to Latin America told Bonner, "I'm not going to get caught in the same trap that you did." The whole episode, said another *Times* foreign correspondent, "had an intimidating effect on the foreign desk."[90]

Is it appropriate for a press critic to give financial assistance to a plaintiff in a libel suit as AIM did in Dr. Carl A. Galloway's lawsuit against CBS's *60 Minutes* in 1983?[91] According to Richard Labunski's *Libel and the First Amendment: Legal History and Practice in Print and Broadcasting*, Galloway sued over a December 9, 1979, *60 Minutes* broadcast, "a segment reported by correspondent Dan Rather entitled 'It's No Accident.' It examined an insurance fraud scheme in which a number of individuals at a Los Angeles clinic, including Dr. Carl Galloway, allegedly bilked insurance companies through the use of phony medical claims."[92] AIM's $5,000 contribution to Galloway's libel action was not publicly known until the *New York Times* revealed it in a June 7, 1983, story, three days after a jury ruled in CBS's favor.[93] In a June 21, 1983, letter to the *Times*, Irvine responded,

> In her June 7 news article on the decision in the Galloway suit against CBS, Sally Bedell Smith stated that I had contributed $5,000 to Dr. Galloway. It should be made clear that the contribution was from Accuracy in Media (AIM) and not from me personally...Mrs. Smith implied that I had "an ideological ax to grind." I can't see anything ideological in the Galloway case. It is probable that AIM will also assist John Farley and Frank Possert, two former New Jersey police officers who also have a libel suit against CBS and Dan Rather, which may be going to trial before long. This is not an ideological case either. AIM is giving assistance because the financial burden of seeking redress for damage done to reputations by giant corporations such

as CBS is too heavy for individuals of modest means to bear alone...Accuracy in Media has no desire to encourage libel suits, which we view as an expensive and cumbersome way of solving the problem. We would much prefer to see the media show a greater willingness to undo the damage they have wrought by admitting their errors promptly and with good grace. We would also like to see them take greater pains to avoid the kinds of errors that lead to libel suits.[94]

Though an unorthodox tactic for a media watchdog, AIM's financial support of Galloway was not presented to CBS as a warning, but rather as a statement of fact, e.g., we will end our financial support of Galloway only when you give Galloway what he wants. Even if that had been the case, CBS has no legitimate right to limit the sources of a libel plaintiff's funding, and AIM has a legitimate right to aid such plaintiffs.

In an article in *The Nation* in 1986, Massing, citing episodes such as AIM's campaign against Bonner, made a case that the organization was losing its effectiveness: "Today, AIM's zest for venom and vendetta has reduced its credibility to an all-time low, so that even its occasional well-founded complaints go unattended."[95] After the 1980s, AIM did not pull off coups comparable to the "Vietnam: Op/Ed" nor did any more of its campaigns lead to the demotion or dismissal of a journalist. For example, AIM led an unsuccessful campaign coalition of conservatives to get CNN and its Baghdad correspondent, Peter Arnett, removed from the Gulf War in 1991. Irvine, who said CNN was aiding Saddam Hussein's propaganda war, encouraged AIM's members to pressure CNN advertisers.[96] Still, Irvine stayed in the news. He co-wrote a media column for the *Washington Times* in the 1990s, which was syndicated to some 100 papers. And he certainly was not losing clout with political conservatives in the news business. One, Joe Robinowitz, a news director of Fox's WTTG-TV in Washington, D.C., was fired after the *Washington Post* revealed that an unsent computer memo showed he had planned to consult with Irvine and others about replacing reporters because of their political views.[97] Beyond the politically conservative, Irvine still was recognized as a leading press critic, even as he insisted that the Clintons were complicit in the 1993 death of Vincent W. Foster, Jr., the deputy White House counsel, though they were cleared by several investigations.

CONCLUSION

Reed Irvine's AIM was an effective press critic because its activism led to an unprecedented program change at PBS, the reassignment of a reporter at the *New York Times*, because he pioneered the concept of the citizen media watchdog organization, marshalling the public opinion of thousands of subscribers in his campaign efforts, and because he inspired a movement. In its obituary of Irvine, the *Times* noted, "Ideologically, [AIM] paved the way for the tide of conservative talk shows, Web sites and news programming that would follow decades later."[98] L. Brent Bozell III founded another conservative media watchdog group, Media Research Center, in 1987. He credits Irvine with "inventing the field of professional conservative media criticism."[99] Finally, AIM's "Impeach Dan Rather" campaign—a petition drive to ask the CBS board of directors to impeach Dan Rather launched in early 1988—faltered, only to be reignited by conservative bloggers whose fact-checking led to Rather's resignation in March 2005. Within two weeks of the September 8, 2004, airing of the *60 Minutes Wednesday* segment "For the Record," in which CBS news reporters unwittingly presented forged documents as part of their case concerning President George W. Bush's Texas Air National Guard service, AIM members joined bloggers in a protest outside CBS News offices in Washington, D.C.

AIM editor Cliff Kincaid justifiably crowed about Dan Rather's predicament: "AIM founder Reed Irvine's 'Can Dan' campaign against Dan Rather, launched 16 years ago, appears to be on the verge of success."[100] Then in the type of overreaching rhetoric that tends to undermine AIM's credibility as responsible critic in the eyes of many, Kincaid literally claimed that CBS, and *USA Today*, had conspired to commit criminal fraud "that CBS had been caught in the middle of a criminal conspiracy that was seeking to use forged documents to bring down an American president.[101] But based on the words Kincaid used—the current attorney general—or at least the FBI—*might* have an interest in the "Rathergate" matter—his comments were not a threat even if he had connections with legal enforcement. He merely made a legal argument.

Five months later, an independent review panel, headed by Republican Dick Thornburgh, a former U.S. attorney general under George H. W. Bush, and Louis D. Boccardi, a former president and chief executive officer of the Associated Press, concluded that CBS had not adhered to basic journalistic steps consistent with accurate and fair reporting. Yet it was "not able to reach a definitive conclusion as to the authenticity of the so-called forged documents.[102] As of this March 2008 writing, no prosecutor had charged CBS with a conspiracy to commit fraud.

CHAPTER 3

Let a Thousand Bloggers Swarm

Late Tuesday morning September 21, 2004, a small band of "pajamahadeen" came out of the blogosphere and into full public view on the sidewalks of Washington, D.C. There, in front of a red brick building that houses a CBS News bureau, the pajamahadeen stood, marched, and chanted, "Hey, hey, ho, ho. Rather, Mapes and Heyward got to go!" "What did Rather know and when did he know it?" "Can Dan!"[1] A few wore even pajamas and bathrobes.[2] They were, of course, calling for the dismissals of anchorman Dan Rather, news producer Mary Mapes, and News President Andrew Heyward of CBS.

For some time, it had been fashionable for many in mainstream media (MSM) to dismiss their right-wing critics in the blogosphere as little more than lonely guys sitting at home in their pajamas, harping about trivial reporting errors and liberal conspiracies in the MSM. That is pretty much how Jonathan Klein, a former vice president of CBS News, unwisely dismissed them on a September 10 airing of *The O'Reilly Factor*: "It's an important moment because you couldn't have a starker contrast between the multiple layers of checks and balances [of the mainstream media] and a guy sitting in his living room in his pajamas writing."[3]

So blogger Jim Geraghty at the *National Review Online*, among others, reclaimed the putdown, fusing it with the word Muhjahadeen, warriors who wage jihad. "The Pajamahadeen have accomplished much, but there is still much to be done before we complete the toppling of the Sauronic Big Eye of CBS,"[4] Geraghty wrote in a September 17, 2004, "Communique to the Pajamahadeen."

What the pajamahadeen were protesting, "the important moment" Klein alluded to and the accomplishment Geraghty referenced, was the controversy swirling around the 60 *Minutes II*, later renamed 60 *Minutes Wednesday*, airing of "For the Record" on September 8, 2004. The report raised doubts about whether President George W. Bush fulfilled his obligations to the Texas Air National Guard service. The story relied to a large extent on four memos purported to be typed and written by one of Bush's guard commanders in the early 1970s, Lt. Col. Jerry Killian. Rather, the correspondent for the segment, explained their significance at the top of the segment: "Did then Lieutenant Bush fulfill all of his military commitments?. . . Tonight, we have new documents and new information on the President's military service and the first-ever interview with the man who says he pulled the strings to get young George W. Bush into the Texas Air National Guard."[5]

Blogosphere chatter about the authenticity of the Killian documents spread virus-like before the 60 *Minutes Wednesday* program ended that night at 9 P.M.[6] By the following day, right-wing bloggers' accusations and complaints generated into skilled fact checking and informed analysis about the typography of the documents, igniting, in the words of the independent review panel that later investigated CBS's handling of the report, "a raging media firestorm in print, on the air and on the Internet about the documents' authenticity."[7] That type of collaborative and rapid blogging has become known as a blog swarm.

The pajamahadeen struck swiftly and effectively. By as early as September 13, a story in the *New York Sun* offered an account of "How Four Blogs Dealt a Blow to CBS's Credibility."[8] A blogger using the pseudonym "Buckhead" first raised the issue of the letter spacing and fonts of the Killian memos to question their authenticity on the *Free Republic*'s online discussion board before the program went off the air: "In 1972 people used typewriters for this sort of thing, and typewriters used monospaced fonts. . . I am saying these documents are forgeries, run through a copier for 15 generations to make them look old."[9] (Soon after, the MSM revealed Buckhead to be Atlanta litigator Harry W. MacDougald, a Republican who helped draft a petition urging the Arkansas Supreme Court to disbar then-President Bill Clinton.[10])

On September 20, after nearly two weeks of defending the authenticity of the documents, Heyward and Rather apologized for airing the story.[11] The apologies, however, did not mollify the pajamahadeen. Conservative media watchdogs had targeted Rather as early as 1988 when Accuracy in Media (AIM) founder Reed Irvine launched a campaign to get Rather off the air.[12] They would not be sated with contrition. There was, as Geraghty urged, still much to be done. Emboldened, the pajamahadeen abandoned their keyboards—for one late morning—and took to the streets. MacDougald, aka Buckhead, was not among the pajamahadeen and others calling for the dismissals of Rather, Mapes, and Heyward on September 21. However, other Freepers—as bloggers using *FreeRepublic.com*, an online site for grassroots conservatism, are fond of referring to themselves—were. The Freepers in attendance had names gangsta rappers might envy: staytrue, BillF, sauropod, hellinahandcart, bmwcyle, tellw, Nina0113, TBP, and kristinn. *Free Republic* spokesman Kristin Taylor is kristinn; the identities of the others are unknown. In photographs of the protest posted on the *Free Republic* Web site, Taylor wore blue plaid pajamas and a red bathrobe.[13] AIM representatives joined the protest, led by AIM editor Cliff Kincaid.

The following day, CBS announced that an independent review panel consisting of Dick Thornburgh, former governor of Pennsylvania and U.S. attorney general under President Ronald Reagan and President George H. W. Bush, Louis D. Boccardi, retired president and chief executive officer (CEO) of the Associated Press, assisted by Washington, D.C.–based law firm Kirkpatrick & Lockhart Nicholson Graham LLP would conduct a probe to help identify the errors in the news gathering and actions CBS might take regarding journalists and reporting procedures.[14] (Meanwhile, the Freepers, at least three pajama-clad, returned to protest in front of CBS in Washington, D.C., on September 26.[15])

In early January 2005, CBS management followed the advice of the independent review panel that found "a widespread breakdown of fundamental processes at 60 *Minutes Wednesday*," offering six recommendations for change.[16] Management asked Senior Vice President Betsy West, who supervised CBS News primetime programs; 60 *Minutes Wednesday* Executive Producer Josh Howard; and Howard's deputy, Senior Broadcast Producer Mary Murphy, to resign. The broadcast company fired the producer of the report, Mary Mapes.[17] Rather already had announced in November that he planned to step down as anchor of the *CBS Evening News* in March 2005.[18] (Rather filed a lawsuit against CBS on September 19, 2007, seeking at least $20 million in compensatory damages, alleging, among other things, network executives had made him a "scapegoat" in an attempt to placate the Bush administration and challenging the fairness of the panel because of Thornburgh's close affiliation with the elder Bush.[19])

Never had a crowd-sourced, fact-checking campaign proven so effective at holding a news outlet accountable as it did when right-wing bloggers at *Free Republic, Instapundit, INDC Journal Blog, Allahpundit.com, Powerline.blog.com,* and *Little Green Footballs* collaborated in an investigation of Killian documents. No press criticism has led to such significant changes in a news organization's personnel, practices, and policies. The scandal many called Rathergate marked a turning point, not just for CBS, but also for the entire MSM, largely because of the potential impact of the 60 *Minutes Wednesday* report. Because CBS News went after a target as big as the U.S. president, particularly within a month before voters would go to the polls to vote to reelect him, the stakes were huge for the target, the news organization, and, to a lesser degree, the pajamahadeen. It was a pivotal moment that would determine the credibility of the president, CBS, and the pajamahadeen. In the end, the conservative bloggers won and won big. Afterward, it was clear that the MSM could no longer afford to summarily dismiss or ignore the pajamahadeen.

About three years earlier, the MSM had been warned about this shift in power between it and the public. On September 18, 2001, blogger Ken Layne announced to the MSM, then referred to as Big Media, that "we can Fact Check Your Ass. We have computers. It is not difficult to Find You Out, dig?"[20] Eerily, seven days before CBS aired "For the Record," University of Tennessee College of Law professor and blogger Glenn Harlan Reynolds of *Instapundit* wrote the following in a *Wall Street Journal* op-ed piece: "But so long as the mainstream media are lazy, and biased—and strongly in favor of a Democrat—the fact-checking and media-bypassing power of the blogosphere is likely to disproportionately favor Republicans. That's not so much a reflection on blogs, alas, as it is a reflection on big media."[21]

Bloggers, including those who post replies and queries critiquing news reports on Weblogs and discussion boards are quintessential citizen press critics. By citizen press critic I mean a news consumer or an individual whose community or self is the subject of news coverage and one who comments publicly about a news outlet's performance and content. Thus, an outlet distributing news to an international audience creates citizen press critics in other nations who presumably have a stake in the accuracy and reliability of its content. It follows then that outlets distributing content on the Web may reach a worldwide audience. Typically, citizen press critics do not need to be experts in the history, practice, and ethics of journalism, nor practitioners. It is not necessary for them to be literate if broadcast content is at issue. However, they may and often do have expertise in the particular topic or first-hand knowledge of an event covered by a news outlet.

Finally, citizen press critics need not be free of ideological or partisan bias. On the contrary, it is often their pursuit of an agenda to reform news media that propels them to engage in public dialogue about news media performance. Bloggers who raised doubts about the veracity of the Killian documents were politically conservative Republicans, and their hatred of Rather was oft repeated and well known.

In his seminal work, *Watching the Watchdog: Bloggers as the Fifth Estate*, communication scholar Stephen D. Cooper identifies four genres of media criticism practiced in the blogosphere: accuracy, framing, agenda-setting/gatekeeping, and journalistic practices: "Blog criticism of accuracy concerns factual evidence mentioned in reporting. Framing concerns the interpretations or meanings of facts and events. Agenda-setting/gatekeeping concerns the newsworthiness or importance of particular events and issues. Criticism of journalistic practices concerns the working methods of professional journalists and news outlets."[22] Arguably, the strongest case a press critic can make against a mainstream news outlet is to show that a report is most likely false because key documentary or human sources relied upon by the reporter lack credibility, were erroneous, or were fraudulent. Generally, in an objective report, a news consumer should be able to verify information a reporter asserts is factual. Still, accuracy audits used by newspapers in the 1970s show "the proportion of stories with errors has ranged from 40 percent to 60 percent."[23] Nevertheless, "accuracy is the foundation of media credibility."[24]

Accordingly, the general policy of "CBS News Standards" states, "Credibility is essential to every news organization. It is a bond between us and our viewers and listeners. Nothing erodes the bond faster than viewers or listeners thinking that we have an axe to grind or that we are beholden to anyone or anything other than fairness and the truth."[25] Accusations of bias—distorting facts or slanting the presentation of a set of facts to favor an individual, ideology, place, class, or political party—hold little weight when a news report's sources of information are credible. Critics may still accuse an outlet of framing the facts in a biased way, but news organizations typically do not acknowledge such complaints as meritorious. In contrast, when the pajamahadeen collectively made a compelling case against the legitimacy of the Killian documents based on verifiable information, the MSM outlets investigated their claims. For instance, two of the four experts first consulted by 60 Minutes Wednesday, Emily Will and Linda James, told ABC News' World News Tonight on September 14 that CBS journalists ignored the concerns they raised about the legitimacy of the Killian documents.[26] Similar reporting by CBS's rivals intensified the pressure on those involved in the September 8 broadcast to produce more evidence to support their claims.

Though Rather served as the correspondent for that broadcast, his direct involvement was limited during the bulk of an investigation started in 1999, dropped after the 2000 presidential election, and resumed in mid-2004. Mapes and her staff conducted the overwhelming majority of the reporting. As the review panel noted, many other news organizations and reporters pursued the same investigation of Bush's service in the Air National Guard during the Vietnam era.[27] About a week before the broadcast, Mapes had the following key sources: Ben Barnes, the former speaker of the Texas House of Representatives, former lieutenant governor of Texas, and a Democrat who said he gave Bush preferential treatment by recommending him to the head of the Texas Air National Guard. Lieutenant Colonel Burkett (Ret.) of the Texas Army National Guard (TexANG) gave the documents believed to be from the files of Lieutenant Colonel Killian, Bush's commander when he served from May 1968 to October 1973. (The broadcast failed to reveal that Burkett was the source of the documents. The review panel noted that previous reporting by other news organizations showed Burkett to be an extremely unreliable source.)[28] From September 2 to 8, Mapes and her staff scurried to confirm the authenticity of a total of six documents that Burkett gave them from September 2 and 5. The independent review panel pointed to this last minute rush as one of the serious deficiencies in the investigative reporting and vetting process:

> Attempts at this confirmation included: an on-camera interview of one person who had served in the TexANG in an administrative position but had no personal knowledge of the documents or Lieutenant Bush's service; seeking the opinions of four handwriting and document examiners; discussing the documents with Lieutenant Colonel Killian's former commanding officer over the telephone; speaking with

Lieutenant Colonel Killian's widow; and providing the documents to the White House for comment.[29]

Before Buckhead aka MacDougald wrote the 47th posting about the CBS program, the first to raise the point about the typewriter fonts,[30] the preceding postings consisted of rants, sarcasm, invectives, and conspiracy theories. Then and later, similar postings flooded the right-wing blogosphere. But a more restrained, fact-based query, offering verifiable evidence, persisted that would prove effective in raising legitimate doubts about the documents, prompting the MSM to pick up the inquiry within two days of the broadcast. One can reasonably disagree with their conclusion that the documents were forged. Notably, the independent review panel failed to reach a conclusion about the documents' genuineness.[31] The bloggers' reporting and analysis, however, certainly demonstrated that recognized handwriting and computer typography experts could be located within four days and that their conclusions should have given pause to a conscientious investigative reporter, if merely for self-preservation.

Powerline.blog.com—penned by conservatives John H. Hinderaker, a Minneapolis litigator, another lawyer in the same city, Scott W. Johnson, and Washington, D.C., attorney Paul Mirengoff, all Dartmouth College graduates—posted a 2,779-word analysis and report at 7:51 A.M., the next day. Johnson was the author and the crowd-sourced report included a copy of a "genuine typed memo of September 6, 1973" juxtaposed with a copy of one of CBS's memos: "On the left is Killian's genuine typed memo of September 6, 1973. No superscript, and an authentically 1970's [sic] look. On the right is CBS's fake August 18 memo. Note the superscript, and the generally modern, word-processed look."[32]

That afternoon *Powerline.blog.com* and *Little Green Footballs* blog linked, allowing them to share their information. According to *The Weekly Standard,* Charles Johnson, who runs *Little Green Footballs,* "had seen both Buckhead and *Power Line* and decided to run a test. A desktop publishing pioneer and webpage designer in his day job, Johnson opened Microsoft Word and without changing any of the default settings—tabs, margins, font—created an eerily similar replica of one of the memos in just a few minutes, and posted it at 1:24 P.M."[33] The *New York Sun* also credits Johnson with posting "the first of what would be almost a dozen tests over the next few days on the CBS documents, all of which showed remarkable similarities between the allegedly typewritten documents and documents produced by Microsoft Word."[34]

During the afternoon following the broadcast, William Ardolino tracked down a forensic document examiner named Dr. Philip D. Bouffard, who according to Ardolino said, "he's pretty certain that it's a fake."[35] In a cautiously written report, Ardolino offered the expert's qualifications, including that, among other credentials, "Dr. Bouffard is one of the top two experts in forensic document examination (regarding typefaces) in the country."[36] He concluded, "I hesitate to render verdicts, but based on an initial visual analysis by one of the country's foremost forensic document analysts that specializes in old typefaces, it looks like CBS was duped."[37]

On September 12, another blogger, Joseph M. Newcomer, insisting that he was not a George Bush fan, but a pioneer in electronic typesetting—he cited a co-authored 1972 work as credentials, and his Web site offered other verifiable professional achievements and affiliations—posted an illustrated, 7,000-word analysis. He concluded that the documents were forgeries.

> This letter concentrates only on the raw technology of the fonts and printing. It does not address many of the issues others on the Internet have raised, such as the incorrect usage of military titles and abbreviations, incorrect formatting relative to prevailing 1972 military standards, etc. I am not qualified to comment on these. All I can say is that the technology that produced this document was not possible in 1972 in the sort of equipment that would have been available outside publishing houses, and which required substantial training and expertise to use, and it replicates exactly the technologies of Microsoft Word and Microsoft TrueType Fonts.[38]

CBS had its defenders in the blogosphere, notably "Hunter" on *Dailykos.com*.[39] And some Democrats, as George Stephanopoulos reported, wondered whether the documents were part of a Republican setup.[40] As part of its effort to verify, CBS gave the documents to the White House before the broadcast.[41] So the theory was that the White House, believing the memos were dubious, sent them to Republican operatives, but did not tell CBS of its suspicions.

That conspiracy theory could be summarily dismissed if not for the fact that the Atlanta litigator MacDougald, a longtime Republican activist, asserted that the memos were forgeries before the program went off the air and did not reveal himself to be Buckhead until after the *Los Angeles Times* outed him, as Mary Mapes notes in her book, *Truth and Duty: The Press, the President, and the Privilege of Power*.[42] Before the publication of Mapes's book, MacDougald offered a lengthy response on *FreeRepublic.com* to those who questioned whether he received the documents in advance of the broadcast. He said he could spot the alleged flaws in the memos because of his interest in computers dating back to 1979 and because of his handling of thousands of documents during his career as a lawyer: "I relied upon no one and nothing other than what I already knew and what I saw when I looked at the documents."[43]

Beyond Rathergate, some blogosphere denizens contend that anonymous and pseudonymous bloggings are unethical. The argument holds that anyone engaged in public discussions as well as the targets of public critiques or accusations should have enough knowledge about the motives and affiliations of discussants so as to feel free from possible coercion. It is far too easy, those who call for full transparency argue, for a participant in a blog discussion to spew hate, lies, threaten harm, or post another blogger's home and office number with intent to harass. *Powerline.blog.com*'s Hinderaker, who defended MacDougald— "He preferred anonymity for professional reasons..."[44]—experienced just how insidious blog swarming can be. Hinderaker posted an item defending James Dale Guckert, who used the pseudonym Jeff Gannon when he worked as a reporter gaining access to White House press conferences. Guckert had worked as a gay prostitute, and his employer Talon News had close ties to GOPUSA (Grand Old Party USA), liberal bloggers revealed.[45] In response to Hinderaker's defense of Guckert, bloggers published his office phone number and e-mail address, "prompting a deluge of harassing phone calls and emails."[46] When Hinderaker published an item saying left-wing bloggers should stop assaulting a White House reporter alleged to have worked as a gay prostitute, his blog brethren went on the assault, publishing his work phone number and prompting a deluge of harassing phone calls and e-mails. "My secretary was crying" because callers kept swearing at her, he says. "Then we started getting calls at the house. My wife wanted to hire a bodyguard."[47]

To cope with such misconduct, Tim O'Reilly, CEO of Sebastopol, California's O'Reilly Media, and others attending the O'Reilly Emerging Tech Conference in 2007, proposed a "Bloggers Code of Conduct." O'Reilly proposed that those who run blogs should consider eliminating anonymous comments: "When people are anonymous, they will often let themselves say or do things that they would never do when they are identified. There are important contexts in which anonymity is important, for example, for political speech in repressive regimes. But in most contexts, accountability via identity changes how people behave. Requiring a valid email address for comments won't prevent people who want to hide their identity from doing so, but it's one more indication that accountability is valued."[48]

No one, however, could reasonably construe MacDougald's pseudonymous posting as a call for others to threaten CBS journalists. He merely related a set of alleged facts about typewriters and computers, from which he concluded that the documents were forgeries. But notions of accountability argue that he should have disclosed his name or political background given his affiliation with two prominent conservative legal groups, the Federalist Society and the Southeastern Legal Foundation, and his role in drafting the Foundation's petition in 1998 that led to the five-year suspension of Clinton's Arkansas law license for giving misleading testimony in the Paula Jones sexual-harassment case. Had the 60 Minutes Wednesday report stood up under scrutiny, an anonymous accuser would not have had to issue an apology or acknowledge an error. The blogger could adopt a new online persona and continue to post wild accusations, damaging the reputations of others. Moreover, how does one know that veiled bloggers are not assuming multiple pseudonyms to generate a misleading appearance of public consensus?

Yet under a constitutional concept of democratic discourse, anonymous and pseudonymous postings are generally legitimate and in certain circumstances vital to the exercise of free speech. The U.S. Supreme Court has long held that anonymous speech has an expressive value both to the speaker and to society that outweighs public interest in disclosure under most circumstances.

Most recently, in *McIntyre v. Ohio Elections Commission,* the Court ruled the freedom to publish anonymously is protected by the First Amendment, extending that protection to the advocacy of political causes.[49] The case involved a woman who distributed campaign literature that did not contain her name or address. She signed leaflets as "Concerned Parents and Tax payers."[50] Though it did not address bloggers, the Court's reasoning is instructive in understanding why bloggers who use pseudonyms pose little danger to legitimate public discourse in a democracy. Noting that the United States and Europe have long traditions of published writers using pseudonyms, the Court turned to the use of pseudonyms by advocates in the seminal U.S. Constitutional debates.

> That tradition is most famously embodied in the *Federalist Papers,* authored by James Madison, Alexander Hamilton, and John Jay, but signed "Publius." Publius's opponents, the Anti-Federalists, also tended to publish under pseudonyms: prominent among them were "Cato," believed to be New York Governor George Clinton; "Centinel," probably Samuel Bryan or his father, Pennsylvania judge and legislator George Bryan; "The Federal Farmer," who may have been Richard Henry Lee, a Virginia member of the Continental Congress and a signer of the Declaration of Independence; and "Brutus," who may have been Robert Yates, a New York Supreme Court justice who walked out on the Constitutional Convention.[51]

The Court reasoned that anonymity shields an individual from retribution or social ostracism for voicing an unpopular view, revealing secret wrongdoing, breaking a taboo, or advocating dissent. It acknowledged, however, that the prevention of fraud and libel is a legitimate social interest that should be weighed against free speech interests when considering the value of anonymous speech. But, it said, the state law in question went too far by requiring advocates to provide their true identities: "The right to remain anonymous may be abused when it shields fraudulent conduct. But political speech by its nature will sometimes have unpalatable consequences, and, in general, our society accords greater weight to the value of free speech than to the dangers of its misuse."[52]

Even if MacDougald were the operative in a Karl Rove–engineered plot, would it have made a difference regarding the credibility of MacDougald's assertion? Not likely. The motives of the Freepers and the pajamahadeen were transparent regardless of their use of names such as staytrue, BillF, sauropod, hellinahandcart, bmwcyle, tellw, Nina0113, TBP, kristinn, or Buckhead. They wallow in their contempt for the so-called liberal media and Dan Rather, in particular, to such a degree that they attribute to Rather and Mapes the worst motives, despite the fact that CBS gave the memos to the White House in advance of the broadcast. (If Rather and Mapes were so poisoned against Bush and Republicans, what was the devious purpose behind giving the White House a chance to make its case to CBS to prevent the broadcast?)

Operating at such a fever pitch, MacDougald and others who used colorful pseudonyms did not need the White House to orchestrate a campaign to discredit CBS's report. Moreover, MacDougald's assertion was tested by other bloggers, and anyone disputing their findings was free to conduct their own tests, post their findings, and make countervailing arguments in the MSM or in the blogosphere. Quoting a New York court from an earlier case, the Court in *McIntyre* described an obligation "the common man" has in sizing up the merits of an argument taking place in a public forum under a Constitutional concept of democratic discourse: "People are intelligent enough to evaluate the source of an anonymous writing. They can see it is anonymous. They know it is anonymous. They can evaluate its anonymity along with its message, as long as they are permitted, as they must be, to read that message. And then, once they have done so, it is for them to decide what is 'responsible,' what is valuable, and what is truth."[53]

All the same, Rather's lawsuit against CBS and its owner Viacom raises the possibility that CBS and Viacom were coerced into taking action against their employees. They claim, in part,

> In fact, the Panel was not selected by CBS with a desire that it be independent. It was designed to give the appearance of fairness, when in fact its conclusions were preordained to find fault with the Broadcast and those persons responsible for it, and provide a basis for CBS to: diminish the career and reputation of such persons; divert public attention from the accurate facts reported in the Broadcast concerning President Bush's service (and lack thereof) in the TexANG during the Vietnam War; and enable CBS and Viacom to curry favor with the White House by demonstrating its intent to minimize CBS News' criticism thereof.[54]

As of this March 2008 writing, the author had no knowledge of the truth or falsity of Rather's claims. But even if the claims are true, there is no evidence that the White House pulled the strings of the pajamahadeen. Consequently, their campaign cannot be seen as coercive.

The panel found that *60 Minutes Wednesday* failed to verify the documents, did not interview the original source of the documents, and provided a vociferous defense of the story without adequately probing the questions that were being raised about its accuracy. That defense, the panel found, included inaccurate press releases. The panel ascribed the failure to follow fundamental newsgathering and verification procedures at CBS to "the combination of a new *60 Minutes Wednesday* management team, great deference given to a highly respected producer and the network's news anchor, competitive pressures, and a zealous belief in the truth of the segment."[55]

Did a liberal bias drive Rather, Mapes, and others to rush the story out in time to affect the election? The panel said certain actions could support such charges, but it also said it "cannot conclude that a political agenda at *60 Minutes Wednesday* drove either the timing of the airing of the segment or its content."[56] In fact, Rather and *60 Minutes* made similar mistakes on a nonpolitical probe, the December 9, 1979, *60 Minutes* "It's No Accident," that led one of the targets,

Dr. Carl A. Galloway, to file a libel action in 1980.[57] Rather and his producer failed to get authentication of a signature (Galloway's) on medical records Galloway said were phony. At trial, Rather testified "he never had any doubt about the authenticity of the doctor's signature on the bogus medical report."[58] Rather and his producer also left several unreturned messages with Galloway, a failure Rather considered an admission of guilt by Galloway, though he never met or talked to Galloway while preparing the report.[59] On June 6, 1983, a Los Angeles jury ruled in favor of Rather, 60 Minutes, and CBS. By a 10–2 vote the jury concluded that the news organization's reporting and verification efforts did not constitute reckless disregard for the truth, the liability standard a public figure must prove in a libel case under New York Times v. Sullivan.[60] In effect, the jury voted its approval of Rather and 60 Minutes' reporting and verification procedures. The 60 Minutes "It's No Accident" broadcast shows that Rather and 60 Minutes did not need political or ideological motivation to broadcast a story that was not thoroughly verified. But libel standards of culpability mean little in the court of public opinion in which bloggers prosecute.

Based on the panel's findings CBS President Leslie Moonves dismissed Mapes, largely because she failed to tell "the people in charge of vetting the piece... that while four people were given some documents to authenticate the handwriting and the typography, two experts were discounted when they raised objections, and all four experts warned that documents could not be authenticated from Xeroxed copies... only one expert had tentatively authenticated only one signature which seemed to match a known sample."[61] Howard, Murphy, and West were asked to resign, and Esther Kartiganer, senior producer in charge of reading scripts and unedited transcripts, was offered a reassignment.[62] Moonves quickly put in place eight reforms, including the creation of a position of Senior Vice President of Standards and Special Projects as the panel had recommended.[63]

Meanwhile, as the blogosphere was sizing up the panel's findings and CBS's reaction to them in early 2005, Rony Abovitz posted a report on January 28 that led to CNN's chief news executive Eason Jordan's resignation on February 11.

Abovitz is not a member of the pajamahadeen. He is a biotech company founder and, in his words, an independent thinker "with a pretty liberal outlook"[64] and "definitely not a Republican."[65] Call him "Joe Citizen" blogger, or, as the American Journalism Review (AJR) did, "an accidental blogger and an accidental media critic."[66] AJR also described him as a "34-year-old, babyfaced, tousle-haired self described geek, who sees himself as neither liberal nor conservative and is suspicious of power in general."[67] Abovitz denies that he sought Jordan's dismissal. Regarding his intent when he filed his January 28, 2005, posting on ForumBlog.org that incited right-wing bloggers to swarm, leading to Jordan's fall, Abovitz says, "I had no idea that this was going to be a big story."[68] Still, Washington Post media critic Howard Kurtz distinguished Abovitz's feat as unique. Noting that the impact of previous blog swarms was bolstered by the MSM's coverage, Kurtz observed that Jordan's fate was sealed almost solely by the pressure applied by "a relentless campaign by online critics."[69]

Abovitz attended the World Economic Forum conference that month in Davos, Switzerland, because the Forum had selected him as one of its 29 technology pioneers. According to a news release, the Forum provides "a collaborative framework for the world's leaders to address global issues, engaging particularly its corporate members in global citizenship."[70] It selected Abovitz's Z-KAT company, a leader in the field of computer-assisted minimally invasive surgery, as a pioneer. Forum organizers invited attendees to blog the event. But technically, Abovitz should not have filed the 1,093-word report on what he witnessed at the "Will Democracy Survive the Media?" session. The *AJR* and the *New York Times* reported that the session was "off the record"; the press was barred from reporting on it.[71]

As an ethical matter, journalists should generally honor such a request. But there are exceptions. The Society of Professional Journalists' Code of Ethics Conduct, for example, advises journalists to "[r]ecognize that private people have a greater right to control information about themselves than do public officials and others who seek power, influence or attention. Only an overriding public need can justify intrusion into anyone's privacy."[72] Perhaps that explains why journalists attending the session did not report Jordan's remarks.

Abovitz, however, chose to believe, according to the *New York Times*, that the MSM journalists there did not report Jordan's remarks "because journalists wanted to protect their own."[73] Abovitz insists he knew nothing about reporting restrictions. Furthermore, according to Abovitz, the cameras and lights at the session indicated to him that news media were covering it.[74]

Bloggers could post comments for a lifetime and never have the impact Abovitz did from his first posting. According to Abovitz's posting, David R. Gergen of Harvard University's John F. Kennedy School of Government moderated a panel discussion in which "Richard Sambrook, the worldwide director of BBC radio, U.S. Congressman Barney Frank, Abdullah Abdullah, the Minister of Foreign Affairs of Afghanistan," and Jordan participated. "The audience was a mix of journalists, WEF attendees (many from Arab countries), and a US Senator from Connecticut, Chris Dodd."[75] Abovitz's lead read, "This fiery topic became a real nightmare today for the Chief News Executive of CNN at what was an initially very mild discussion at the World Economic Forum titled 'Will Democracy Survive the Media?'"[76] In the third paragraph, he got to the core of the controversy.

> During one of the discussions about the number of journalists killed in the Iraq War, Eason Jordan asserted that he knew of 12 journalists who had not only been killed by US troops in Iraq, but they had in fact been targeted...Due to the nature of the forum, I was able to directly challenge Eason, asking if he had any objective and clear evidence to backup these claims, because if what he said was true, it would make Abu Ghraib look like a walk in the park. David Gergen was also clearly disturbed and shocked by the allegation that the U.S. would target journalists, foreign or U.S. He had always seen the U.S. military as the providers of safety and rescue for all reporters. Eason seemed to backpedal quickly, but his initial statements were

backed by other members of the audience (one in particular who represented a worldwide journalist group). The ensuing debate was (for lack of better words) a real "sh—storm"...To be fair (and balanced), Eason did backpedal and make a number of statements claiming that he really did not know if what he said was true, and that he did not himself believe it. But when pressed by others, he seemed to waver back and forth between what might have been his beliefs and the realization that he had created a kind of public mess.[77]

The incendiary nature of Jordan's remarks would appear obvious in the context of the Iraq War and highly partisan politics at home. Worse, two years earlier, Jordan wrote in the *New York Times* "that he saw and heard awful things that he could not report [when Saddam Hussein was in power] because doing so would have jeopardized lives of Iraqis, particularly those on CNN's Baghdad staff."[78] Some journalism ethicists defended Jordan's decision. Even *Fox News* media analyst Eric Burns said "he 'commended' Mr. Jordan, if he had indeed protected innocent people from harm."[79] But to some conservative bloggers, Jordan's earlier remarks marked him as anti-American. Jim Geraghty's February 1, 2005, posting on the Davos comments reveals such a prejudice: "Yes, this is the same Eason Jordan who wrote in *The New York Times* that CNN reporters in Baghdad witnessed abuses, including torture of Iraqis by Saddam's secret police, and did not report this to viewers in order to keep CNN's Baghdad bureau open."[80] An accurate account of the op-ed piece would have included Jordan's claim to want to keep Iraqi staffers from harm. Geraghty insinuated that Jordan is guilty of treason. Other bloggers were explicit in raising such an accusation.

Under the ethical principles guiding most of the MSM news outlets adhering to objectivity, patriotism is not a valid criterion for judging media performance. Journalists' first loyalty is to citizens, not the government. Professional ethical codes advise them to seek the truth and avoid siding with factions. Accordingly, ethicists James B. Murphy, Stephen J. A. Ward, and Aine Donovan argue, "Even in times of war and insecurity, responsible journalism must not allow a narrow patriotism to undermine its commitment to truth telling. Journalists best fulfill their civic role by adopting the perspective of a democratic patriotism. Democratic patriotism requires journalists to provide critical perspectives and tough-minded reportage to help the public evaluate military policy and calls for war."[81] Many of the MSM organizations, however, have failed to articulate these standards to the public. Worse, some news television networks engaged in flag waving during the first months of the invasion of Iraq. Consider the anchor people's American flag pins. Others simply never made the case emphatically enough even as they were accused of treason by right-wing bloggers.

Geraghty, blogging for the *National Review,* was one of the first bloggers in the United States to post comments about the brewing controversy over Jordan's comments. In a February 2, 2005, 10:14 A.M., posting, Geraghty offers, "Maybe I'll be proven wrong, but I suspect Eason Jordan's comments will be the next big blog-storm."[82]

In a February 1 blog, Roger L. Simon asked, "Is This Treason?" He, however, concluded, "Well, I guess he stopped short of treason by backpedaling (at least as far as I understand the law), but I wonder what CNN's advertisers will think of their continued sponsorship of this network with its bizarre Chief News Executive and his vicious and obviously unsubstantiated allegations. If I were they, I'd be running for the hills."[83]

Glenn Reynolds's February 1, 2005, posting on his *Instapundit.com* was succinct and apparently accurate, alluding to Jordan's 2003 revelation: "HAVING KEPT HIS MOUTH SHUT on things he knew were true, it would behoove Eason Jordan not to blather about things that he doesn't know are true. Really."[84]

According to *Powerlineblog.com*, CNN tried to quell the brewing discontent by e-mailing the following statement to bloggers on February 2: "Many blogs have taken Mr. Jordan's remarks out of context. Eason Jordan does not believe the U.S. military is trying to kill journalists. Mr. Jordan simply pointed out the facts: While the majority of journalists killed in Iraq have been slain at the hands of insurgents, the Pentagon has also noted that the U.S. military on occasion has killed people who turned out to be journalists. The Pentagon has apologized for those actions."[85]

Meanwhile, blogger Michelle Malkin, another conservative, kept pushing the story. In at least 12 postings from February 6 to February 11, she echoed the comments of most conservative bloggers: The Forum should release the transcript and video of the discussion. The MSM refuses to cover the controversy. What did Jordan really say? CNN is biased against the US military.[86] Combined, such queries and accusations added up to one allegation: The Forum, the MSM, and CNN, in particular, were engaged in a vast conspiracy to hide the truth. Here is how Hugh Hewitt put it in *The Weekly Standard* on February 3, 2005:

> The account of Jordan's remarks—including his backpedaling and the crowd's reactions—is available at *ForumBlog*. Thus far no major media outlet has demanded an accounting of Jordan, but the idea that a major figure from American media traffics in such outlandish and outrageous slanders on the American military deserves attention and criticism, not indifference. It is no wonder that anti-American propaganda gains traction in the world when American news executives set fantasies such as this one in motion. If Jordan had no grounds for peddling this grassy-knoll garbage, he should be fired. If he did have even the flimsiest of grounds, he ought to share his evidence and let the public decide whether his judgment is as flawed as it was when he covered for Saddam all those years.[87]

Abovitz believes CNN and the Forum mishandled the matter by trying to "whitewash" it.[88] He says if CNN management believed the tape could clear him by showing that he misspoke, "it seems weird that they did not want to play the tape."[89] The Forum, however, was under no obligation to release the video or transcript because it is a private entity that had promised participants that the session was "off the record." The *Financial Times* (London) explained that the "session was operating under the 'Chatman House rule'—you can tell anyone what you heard there, but not who said it."[90] And some participants, notably Congressman Barney Frank, confirmed the reliability of Abovitz's report to Malkin that Eason initially said some in the U.S. military deliberately targeted journalists and that he quickly modified his statement. According to Malkin's Feb. 7 posting, Frank explained "that [Jordan] wasn't saying it was the policy of the American military to target journalists, but that there may have been individual cases where they were targeted by younger personnel who were not properly disciplined."[91]

As for the MSM's alleged conspiracy to intentionally ignore the controversy, CNN and Jordan mismanaged the crisis by not publicly responding until February 8, the February 2 e-mail to bloggers notwithstanding. Yet, there is little evidence of a willful blackout of the controversy by the MSM. According to a search of a LexisNexis news database, the *Pittsburgh Post-Gazette* and the *Riverside (CA) Press-Enterprise* published editorials highly critical of Jordan on February 6. The *Fox News Network*'s first coverage of the controversy was on February 8. The *Wall Street Journal* first mentioned it in an editorial by Bret Stephens on February 10. Were the right-leaning *Fox News* and the *Wall Street Journal* editorial page part of the alleged conspiracy or just simply late to the story?

The controversy that the right-wing bloggers stoked took its toll on February 11. According to a CNN report, Jordan resigned, "saying the controversy over his remarks about the deaths of journalists in Iraq threatened to tarnish the network he helped build...'I never meant to imply U.S. forces acted with ill intent when U.S. forces accidentally killed journalists, and I apologize to anyone who thought I said or believed otherwise.'"[92]

Some have publicly speculated that CNN management eased Jordan out. What is known with certainty is that Jordan attributes his departure to the blogosphere discourse. So what was Jordan's failure as a news executive that warranted his departure? *Slate* media critic Jack Shafer said he believed that CNN dismissed Jordan and was right to do so.

> If Jordan ever harbored thoughts that U.S. forces had targeted journalists, a position that could be supported by the Kurtz story, then it was his duty as a newsman to pursue the story by assigning a CNN investigative team to it. If he did, I'd love to see the results. But it's fairly obvious that he didn't. Jordan's dereliction is less a mistake than it is proof of brain rot. The supreme editor of a news organization can't expect to make unsupportable inflammatory statements and maintain the respect of his truth-seeking troops at the same time. CNN did the right thing to show him the door. I would have done the same.[93]

Consider, however, the position the *Wall Street Journal* (WSJ) editorial page took on Jordan's departure. WSJ editorial writers are, as the half-joke goes, to the right of Attila the Hun. Yet they did not believe Jordan was guilty of a transgression that merited dismissal.

It has been a particular satisfaction to the right wing of the so-called "blogosphere," the community of writers on the Web that has pushed the Eason story relentlessly and sees it as the natural sequel to the Dan Rather fiasco of last year. But Easongate is not Rathergate...the worst that can reasonably be said about his performance is that he made an indefensible remark from which he ineptly tried to climb down at first prompting. This may have been dumb but it wasn't a journalistic felony...No doubt this point of view will get us described as part of the "mainstream media." But we'll take that as a compliment since we've long believed that these columns do in fact represent the American mainstream. We hope readers buy our newspaper because we make grown-up decisions about what is newsworthy, and what isn't.[94]

Postscript: Jordan resurfaced as the CEO of Praedict, "a group of well known professionals who have come together from media, marketing, and military backgrounds," offering news and analysis on *IraqSlogger.com*.[95] About the time he started the Web site, Jordan invited Malkin, one of his fiercest blogosphere critics from the Davos session controversy, to go with him to Baghdad to solve the mystery of Jamil Hussein.[96] By mid-December 2006, Hussein's existence had ballooned into yet another right-wing blogger crusade alleging fabrication and cover-up.

The controversy stemmed from a November 25, 2006, Associated Press (AP) story that reported, among other events in Baghdad, that "rampaging militiamen burned and blew up four mosques and torched several homes in the capital's mostly Shia neighborhood of Hurriyah, police said. Iraqi soldiers failed to intervene in the assault by suspected members of Shiite Mahdi Army militia or subsequent attacks that killed a total of 25 Sunnis, including women and children, said police Capt. Jamil Hussein."[97]

Malkin first questioned the accuracy of the AP account in a November 27 posting: "But did the killings the AP alleges took place really happen? Look, there's no denying blood is flowing in Iraq. But how much and whose and at whose hand? Self-appointed "spokesmen" in Iraq are skilled in the art of media manipulation. They—like many in the American media—have a vested interest in exaggerating the violence as much as possible."[98] She was the most prodigious among right-wing bloggers about the AP coverage of Baghdad, posting 24 reports from November 27 until January 31, 2000.[99]

By January 4, 2007, there was no reason for Malkin to join Jordan in a quest to find Hussein. That is because Hussein did exist and faced arrest for speaking to the media, the AP reported on January 4.

The Interior Ministry acknowledged Thursday that an Iraqi police officer whose existence had been denied by the Iraqis and the U.S. military is in fact an active member of the force, and said he now faces arrest for speaking to the media.

Ministry spokesman Brig. Abdul-Karim Khalaf, who had previously denied there was any such police employee as Capt. Jamil Hussein, said in an interview that Hussein is an officer assigned to the Khadra police station, as had been reported by The Associated Press.

The captain, whose full name is Jamil Gholaiem Hussein, was one of the sources for an AP story in late November about the burning and shooting of six people during a sectarian attack at a Sunni mosque.[100]

In a profile of Malkin, the *Washington Post*'s Kurtz said, "Malkin reported the news and expressed regret."[101] But her January 4 posting, "Jamil Hussein Development: 'Faces Arrest?'" contains no apology or words of regret from her.[102] Rather, Malkin linked to comments she made the previous day:

> The "Jamil Hussein" story is one important item on our agenda, but not the only one. As Curt and other bloggers on this story have noted from the beginning, Jamilgate isn't just about "Jamil Hussein." Bryan and I plan to do as much on-the-ground reporting as we can to nail down unresolved questions—not only about Jamil Hussein and the Hurriya six burning Sunnis allegations, but also about the AP four burning mosque story discrepancies and the many other AP sources that our military has publicly challenged—including "Lt. Maitham Abdul Razzaq" and more than a dozen police officers listed by U.S. military spokesman Navy Lt. Michael Dean.[103]

As the *New York Times* reported, other right-wing bloggers refused to retract their accusations or express regret for Hussein's predicament: "The Flopping Aces blog….accused The A.P. of 'whining,'…Dan Riehl…remained defiant. 'I don't see that bloggers have anything to apologize for, nor do I see this story being at an end.'"[104]

CONCLUSION

This chapter examined three campaigns citizen press critics waged against news personnel at CBS, CNN, and the Associated Press. The critics evaluated the performance of the MSM from a politically conservative perspective. A central tenet of their critique is that the MSM covers events with a so-called liberal bias. Specific to the controversies addressed here, these conservative bloggers appear to believe that many in the MSM opposed President Bush's policies and sought to depict the war in Iraq in a negative light. Consequently, the bloggers campaigned against accuracies and omissions in the MSM sometimes by conducting their own research and reporting. The bloggers' critiques fall under the genres of accuracy, framing, and agenda-setting/gatekeeping as outlined by Cooper.[105] Both campaigns proved effective. The critique and activism targeting CBS led to reforms in the news organization's reporting and vetting procedures and personnel there, and a CNN news executive stepped down or was asked to leave. The campaign waged against AP was ultimately not successful by the standards set by the two previous campaigns. Yet, AP felt pressure to respond to the critiques to prove their suspicions incorrect, which is still some measure of a critic's effectiveness.

Yet, many of the bloggers tactics—the use of anonymity, pseudonymity, unsubstantiated speculation, trafficking in rumors, spinning facts to suit one's bias, and the reluctance to admit errors—are many of the same ethical lapses such critics fault the MSM for practicing. Unprincipled critics risk a loss of credibility, if not among their constituents, then certainly among a wider audience. To paraphrase the U.S. Supreme Court in *McIntyre*, it is for the public to decide what is responsible, valuable, and truthful.[106]

Likewise, under a constitutional concept of democratic discourse, the MSM is obligated to make its case to the public in general and case by case by openly questioning the trustworthiness, accuracy, credibility, and ethics of such bloggers, and by emphasizing its record as credible gatekeepers. As noted earlier, the *Wall Street Journal*'s editorial writers, anticipating that they would be smeared by their fellow travelers, made such a case to their readers: "We hope readers buy our newspaper because we make grown-up decisions about what is newsworthy, and what isn't."[107]

CHAPTER 4

Ben H. Bagdikian: Ahead of the Curve

"This is an insider's book, written by one wise in the ways of the media. Compared to him, other insiders seem like ostriches with their heads buried in the shifting sands of change." So wrote then–Stanford University professor Edwin B. Parker in 1971 about Ben H. Bagdikian's *The Information Machines: Their Impact on Men and the Media*.[1] Ben H. Bagdikian, the media savvy author, however, was preoccupied with other matters when the book was published that year.

That June, a former RAND Corporation colleague, Daniel Ellsberg,[2] gave Bagdikian copies of secret government documents that led to the now celebrated Pentagon Papers case—well, celebrated by many journalists and free press advocates—in which the *Washington Post* and the *New York Times* argued successfully before the U.S. Supreme Court that they had a First Amendment right to publish the classified government documents.[3] Bagdikian was then assistant managing editor of national news at the *Washington Post*.[4] He had been a visiting scholar in RAND's social science department working on nongovernmental and nonclassified work, and that is where he did the research and writing that led to *The Information Machines*.

An award-winning journalist,[5] independent scholar, former dean of the Graduate School of Journalism at University of California at Berkeley, and media critic, Bagdikian is perhaps best known as the author of *The Media Monopoly*, first published in 1983, and now in its current incarnation, *The New Media Monopoly* (2004). Yet the words Parker chose to describe Bagdikian and the significance of his lesser-known study of media technologies aptly sizes up why his writings have spurred changes in the newspaper industry and inspired a generation of media scholars and a media reform movement.

"Bagdikian dares to look the future in the eye and report clearly what he sees," Parker declared, noting that journalists "will appreciate the careful job of reporting" and scholars "will be hard pressed to match the balanced perspective he brings."[6] Parker said Bagdikian had set the foundation for study of the communication revolution, concluding, "There is still room for others to provide more depth and to keep a continuing finger on the pulse of the communication revolution. But those tasks should be easier now that a pioneer has led the way."[7]

Twenty-five years later, the *Journal of Broadcasting & Electronic Media* selected *Information Machines* as one of the 12 most important electronic media books since the journal's inception in 1956: "It was a widely cited study for a number of years. Looking back a quarter-century, the author did pretty well in suggesting the likely power to be wielded by increasingly centralized media institutions."[8]

As a media critic, Bagdikian has been farsighted, inspirational, influential, long lasting, and a forerunner. "[A]lmost from the start" of his professional journalism career as a reporter at the *Springfield (MA) Morning Union* in 1941, he has taken the "time to look at the news process through research and media criticism."[9] He published his "first national media criticism"[10] in 1950, winning that same year a George Foster Peabody Award for a "Series of Articles Analyzing the Broadcasts of Top Commentators," as a reporter with the *Providence (RI) Journal-Bulletin.*[11] Apparently, the 30-year-old reporter had a knack for media criticism as the Peabody committee described him as "a brilliant young reporter...who in a series of lively articles carried out the most exacting, thorough, and readable check-up of broadcasts by Walter Winchell, Drew Pearson, and Fulton Lewis, Jr....Here was criticism of the very highest order, and as readable as it was accurate."[12] His byline first appeared in the *Columbia Journalism Review*'s third issue in 1962, for which he wrote the column "Letter from Washington" until 1967.[13]

Though accomplished as a journalist and media critic by the mid-1960s, Bagdikian had not yet written the works and engaged in the projects that would elevate him to the status of arguably the most influential journalism and media critic in the post–World War II era. He jokes that he was still derisively referred to as "an alleged critic," "self-appointed," or a "so-called critic" by *Editor & Publisher* back then.[14] Few visionaries have the fortune to see their concepts bear fruit. Some have the misfortune to see their predictions come true. For this journalist/media critic, prescience has been a mixed blessing.

Bagdikian is the kind of press critic that journalists trolling in the trenches or basking in the Beltway's big lights find difficult to summarily dismiss, largely because his newspaper experience is quite typical yet his achievements as a journalist are distinguished. He has newsroom "cred." He is an everyman journalist who recalls the days when the daily newspaper was king, that when "an editor went through the swinging door to the composing room it added the noise of great linotype machines turning words on paper into letters in metal."[15] He suffered through the low pay, long hours, and fickleness of management at low- and mid-level newspapers. He was a union man. In 1954, he fell out of favor with management at the *Providence Journal-Bulletin* for his efforts to unionize, toppling from his star reporter status: "I suppose the paper's law firm had warned them not to fire me but to make life for me so miserable that I would quit voluntarily and be a warning to other reporters harboring thoughts of joining the union."[16]

In March 1956, he escaped from the newsroom by winning a $5,000 Ogden Reid Fellowship, which dramatically changed management's estimation of him. When he returned from Europe to the *Providence Journal-Bulletin,* he learned he had been one of four finalists for a Pulitzer Prize in foreign reporting. He was a hot prospect; four other papers wanted to hire him.[17] Apparently, he grew skillful in grant writing. In 1961, he earned a John Simon Guggenheim Memorial Foundation fellowship.[18] Later he worked as a contributing editor for *The Saturday Evening Post.*[19] Professional journalists admire, respect, and no doubt envy him for being a part of a Pulitzer Prize winning team in 1953 and, of course, for his fortune at being able to help shape history and the *Washington Post*'s free-press position in the Pentagon Papers case.

This is a man who rolled up his white-shirt sleeves in the *Washington Post* newsroom beside newspaper icon Ben Bradlee. *Post* owner Katherine Graham asked him to join the paper in 1970. Bagdikian's critique of the *Washington Post* in the *Columbia Journalism Review*—"What Makes a Newspaper Nearly Great?"—inspired Graham to hire him.[20] "The *Post* is irritating because it comes within a lunge of greatness as a newspaper but it is not great," he wrote, identifying its shortcomings as too often failing to get basic facts correct and inconsistency on the part of editors to give news reports their appropriate length and placement in the paper.[21]

Bradlee, once, in traditionally macho newsroom fashion, praised Bagdikian— "I've got to hand it to you, buddy. You've really got big ones"[22]—for spending six days in a maximum security prison solely to gain a first-hand perspective on prison life. He turned the *Post* prison series into a book, *The Shame of Prisons,* co-authored with Leon Dash, also of the *Washington Post.*[23] Eventually, the two Bens would have a falling out.

He is the stuff of free press legend. Listen to the famed journalist turned author David Halberstam praise the pivotal role Bagdikian played in persuading Bradlee to defy the Nixon administration and publish the Pentagon Papers; note how the perspective Bagdikian had gained as a press critic of more than 20 years at that time helped him see that the bigger picture eluded Bradlee.

> Meanwhile, Bagdikian was being very very eloquent and forceful. If this kind of fight for a free press was somewhat new and alien to Bradlee, it was as if Bagdikian, press critic and scholar, had been waiting all his life for it. He was telling the lawyers that other newspapers did not have to feel bound by the government's decision, that each paper had to follow its own destiny. The *Post* had some of the most serious and professional journalists in the country, they had covered this story for more than a decade,

they were more than competent to judge what damaged and what did not damage national security. As for the *Times*, if the *Post* did not print now it would seem to be failing to support the *Times* and taking the government's side against it. The best way to help the *Times* was to publish the Papers, rather than to let it stand alone. Then he stopped and said, and it affected everyone in the room: "The only way to assert the right to publish is to publish." Bradlee had never admired Bagdikian more.[24]

Bagdikian set the cornerstone for his legacy as a media critic in 1966–1967. Much of the concept was laid out in a 1967 *Esquire* magazine article, "The American Newspaper Is Neither Record, Mirror, Journal, Ledger, Bulletin, Telegram, Examiner, Register, Chronicle, Gazette, Observer, Monitor, Transcript, Nor Herald of the Day's Events,"[25] later revised as "What's Wrong with the American Press," a chapter in Bagdikian's *The Effete Conspiracy and Other Crimes by the Press.*[26] In both articles, Bagdikian talked about the three areas of news media accountability and reform where eventually he would have the most impact: media ownership, news councils, and news ombudsmen positions. In *Double Vision*, he writes, "I was enthusiastic because I had first called for such [an in-house ombudsman-critic] in a 1957 magazine article."[27] (He later explained that he had suggested in a publication that newspapers place "public representatives" on their boards of directors ten years before he wrote the *Esquire* article, but he could not recall the publication's name.[28]) Many, however, point to the *Esquire* article as the impetus for the modern news ombudsman.

> Another measure might be local press councils…in which the paper's top leadership would sit regularly with community representatives, not to have a town committee edit the paper but to establish some human relationship between audience and the news establishment…A brave owner someday will provide for a community ombudsman on his paper's board—maybe a nonvoting one—to be present, to speak, to provide a symbol and, with luck, to represent public interest.[29]

It was more than just talk. He was a hands-on news reformer. As president of the Mellett Fund for a Free and Responsible Press, Bagdikian oversaw the first systematic trial of local press councils, a one-year experiment (1966–1967) conducted in Bend, Oregon; Redwood City, California; and Sparta and Cairo, Illinois.[30] It was not the idea that was new; it was the execution. The idea that a nongovernmental, lay citizen group should monitor press performance by addressing citizens' complaints of alleged press irresponsibility had been in the air for some time.

European nations had set up news councils as early as 1916, when Sweden established its Press Fair Practices Commission.[31] Stanford University communications professor Chilton Bush promoted the idea of press councils among California newspaper publishers in the 1930s.[32] In 1958, he launched the Citizens Advisory Council in Santa Rosa, California, to evaluate the performance of the local paper, the *Santa Rosa Press Democrat.*[33]

In the United Kingdom, the Royal Commission on the Press proposed the national press council in 1943; the (Hutchins) Commission on Freedom of the Press call for a national council in 1947 bore no fruit; *Louisville (KY) Courier-Journal & Times* president and editor Barry Bingham, Sr., raised the idea, but nothing materialized.[34] Small-town editor and Harvard University Nieman fellow Houstoun Waring founded the Colorado Editorial Advisory Board, which operated from 1946 to 1952 and was later revived as a press council in 1967.[35] In California, William Townes, *Santa Rosa Press Democrat*, experimented with a local press council in 1950.[36]

Bagdikian noticed that the councils in the United States failed to maintain detailed documentation of the results of their experiments or share them with the industry.[37] The Fund wanted to show the news industry that such councils were capable of improving press performance, establishing communication between the public and the news, all without eroding press independence. So the Fund worked with universities, setting up "independent projects carefully designed and recorded to produce a body of experience available to the whole trade."[38]

In 1972, Stanford University professor William L. Rivers, who administered the experiment in California, contended that it was not until the Bagdikian-led effort "that the press council began to take on its present dimensions"[39] in the form of the continued operation of councils in Oregon and Illinois, the revival of the Littleton, Colorado, council (1967), Honolulu (1970), Minnesota (1970), and the publication of a 1972 report of a Twentieth Century Fund task force calling for a national news council. In *BackTalk: Press Councils in America*, Rivers linked the establishment of the Honolulu Community Media Council to the Mellett Fund experiments.[40]

Outside observers also believed the Fund's experiment made an impact. According to a report for the Freedom of Information (FOI) Center, the "press council movement in this country was given a forward thrust by the Mellett Fund...the first systematic attempt in this country to demonstrate the utility of the community press council."[41] The author of the FOI Center report noted that "the permanent press councils operating in 1969 represented inchings in the direction of acceptance of the idea that an advisory board, set up to evaluate newspaper performance, can be beneficial to both the public and the press."[42]

Norman E. Isaacs, a founder and a chairman of the National News Council (1973–1984) assessed the impact of the Fund's experiment this way: "The results were mixed, but there were enough constructive aspects to sharpen the appetites of the idea's supporters, and two much larger efforts were to surface and succeed. The most important was in Minnesota, where Robert Shaw, the manager of the state newspaper association, was the chief architect and was influential in persuading the organization to adopt a procedure for the hearing of complaints by its Goals and Ethics Committee."[43] The other effort, Isaacs noted, was the Honolulu Community Media Council.[44] A Northwest News Council, created in 1992, operated in Washington and Oregon until 1998.[45] Though only three news councils operated in 2006 in Minnesota, Washington, and Honolulu, councils in Connecticut and California were expected to launch by early 2008.[46] In summer 2007, representatives of the councils agreed to form a National Coalition of News Councils/Forums.[47]

News councils and news ombudsmen investigate public complaints against a news outlet, but the key distinction is that the latter is a paid employee of the outlet. In the United States, news ombudsmen look upon Bagdikian as something of a founding philosopher. The Organization of News Ombudsmen, for example, traces its origins to Bagdikan's appeal in *Esquire:* "It was an editor of The *Washington Post* who sounded the first call for a newspaper ombudsman in North America."[48] Later that year, June 11, 1967, the *New York Times'* A.H. Raskin proposed that newspapers create departments of internal criticism, serving as public protectors.[49] But perhaps because he was first or because he served as the *Post*'s second ombudsman (1971–1972), Bagdikian seems to loom larger than Raskin[50] among ombudsmen advocates.

The concept of ombudsman is Swedish.[51] What publication first created a news ombudsman position and in what nation is a matter of some debate, though. Japanese newspapers operated content checking systems as early as 1922; some say the *New York World* set up a checking system called the Bureau of Accuracy and Fair Play in New York City in July 1913; others say such checking systems did not perform the same function as news ombudsman and insist the first news ombudsman in the United States was appointed in June 1967 to serve readers of the *Louisville (KY) Courier-Journal* and the *Louisville (KY) Times*, responding to Bagdikian's and Raskin's proposals.[52]

The *Washington Post* was the second paper in the United States to create an ombudsman position, and Bagdikian was the second editor to hold the post there, after Richard Harwood, an assistant managing editor, who assumed the job in September 9, 1970.[53] The job required Bagdikian to assume three roles —complaints editor, internal monitor, and media education writer—while maintaining his title as assistant managing editor. From the start, the multitasker had reservations: "I didn't think a critique of the paper was best done by someone with a title that implied some control over the content being criticized."[54] Ultimately, he was right. He could not square his role of honest critic on the public's behalf with his obligations as management.

In *Double Vision*, he recounts how Bradlee scolded him for positing "what may have been an unwise hypothetical question" to members of the Congressional Black Caucus at a Harvard University symposium to demonstrate that media's primary purpose was profit, not racism: "[D]id they suppose . . . that blacks would get a paper's attention more readily by calling it racist or threatening to boycott it?"[55] After Bradlee read an Associated Press wire account of the symposium in which the question was not characterized as hypothetical, he exploded, "That's more than I can take! You've been disloyal to the paper and you've been disloyal to me."[56] Months later, in August 1972, Bagdikian resigned, telling *Time* magazine, "There's a feeling here that I should be loyal to the management. When they first put me in this job, they assured me that my first loyalty would be to the readers."[57]

In *News Ombudsmen in North America: Assessing an Experiment in Social Responsibility*, Neil Nemeth describes the bind Bagdikian found himself in as the "classic ombudsman's dilemma: does he work for the readers or the newspaper?"[58] Steven Brill, the founder of the short-lived *Brill's Content*, put in place a solution to that dilemma. He hired Bill Kovach and then Michael Gatner as ombudsmen and gave them guaranteed contracts to shield them from possible pressure—perceived or real—from management that might mute their criticism of their boss.[59] Today, the *Post* protects its ombudsman by providing a two-year contract, with access to editorial management and independence from it and the right to write an uncensored column that appears in a prominent space in the paper, which Geneva Overholser, ombudsman there from 1995–1998, contends "The *Post*'s model is far stronger than most of the 40 or so others among America's 1,500 daily papers."[60]

Studies show that ombudsmen can improve the accuracy and fairness in reporting and bolster a news outlet's standing with its readership by mediating disputes between the public and the outlet's editors and journalists. Yet, ombudsmen have little or no effect upon improving an outlet's policies, spurring substantive and systematic discussion about an outlet's mission, or ferreting out deception.[61] Nevertheless, by 2007, about 40 news outlets in the United States employed ombudsmen or public editors, including latecomers *New York Times*, CBS Television, and ESPN, the cable sports network. Long opposed to hiring an ombudsman, the *Times* brought its "public editor" on board in July 2003 only after the Jayson Blair journalistic fraud scandal led a 28-member committee headed by Allan M. Siegal, *Times* assistant managing editor, to recommend such an adoption.[62] CBS Public Eye is a blog where a small staff posts answers, analysis, and explanations to queries and complaints from the public. Its staff says it was not set up as a response to the National Guard memo disaster at *60 Minutes: Wednesday* and the January 2005 Thornburgh-Bocardi report.[63]

Forty years later, Bagdikian can take satisfaction in his role in the MSM's adoption of ombudsmen and the revival of the news council effort, but he looks upon his role as "the chicken little of media criticism"[64] with mixed emotions. His calls for greater journalism accountability by news councils and ombudsmenship were calls to action. His writings about media consolidation, however, were warnings and hopes for intervention and cessation. Most of his predictions came true, but it was not until 2003 that the media reform movement mobilized to put the brakes on media consolidation.

Bagdikian has written about consolidation of media ownership and its impact on content and democracy since the early 1960s. He started with examinations of newspaper ownership, management, and chain building. James Boylan, *Columbia Journalism Review* (*CJR*) founding editor, recalls, "There was a looming peril of the absorption of journalism into corporate conglomerates; Bagdikian issued one of the first warnings, in 1967."[65] Bagdikian's precise words in the spring 1967 *CJR* were, "Nevertheless, diversification and conglomerates seem destined to grow: they make too much fiscal sense. In the process more news operations will become appendages to conventional business."[66]

There he was in the summer of 1967 testifying before the U.S. Senate Anti-Monopoly Subcommittee "in which I had opposed special privileges for newspapers, in this case exemptions from antitrust laws."[67] That year Senator Carl Hayden of Arizona and 14 other senators co-sponsored the Failing Newspaper Act. That proposal became the Newspaper Preservation Act of 1970, providing an exemption allowing a newspaper owner to merge or form a joint ownership to prevent a competitor from going out of business. Bagdikian suggested that dying papers be put up "for sale at a fair market price to independent buyers"[68] as an alternative to awarding an exemption.

In 1967 he was at RAND, drawing upon experts to analyze new media technologies and crystal ball gazing. *The Information Machines,* an outcome of the RAND project, is a statistical and factoid-dense historical and economic analysis of the newspaper industry confronted by the challenges of the new technologies of computers, cable television, and satellite transmission. "Newspapers today make 12 to 15 percent profit on assets after taxes, which is quite respectable,"[69] Bagdikian notes. (In 2005, the average profit of newspapers owned by 13 publicly traded companies was just below 20 percent.[70]) His is not an ideologically mired condemnation of monopoly power in the newspaper business. Bagdikian's conclusions are steered by economic data and empirical observation, allowing him to make meaningful distinctions: "Thus, monopoly has been a mixed phenomenon for the reader, diminishing the opportunities for diversity and tempting papers to choose less expensive news, but at the same time permitting a less sensationalist handling of information."[71]

Writing in such publications as the *CJR, Quill, Neiman Reports,* and the scholarly *Journal of Communication* in the 1970s, Bagdikian continued his political economic analysis of newspaper industry trends.[72] That line of inquiry culminated in *The Media Monopoly.* Along with the updated editions of the book, he also reported in a 1989 article in *The Nation* that a handful of private organizations claimed that by the 1990s, "five to ten corporate giants will control most of the world's important newspapers, magazines, books, broadcast stations, movies, recordings and videocassettes."[73] Many have acclaimed this as a prediction, as though he intuited it rather than reporting what owners revealed to him. Nevertheless, it has proven disturbingly accurate. In the *Nieman Reports,* for example, Norman Solomon observed, "In 2000, half a dozen corporations own media outlets that control most of the news and information flow in the United States."[74] That the assertion has now taken on legendary status testifies to Bagdikian's near reverence among media reform advocates. Here is how David Croteau and William Hoynes, sociologists who conducted empirical studies for the media watchdog group Fairness & Accuracy in Reporting, assess Bagdikian's work on media ownership:

> Bagdikian…has provided the best-known examination of the concentration of media ownership. While Bagdikian is not a sociologist, his work is full of sociological questions about the relationship between ownership and diversity. His most

important contribution is the way he draws connections across the various media, showing how, for example, companies that are giants in the music industry have a similar position in film. The combination of ownership concentration and growing horizontal integration leads Bagdikian to conclude that the absence of competition in the media industry will lead inevitably to homogeneous media products that serve the interests of the increasingly small number of owners.[75]

Radical Mass Media Criticism places Bagdikian in the pantheon with Edward Herman, Noam Chomsky, and Robert W. McChesney as writers of the "most internationally resonant work on the political economy of the mass media in the US," and *The Media Monopoly* as one of the "key works" in that field of analysis.[76] Media scholar McChesney, president and co-founder of Free Press, a leading national media reform organization, gives credit to *Media Monopoly* for laying the groundwork for much of his analysis in his study, "The Problem of Journalism: A Political Economic Contribution to an Explanation of the Crisis in Contemporary US Journalism."[77] As big media companies ballooned into even bigger conglomerates by 2000, Ben H. Bagdikian became the man journalists, activists, scholars, media critics, and even a U.S. senator quoted as an authority on media ownership's impact on content and civic engagement.

Bagdikian's *Media Monopoly* and related writings have helped inspire the current media reform movement led by such groups as Fairness and Accuracy in the Media, Consumers Federation of America, Prometheus Radio Project, Reclaim the Media, and Free Press, which galvanized thousands of U.S. Americans to oppose the Federal Communication Commission's (FCC's) attempt to relax its media ownership rules, and the widespread public opposition to the FCC's June 2, 2003, vote, allowing further consolidation within broadcast and between broadcast and print outlets. Corporate news outlets could not ignore that opposition to media mergers had gone mainstream as the *Financial Times (London)* observed, "The FCC rules sparked bipartisan criticism from lawmakers and opposition from groups as diverse as the National Rifle Association and the National Organization for Women. Critics argued that the FCC vote would concentrate too much power in the hands of media moguls."[78] By voting 3–2 to relax media ownership restrictions, the Republican-dominated "FCC basically ignored nearly two million people of all political persuasions who registered their opposition," University of Pennsylvania Law Professor C. Edwin Baker noted.[79]

In September 2003, U.S. Senator Robert C. Byrd gave a speech opposing the FCC's vote because, he said, "I fear that it will strangle voices that disagree with corporate interests at virtually every level of news and commentary."[80] He quoted passages from the first and sixth editions of *The Media Monopoly*, making the point that with each new edition, Bagdikian recorded a smaller number of corporations dominating the media. "The sixth edition, published in 2000, documented that just six—six!—corporations supply most of America's media content," Byrd remarked, adding, "The June 2 vote by the Federal Communications Commission threatens to expand the influence of these few corporations even further, stretching their hands around a larger number of local television and radio stations, scarfing up newspapers and Internet news outlets."[81]

Communications scholar Nancy Snow contends Bagdikian does not get full credit for his prescience: "Nowadays he's seen as just one among a crowd of media reform scholars who criticize the conglomerization of news when he should be credited for daring to predict the obvious trend in the news media toward concentration at a time when no one else was looking at the media system as a whole."[82]

Perhaps. In his late 80s—he was born January 30, 1920—he is hardly forgotten or ignored. *Editor & Publisher* sought him out to comment on William Dean Singleton's MediaNews Group control of 44 San Francisco Bay–area newspapers in June 2006.[83] Surprisingly, *Variety*, the movie trade book, asked him in 2007 to opine about why the movie industry had tended to avoid making movies about the Iraq war.[84] Late that year the *Washington Post* interviewed him for an assessment of the impact of Rupert Murdoch's bid to buy the *Wall Street Journal:* "If Murdoch gets control of the *Wall Street Journal* and Dow Jones and if he follows the pattern of his past acquisitions, he will use the *Wall Street Journal* to serve his own purposes, financial and political."[85]

In *Media Concentration and Democracy*, Baker's 2007 defense of the merits of restricting ownership concentration, the law and communications professor describes Bagdikian as "the most readable critic of media concentration… analytic in his objections to concentration"[86] and "probably the most quoted, certainly one of the most acute, commentators on media ownership."[87]

In 2006, the Society of Professional Journalists credited Bagdikian, "the Paul Revere of the journalism world" as it dubbed him, for alerting "the country years before about the increased concentration of media consolidation and the effects it would have on the quality of journalism as a whole," and its president David Carlson added, "We owe Ben a tremendous amount of gratitude for calling attention to and maintaining in the public eye what has become one of the most significant journalistic trends of this generation."[88]

Little of Bagdikian's news media criticism had immediate and direct impact on news organizations' performance. No news or public affairs show was canceled as a result of his commentary. No news media personality, news executive, or journalist resigned because of a public outcry that he ignited. By his own account, he had called for the creation of a representative for the public at news organizations ten years before the first news ombudsman was hired in 1967, so his call for news outlets to hire ombudsmen took quite some time to nudge news organizations in that direction. The Mellett Fund experiments bore fruit quickly, but not inside newsrooms. None of that, however, diminishes his stature as an effective press critic. Consider that in 1967, his expertise as an analyst on news media economics qualified him to testify before the U.S. Senate about the merits of a major piece of newspaper-business-related legislation,[89] and that 36 years later, a U.S. senator would quote him as an expert on media consolidation.[90] Politicians, scholars, activists, and members of the press quote him as an authority on media economics. His landmark book, *Media Monopoly*, has been selling for more than two decades. Scholars such as McChesney and Baker cite him because his standards of inquiry and analysis have proven credible and extrapolative.

So, in late summer 2007, as Bagdikian fires off commentary on politics and media from his home in Berkeley, California, he does not move as fast as he used to. That might not be all that bad. Now, just about everyone else can catch up and get to where he had arrived decades ago.

CHAPTER 5

The Washington News Council: Third-Party Intervention

Claude-Jean Bertrand has "sung the praises" of press councils "in articles published in many languages and [has] never stopped lecturing on the topic" for about 25 years.[1] Nevertheless, Bertrand acknowledges in his 2003 work, *An Arsenal for Democracy: Media Accountability Systems,* that "councils have not reached their assigned goals...nowhere could a council pride itself on having clearly participated in the progress of the media."[2] Given that poor tally, the Washington News Council's May 2007 *Reporting on Yourself: An Independent Analysis of* The Spokesman-Review's *Coverage of and Role in the Spokane River Park Square Redevelopment Project*[3] stands out as perhaps a singular achievement by a press council.

Reporting on Yourself is the Council's independent investigation of the *Spokane (WA) Spokesman-Review*'s coverage from 1994 to 2005 of a major mall development plan in downtown Spokane, Washington. In early 2006, the *Spokesman-Review* asked the Washington News Council to tell it what its owner, editor, and staffers had done wrong during those 11 years of coverage.

The Spokane-based daily's coverage of the project had become a lighting rod for accusations of conflict of interest as early as 1995 when a columnist in a rival weekly, the *Spokane (WA) Pacific Northwest Inlander,* questioned the paper's coverage of the River Park Square (RPS) shopping mall project.[4] The problem was ownership. The Cowles family of Spokane owned "roughly half the city" during that period, along with the development company that built the mall, an NBC affiliate, KHQ-TV, and the only daily in town, the *Spokesman-Review*.[5]

Rival media and many of the paper's readers argued that the *Spokesman-Review*'s coverage heavily favored its owner's effort to sell a renovated parking garage to the city for $26 million, when city appraisers valued it at about $15 million.[6] From May 1994 to 2005, "the RPS redevelopment touched off a torrent of controversy in Spokane, spawning nearly two dozen lawsuits and an IRS investigation. It tore apart the city's political structure and pulled down its bond rating. The *Spokesman-Review*'s coverage of RPS raised questions about the paper's editorial judgment, ethics, and impartiality that persist today."[7]

The bulk of the paper's River Park Square coverage was published during editor Chris Peck's watch, and he wrote columns on the subject that came under fire. The Council's 2007 report blamed Peck, by then the editor of the *Memphis (TN) Commercial Appeal*, for many of the newspaper's ethical lapses.[8] Ironically, Peck, president of the Associated Press Managing Editors (APME) in 2001, co-founded the association's National Credibility Roundtables, a series of newspaper management-reader discussion groups about local news coverage; chaired the American Society of Newspaper Editors (ASNE) ethics and wire content committees; and hosted two ASNE ethics and wire content committees. Under Peck's leadership the *Spokesman-Review* hosted the first roundtable discussion in January 2001.[9] There, *Spokesman-Review* publisher William Stacey Cowles, his editors and staffers, other journalists, readers, and local critics debated and discussed the paper's coverage of the development project.

The session was not, however, as unmediated as the give-and-take on a blog or open to the general public. Peck tended the gates. He handpicked the participants, excluding interested parties "with the most extreme stances, either unquestioning defenders or those whose purpose might be disruption."[10] After the session, *Spokesman-Review* editors developed three new guidelines: when the paper covers ownership's dealings, invite an independent columnist to write op-ed pieces about ownership-related issues, discontinue a practice of routinely allowing the publisher to edit copy that concerned the Cowles family, and open up the lines of communication with readers because "it was too late for editors and staffers to change disgruntled readers' minds" once accusations had been widely aired in the public.[11] "Even the harshest critics likely will acknowledge that a newspaper is heading in the right direction when staff discuss coverage in an open, public forum," Peck later concluded.[12]

That proved to be wishful and erroneous thinking. The scandal continued to dog the paper. Spokane-based *Camas Magazine*, one of the paper's harshest critics, devoted itself entirely to writing about the River Park Square scandal, winning journalism awards in 2001, 2002, 2003, and 2004, and placing second to MSNBC in the National Press Club's Online Journalism—Best Site Competition in 2002.[13] The embattled daily ran its own exposé on its role in the coverage in a series that started March 28, 2004.[14] Steven Smith, who replaced Peck as editor of the paper in 2002, promised readers that "as soon as the court cases were resolved, we would authorize an independent audit to determine the validity of accusations that the newspaper had failed to adequately cover the RPS controversy."[15] And Smith notes that the 2004 series—the "internal mea culpa" as he called it—did not quell the doubts among staffers and community.[16]

The *Spokesman-Review* was not the first embattled news outlet to turn to outsiders to assess its performance and help restore its credibility. First Amendment attorney Floyd Abrams investigated the Cable News Network/*Time* magazine "Operation Tailwind" report in 1998.[17] The *Salt Lake (UT) Tribune* paid two journalism professors, Joel Campbell of Brigham Young University and Jim Fisher of the University of Utah, to assess how it handled its firing of two reporters who also worked as paid sources for the *National Enquirer* during coverage of the kidnapping of Elizabeth Smart in 2002.[18] In early 2004, *USA Today* brought in outsiders Bill Hilliard, Bill Kovach, and John Seigenthaler, Sr., as part of a team that said ex-*USA Today* reporter Jack Kelley had "fabricated substantial portions of at least eight major stories, lifted nearly two dozen quotes or other material from competing publications, lied in speeches he gave for the newspaper and conspired to mislead those investigating his work."[19] CBS commissioned former U.S. Attorney General Dick Thornburgh and former Associated Press president and CEO Louis D. Boccardi to write the September 8, 2004, *60 Minutes* report "For the Record" about President George W. Bush's Texas Air National Guard Service.[20] *Technology Review* hired University of California–Berkeley's Graduate School of Journalism professor Susan Rasky to verify the accuracy of ten articles published between December 2004 and March 2005.[21]

But Smith turned to the Washington News Council (WNC); it was apparently the first time a press council has performed such a function. (The Council's executive director and founder John Hamer insists the nature and scope of the report is "unprecedented... There is no 'perhaps' or 'apparently'" about it.[22]) What is not open to interpretation is that the Council's findings and recommendations, published in May 2007, had an immediate impact. In response, the *Spokesman-Review* revised its code of ethics, restructured editors' duties to improve separation of news and editorial, and its publisher William Stacey Cowles publicly committed to maintaining newsroom independence. Smith and Cowles could have done much more; they declined to follow all five of the Council's recommendations. Nevertheless, the Council's critique spurred a reform of the newspaper's ethical standards and management practices and further public debate about a news outlet's civic obligation. And though Smith is "not a fan of the quasi-judicial process"[23] press councils typically engage in, by turning to it he has helped to bolster the Council's status as an authority on news media ethics and performance.

Smith acknowledges that his coolness to news councils raises conflicts for him, as a leading proponent of public or civic journalism: "As a civic journalist devoted to the concepts of transparency and reader interaction, I ought to be more enthusiastic about the news council concept."[24] Among other concerns, "the WNC's corporate sponsors—Boeing and Microsoft"—trouble him because, he says, they are "companies we routinely cover."[25] Generally, he does not like a "process that produces what is essentially a 'verdict' even though it doesn't adhere to rules that govern any real judicial proceeding."[26]

His general aversion to participating in the Council's hearing process is shared by management at many of the leading Washington news outlets, including the *Seattle Post-Intelligencer*, the *Seattle Times*, and the *Tacoma (WA) News Tribune*.[27] A case in point: the *Seattle Post-Intelligencer* declined to participate in what its staff characterized as a hearing conducted by "the self-styled news-media ombudsman organization" about its coverage of a county sheriff's office in 2006.[28] King County Sheriff Sue Rahr filed a complaint with the Council against the newspaper, claiming that a series, "Conduct Unbecoming," that ran in 2005 and 2006, was inaccurate, biased, or misleading in some key aspects. The Council upheld most of Rahr's claims.[29] The newspaper justified its absence from the hearing by arguing that some Council members, including its founder and executive director Hamer, appeared to have conflicts of interest. But Hamer, who does not cast a vote at such hearings, did not involve himself in the proceedings and six Council members recused themselves from voting.[30]

Hamer had been a controversial local figure even before the Council's inception in August 1998[31] because he had "been a vocal media critic with an admitted conservative bent. He co-edited a media watchdog publication called *CounterPoint* and co-wrote a regular column in the *Seattle Weekly* called 'News Watchdogs.'"[32] Consequently, some saw him as "a media-bashing, conservative ideologue."[33] Even Peck, then-editor of the *Spokesman*, wanted little to do with the Council. "Too many activist media critics, including big business leaders and former politicians" were on the Council's board, he said.[34]

Nevertheless, by 2007 two former local newspaper publishers/owners and two working professional journalists sat on the Council, along with representatives from business, government, nonprofits, and education. The Council's central function is the handling of complaints of "serious questions of journalistic fairness, accuracy or balance"[35] by complainants who must agree not to bring legal action against a news outlet. The Council maintains that it asks complainants to resolve their disputes with the news outlet. If resolution is unsuccessful, the Council may decide to convene a formal public hearing, inviting both sides to make their cases.[36] From its 1998 inception to August 2007, the Council handled 24 formal complaints, finding for the complainant only three times, dismissing many for failing to meet its guidelines, or resolving others after informal mediation.[37] According to telecommunication and First Amendment lawyer and professor Shannon M. Heim, generally press councils have been shown to be "an effective mechanism to bypass the complexity of libel law to more efficiently resolve complaints."[38]

When Smith started his search for an independent auditor in the summer of 2005, he sought someone with whom he had no professional or personal ties; that ruled out Bob Steele, for example, a friend and the Nelson Poynter Scholar for Journalism Values. He also was concerned with cost, wanting to pay no more than about $15,000. So in a telephone conversation with John Irby, then an associate professor at Washington State University, he said he needed to find an independent auditor.[39]

Irby, who later joined the *Bismarck (ND) Tribune* as editor, was a Council board member at the time. He suggested that the Council might be willing to perform the task. Why the WNC, considering that apparently it had never performed such a task? Irby says that as a member he had observed that the Council could be "objective" and had the "expertise. It wasn't my intent to make history. I didn't know anyone had the market on what news councils do or don't do."[40]

Irby, Smith, and Hamer first discussed the venture in Spokane in the fall of 2005.[41] Hamer recalls thinking then that the scope of the proposed outside audit—assessing nearly 11 years of news coverage—was "unprecedented" in contrast to similar efforts such as the Thornburgh-Boccardi report.[42] Smith made a formal request at the Council's annual board meeting in February 2006 in Seattle. It was nearly a daylong meeting, that, according to Hamer, Smith asked to attend for about "90 minutes to discuss the audit and answer questions."[43] Hamer recalls that there was a tough back-and-forth between the members and Smith discussing access, openness, independence, costs, and other matters, and some hesitation because Hamer is the Council's only full-time staffer.[44] A board member raised the issue that the newspaper's offer presented a conflict of interest, and additional funding should be sought.

Ultimately, the *Spokesman-Review* paid $15,000 of the investigation's $30,000 total cost.[45] The Council found funding for the rest of the project from the Ethics and Excellence in Journalism Foundation based in Oklahoma City, Oklahoma. It hired Bill Richards, a former *Washington Post* and *Wall Street Journal* reporter, to research and write the report. But before hiring Richards, the Council and the newspaper entered into a binding agreement[46] in August 2006. "We were concerned with autonomy, access and complete independence," Hamer recalls. "We also didn't want the report to be a whitewash or a witch hunt."[47] When the study was completed, the *Spokesman-Review* posted it on its Web site.

Ted S. McGregor, Jr., of the *Pacific Northwest Inlander* said the report was "no whitewash, as current Review editor Steve Smith predicted critics would charge. No, Richards, a veteran journalist, has methodically documented what most had already concluded: *The Review* should have covered the mall's funding plan more aggressively."[48]

Camas Magazine's Tim Connor, a winner of awards for his investigative reports on the River Park Square coverage, said it came close to a whitewash: "The Washington News Council is not a Spokane institution. It just acted like one in the way it handled its critique of the newspaper."[49] Hamer, however, disputes Connor's characterization, calling his charges "utterly without merit."[50] (As Hamer's response to Connor's assessment indicates, the RSP controversy provoked heated debate months after the report's publication. The scope of this work's evaluation, however, does not extend to rendering a judgment of the merits of the study's findings. Rather, it seeks to assess whether the findings persuaded ownership and editorial management at the paper to implement meaningful reforms.)

The report made five sets of findings:[51]

Finding 1

- The newspaper did not investigate thoroughly or in a timely manner and report promptly and forthrightly the financial structure of RPS.
- The newspaper suppressed financial information of importance to decision-makers and the public at-large, but potentially unfavorable to developers.

Finding 2

- Ownership's involvement in news stories it deemed sensitive was inappropriate.

Finding 3

- A news editor overseeing the reporting of a controversial issue involving the owners of the newspaper should not advocate a particular outcome.

Finding 4

- The *Spokesman-Review* suffers from the potential for self-censorship of the news product by reporters and editors.

Finding 5

- The same attorney simultaneously influenced decisions on related business and newsroom matters.

The report recommended that the newspaper do the following:[52]

- Create a "Cowles Co." beat, staffed by an experienced reporter or hire an ombudsman to oversee Cowles company coverage.
- Allow Cowles company representatives to comment on related stories in the same way it allows other sources or subjects to comment on articles before publication.
- Not allow news editors to write editorials.
- Vest the editor with the authority to make all decisions about news coverage of the Cowles family's business interests.
- Hire a law firm separate from the one used by the Cowles.

Former *Spokesman-Review* editor Peck rejected the Council's findings, noting that he had brought in ethics experts in 2000 to update the code and meet with the staff: "My editors fully comprehended the challenges that came with covering [River Park Square] and the Cowles family during that time. As challenges emerged, we dealt with them...That's why I am puzzled by The Washington News Council's agonizing rehash of River Park Square coverage from a decade ago. It's old news. It's a dead horse. Whatever lessons that needed to be learned from RPS, were learned years ago in the S-R [*Spokesman-Review*] newsroom."[53] Later, he added, "It is a lousy piece of self-serving work that the council is trying to use to raise money and promote itself. Not a good example of what news councils should try to do."[54]

Publisher Cowles's reaction was mixed: "While I reject substantially all of the allegations of influence collected in the News Council's report, I do respect the direction of its recommendations. The moral for me is, it is not enough to operate a newsroom independent of its owners; our newspaper must always take extra steps to help our audience understand that this is indeed the case."[55]

In his response, Smith explained that he was adopting two of the recommendations, that one was already in effect, that he did not have the power to put another one into effect, and why he rejected another. He said that when "circumstances warrant we'll make certain there is an independent, outside editor to assure appropriate, aggressive, fair and balanced reporting. An outside editor can evaluate, arbitrate and suggest and also assure readers the paper is doing its job."[56] He noted that in 2001 the paper had abandoned its policy of allowing the Cowleses to vet Cowles's business-related stories before publication and that "as a matter of policy, we do not allow subjects to review those stories in advance of publication."[57] Smith gave up editorial writing and his seat on the editorial board, as the Council recommended.[58]

Smith, however, reasoned that only the Cowles family had the authority to divest the newspaper from the family's other business interests—Stacey Cowles rejected that recommendation—and he would continue using attorney Duane Swinton to represent the paper in First Amendment matters while the family used him for business litigation. Generally, he reasoned that "[t]he council report was never intended to generate perfect solutions. It was intended to demonstrate the willingness of *Spokesman-Review* staff and the present editorial team to take responsibility for our journalism, past, present and future."[59]

About three months after the report's release—the paper posted it on its own Web site—Smith said that based on evidence such as e-mails from readers, the paper's credibility had been greatly enhanced: "We got a big boost out of this."[60] It is legitimate to conclude then that the Council's report succeeded where the paper's previous efforts of rehabilitation—the 2001 forum, the 2004 series, all the public journalism-inspired "news-is-a-conversation/transparency" blogging[61]—came up short. Apparently, the paper's readers needed to hear what a truly independent, dispassionate, and high-minded observer had to say about the matter.

As currently conceived and operated, press councils are unlikely to persuade media outlets to improve in any substantial or sustained way. That is largely because they do not challenge news media with systematic analysis, regular critiques, an ideological view, offer a vision of an ideal news operation, or draw strength from the public's views on press performance. Public journalism advocates, for instance, offer a vision of a citizen-centric press that engages in a conversation with its audience, as an alternative to the prevailing information model of journalism. Having been persuaded, hundreds of newspapers experimented with public journalism initiatives in the 1990s.[62] Media Matters for

America monitors, analyzes, and corrects what it characterizes as conservative misinformation and bigotry and hate in the U.S. media.[63] Radio personality Don Imus lost his job as a result of its efforts.[64] *Little Green Footballs'* Charles Johnson critiques the so-called liberal media for evidence of bias against conservatives. His scrutiny played a major role in the scandal that led to the resignation of CBS's Dan Rather.[65] But press councils are not social advocates, or choose not to be. Councils, as they currently operate, are reactive. Their core function requires that complaints come to them. It is doubtful that the irregular mediation of complaints against a news outlet that may have little resonance beyond the immediate parties is likely to galvanize public opinion triggering a public outcry that a news organization will find difficult to ignore. The success of the Washington News Council's report, however, suggests a way to make councils more effective in bringing about change: self-initiated, regularly published assessments of news outlet's performances. Perhaps annually? Perhaps after major election campaigns when readers have a large stake in judging news media coverage of candidate performance and campaign issues?

The *Spokesman-Review*'s Smith, a news media reformer himself, appears open to the idea: "I think our audit might suggest a better model for the news council. Abandon the quasi-judicial review process in favor of select media criticism produced by independent journalists and academics under the sponsorship of the council. That is a model I could support."[66]

As with so many "new ideas" about press accountability, the proposed new role for news councils is hardly new. In 1947 the Hutchins Commission on Freedom of the Press recommended the creation of a nongovernmental, independent agency to appraise and report on press performance: "[I]t seems to us clear that some agency which reflects the ambitions of the American people for its press should exist for the purpose of comparing the accomplishments of the press with the aspirations which the people have for it. Such an agency would also educate the people as to the aspirations which they ought to have for the press."[67]

CHAPTER 6

FAIR: Press Criticism from a Progressive Think Tank

Media watchdogs often count any formal response from their targets, even an outright rebuff of their claims, as a sign of some success. Well, at least we got corporate media's attention, they tell themselves. So when one of your frequent targets crowns you as an authoritative source, you surely have arrived as a commanding news media critic. Such was the status of New York–based Fairness & Accuracy in Reporting (FAIR) by May 1996. Almost from its start in June 1986, FAIR peppered the *New York Times* with missives. In December 1986, Martin A. Lee, then its research director, questioned the accuracy of an op-ed piece about Mehmet Ali Agca, the man who tried to assassinate Pope John Paul II.[1] In October 1987, FAIR founder Jeff Cohen lectured the *Times* for its use of "special interests": "The linkage of the Democratic Party to 'special interests' has become an unexamined tenet in the media. But it raises questions: When did you last refer to the 'special interests' who influence or control the Republican Party? Are the Republicans above such interests?"[2]

On January 23, 1988, FAIR sent a questionnaire to senior *Times* editors and correspondents covering Central America, contending that with some exceptions, the newspaper's coverage of Nicaragua "echoed the administration's 'Nicaragua obsession'—emphasizing repressive measures in Nicaragua and downplaying or ignoring more serious human rights abuses elsewhere in Central America."[3] A *Times* editor called the questionnaire an indictment, yet promised that he and his colleagues would study it.[4] In June 1988, Cohen questioned the newspaper's use of the word progressive, asking, "Why is progressive in quotes?"[5] And FAIR's criticism of the Old Gray Lady rarely abated extending into 2007.[6]

In an October 1989 issue of FAIR's *Extra!* Cohen discussed what he meant about the centrist bias of the elite media. The *New York Times* and the *Washington Post* "are the primary propaganda organs of the center, though editorially they've tilted rightward throughout the '80s..." their "centrist propaganda emphasizes system-supporting news, frequently speaking in euphemisms."[7]

Extra! editor Jim Naureckas told the trade book *Folio: The Magazine for Magazine Management* in 1994 that FAIR's "chief preoccupation has been with *The New York Times*—and there's some justification for that. For one thing, I think it's the paper with the most over-inflated reputation in the country. But it also sets the agendas for a lot of reporters, including many at the newsweeklies."[8]

Nevertheless, in a May 19, 1996, article, then-*Times* reporter Constance L. Hays penned a 1,117-word feature on the ten-year-old organization, focusing on its work as a critic of right-wing radio hosts Rush Limbaugh and Bob Grant. Hays concluded that among "a subculture of media-watch groups in New York who criticize Limbaugh and Grant...FAIR—which documents incendiary quotes as well as condemning them—has emerged as the sound bite of authority."[9] (That recognition may say as much about the *Times'* objectivity and fairness as it does about FAIR's reputation as a trustworthy analyst of media performance.)

After a hard-hitting interview with Jeff Cohen in 1999,[10] Pulitzer Prize winning *Los Angeles Times* media critic Howard Rosenberg explained, "In response to those faulting me for being even more obnoxious than usual, when appearing to be especially testy with Cohen...I was hoping to achieve some balance by playing devil's advocate. That's because I agree with him on nearly all issues regarding media."[11] (That endorsement did not sit well with conservative media critic Tim Graham of the Media Research Center in Alexandria, Virginia, who wrote the *Los Angeles Times,* complaining, "Hmm. If The *Times* did not have a liberal bias, would someone from the 'highly conservative' Media Research Center have the pleasure of an interview in its pages as Jeff Cohen of FAIR received...If Rosenberg believes that unlike him, we are here to demand only our opinions are aired, why would he publish only Cohen's, when he admitted a few days later, 'I agree with him on nearly all issues regarding media'?"[12])

Cohen's organization certainly has irked some in corporate media, notably *Washington Post*'s ombudsmen Michael Getler and Deborah Howell. Both used their columns to scold FAIR for its e-mail and phone message barrages. Said Getler in an April 24, 2005, column: "I was inundated with emails and phone messages last week from 700 or so faithful followers of FAIR...I don't like write-in campaigns. I don't like my email queue, and the email of others writing in about things, overwhelmed by hundreds of people saying essentially the same thing, in large part because somebody alerted them to something and suggested what to say."[13] Yet, Getler acknowledged, "On the other hand, even though such campaigns are annoying, and frequently partisan, it doesn't mean that the points raised are not legitimate challenges."[14]

Howell, Getler's successor, however, said FAIR's e-mail campaign was ineffective: "I pay attention to well-thought out emails from local readers...But I can see how email campaigns dilute the influence of those who write. As for me, I must say that email campaigns give me a pain in my right index finger—the one that hits the delete button."[15]

FAIR, however, remains steadfast in its use of electronic communicative activism. Peter Hart, head of the media activism and administration at FAIR, says the group operates on the premise that it is more difficult for corporate media to "ignore thousands of activists than it is to disregard one lone media watch group."[16] Hart argues that Howell's and Getler's responses are indicative of the mainstream media's disdain for the unqualified public to pass judgment on journalism ethics and performance: "While media elites might want us to believe that mass action is somehow less effective, FAIR's twenty years of experience suggest precisely the opposite: Collective activism is the only thing that works."[17]

Certainly a case can be made, as this book does, for the importance of building public opinion to bolster an effort to persuade news management to change its practices. Collective activism, however, is hardly the sole effective tactic used by media watchdog groups, including FAIR. The organization's critiques are widely respected by corporate media because, for the most part, FAIR's staff conveys them as verifiable factual assertions and scientifically sound statistical findings, couching them in the careful language of think-tank experts. On its Web site the group reminds the public, "We maintain a regular dialogue with reporters at news outlets across the country, providing constructive critiques when called for and applauding exceptional, hard-hitting journalism."[18] In 1988, the *Globe and Mail* (Toronto) noted, "Mr. Cohen's group publishes a newsletter that is distributed surreptitiously by sympathizers in the newsrooms of *The New York Times* and other major media."[19] Some, such as the Media Research Center's Graham, see a liberal conspiracy in all that, but FAIR founder Cohen rejects that label: "FAIR is progressive because we stand for structural change. Corporate liberals see a roof with a large hole, and they want to patch it. They don't solve problems. You could call us a left-of-center group. But liberal would not be accurate in describing us. When I first got involved in activism, the liberals were giving us the Vietnam War."[20] FAIR sees a consistent bias operating in the mainstream media (MSM): mostly centrist in its news coverage and center to right in its choice of news sources and pundits. And one of its great successes has been the coverage the MSM has given to the findings of its quantitative studies showing a heavy reliance by PBS's *MacNeil/Lehrer NewsHour*, Ted Koppel's *Nightline*, and National Public Radio (NPR) on political conservative and centrist white male experts, newsmakers, and pundits.

FAIR functions as a media watchdog, activist group, and think tank that adheres to civil libertarian, anticensorship evenhandedness. For example, though the firing of talk show host Bob Grant from ABC-owned WOR Radio in New York in 1996 has been linked to the group's sustained criticism of his on-air antigay and antiblack slurs, its senior analyst Steve Rendall says the group never called for his dismissal. FAIR, says Rendall, paraphrasing U.S. Supreme Court Justice Louis Brandeis's doctrine of counterspeech,[21] would have preferred that the radio station had hired a host to counterbalance Grant's hate speech: "We think the remedy for hate speech is more speech."[22]

The group also can be counted among the leaders in the "media reform" movement, activists on the left who contend that media conglomerates' ownership of the elite journalism outlets makes it difficult for MSM outlets to produce news reflecting a wide diversity of views.[23] The media reform movement traces its roots to famous press critics Upton Sinclair, George Seldes, I.F. Stone, and Ben Bagdikian, all who critiqued journalism based on their analysis of the economic interests of ownership. On the occasion of the group's 20th anniversary, Robert W. McChesney, president and co-founder of Free Press, a national media reform organization, and a leading scholar of the political economy of communication noted, "FAIR provided the foundation for the explosion in media reform activism of the past decade. Today there is an astonishing array of media reform activism, and FAIR's work has been a key reason for its development."[24]

The bylines of more than 100 authors, including Bagdikian, Noam Chomsky, and author and book critic Dan Lazare, have appeared in the group's bi-monthly magazine of media criticism, *Extra!*[25] The group's ten staffers also produce a weekly radio program, *CounterSpin*, which is broadcast on more than 130 stations in the United States.[26] More than 55,000 received its action alerts,[27] which illustrates how it was able to generate enough e-mails and phone calls to raise hackles from Getler and Howell. Its staffers have worked with each other or writers outside the organization to produce several books analyzing media performance, including *Adventures in Medialand: Behind the News, Beyond the Pundits* (1993), *The Way Things Aren't: Rush Limbaugh's Reign of Error* (1995), *Through the Media Looking Glass: Decoding Bias and Blather in the News* (1995), *Wizards of Media Oz: Behind the Curtain of Mainstream News* (1997), and *The Oh Really? Factor: Unspinning Fox News Channel's Bill O'Reilly* (2003). According to its Web site, 80 percent of FAIR's revenue comes from subscriptions to *Extra!* and contributions from supporters, foundation and public charity grants make up 12 percent of its operating budget; the group does not accept corporate funding, governmental grants, or advertising.[28]

In a little more than 20 years of operation, FAIR's efforts have earned it a reputation as an authoritative press critic and media analyst among the MSM, scholars, and its substantial following as measured by the size of its action-alert lists. It has played a major role in promoting the media reform agenda and nudged at least two news outlets, *The MacNeil/Lehrer Report* and *Yahoo! News*, to add diversity to their sources and content. And its founder Cohen, executive director until 2003, is the only nonaffiliated MSM news media critic to appear regularly on national television, including as a co-host of *Crossfire* on CNN, as a weekly *News Watch* panelist on Fox News, and as a commentator on MSNBC, as chronicled in his 2006 book, *Cable News Confidential: My Misadventures in Corporate Media:*[29] "I was inside deep as a progressive media critic has ever gotten. And what I found in places like CNN and MSNBC, the number one fear among the working reporters, producers is of doing anything that would get them or their channel accused of being liberal."[30]

Cohen remembers the moment he became a media critic. He was 19, attending the Winter Soldier Investigation, a gathering of 109 veterans and 16 civilians that took place in Detroit from January 31–February 2, 1971, and was sponsored by Vietnam Veterans Against the War.[31] There he witnessed a mainstream news camera crew pack up and leave rather than take footage of a veteran testifying about war atrocities.[32] First, however, he became a lawyer, practicing for the American Civil Liberties Union (ACLU) of Southern California. In 1978, the ACLU unit sued the Los Angeles Police Department for illegally spying on 144 plaintiffs, including community activists and antinuclear groups; Cohen worked as an attorney on the case. In January 1984, the ACLU won a $1.8 million settlement of that lawsuit from the City of Los Angeles.[33] "That (settlement) gave me some money—roughly $14,000—to travel around Western Europe for a year, where I saw that TV dominated by strong public broadcasting systems delivered smarter news programming and more diverse discussion than our commercial driven TV," Cohen explains.[34] At the outset, Cohen and fellow activists Linda Valentino, Martin Lee, and Andy Breslau operated out of Lee's apartment on Manhattan's West Side, trying with little success to raise money and recruit endorsers.[35]

National attention came early. Within eight months of FAIR's inception, *Newsweek*, the *New York Times*, the *Washington Post*, the *Boston Globe*, *Advertising Age*, the *Christian Science Monitor*, and the *Sydney Morning Herald* (Australia) quoted Cohen or noted FAIR's lead role in an alliance of Leftist activist groups protesting ABC television's planned airing of *Amerika*, a 12-hour, $35 million miniseries that eventually aired in February 1987.[36] The miniseries depicted a Soviet Union–conquered United States of America. Generally, Leftist groups decried it as a propaganda effort to stoke fear among Americans. The United Nations threatened to take legal action to have the director delete or reshoot scenes depicting its Special Services Unit aiding the Soviets in controlling a defeated United States. Consistent with FAIR's adherence to the counterspeech doctrine, Cohen asked ABC to provide "ample airtime for programming and post-'Amerika' panel discussions which supply context and balancing viewpoints" as it had done after the airing of *The Day After*, widely protested by the Right.[37] At the invitation of ABC, Cohen attended a meeting to discuss FAIR's concerns, but little came of the meeting, except additional clout for FAIR.[38]

In the spring of 1988, FAIR entered a new phase, one that proved quite effective in drawing media attention and leading to changes in the operations of ABC's *Nightline* and the Public Broadcasting Service's *MacNeil/Lehrer NewsHour*. Early on, the organization wanted research that would provide quantitative data on the political orientation of *Nightline*'s guest lists. Enter sociologists William Hoynes and David Croteau.

According to Hoynes, the social scientists spent much of that year "reading, coding and analyzing transcripts from 865 *Nightline* programs" covering "a 40-month period from 1985 to 1988."[39] Hoynes and Croteau identified race, gender, nationality, occupation of guests, and "when they appeared on the program, whether they appeared alone, how much they spoke and the topic of each program."[40] The study found that "89 percent of the American guests were male and 92 percent were white," and only 6 percent of the guests spoke for grassroots or minority organizations.[41] On the same day, February 6, 1989, that the organization released a press release on the study's findings—"Are You on the Nightline Guest List?"[42]—*USA Today*, the *San Francisco Chronicle*, and the *Boston Globe* ran stories on the study,[43] signaling that FAIR had reached think-tank status in the MSM's view.

Three days later, *Nightline* host Ted Koppel shot back, "*Nightline* is a news show, not the op-ed page of ABC News. You can't measure content of programs we do simply by looking at names of guests. We have been going to the newsmakers, many of whom are white, conservative males, and challenging their views."[44] There is some evidence to support that the study's finding altered the program's guest list. The following year, Walter Goodman of the *New York Times* reported that it "seems to have encouraged a slight broadening of that program's guest list."[45] Liberal columnist David Nyhan of the *Boston Globe* noted that Koppel's show "made one obvious adjustment after the first blast from FAIR... [Alexander] Haig and [Jerry] Falwell were dumped and [Henry] Kissinger and [Elliot] Abrams made only one appearance each in the next six months."[46]

Though FAIR's May 21, 1990, study, "All the Usual Suspects: MacNeil/ Lehrer and Nightline,"[47] made the *MacNeil/Lehrer NewsHour*'s co-host Jim Lehrer fume—"I didn't work with the right wing and it ain't gonna work with the left"[48]—the organization takes credit for the addition of scholars Noam Chomsky, Edward Said, and *The Progressive*'s editor Erwin Knoll as panelists or guests.[49] Hoynes and Croteau collaborated on the study, an examination of the guest lists from February 6–August 4, 1989.[50] According to the study's findings, 90 percent of the *NewsHour*'s U.S. guests were white and 87 percent were male; among its frequent guests "19 frequent guests (three or more appearances) included nine U.S. officials (six of whom are conservatives)" and was dominated by two conservative think tanks, the Center for Strategic and International Studies and the American Enterprise Institute.[51] Lehrer's ire notwithstanding, *NewsHour*'s executive producer Les Crystal said, "[W]e clearly can and should do better" to seek "a wide range of responsible views and people on the *NewsHour*."[52]

Hoynes's and Croteau's studies received praised from liberal columnists. The *Boston Globe*'s Nyhan, for example, concluded, "FAIR's point, and it seems irrefutable, is that both shows could do a lot better to be more inclusive and less biased toward the official, white, male position. If either program had a female anchor or a nonwhite, you'd probably see some distinctly different results. But that, as they say in TV news, is show business."[53]

The *NewsHour* producers and executives, however, rejected the findings of a FAIR guest list study released in October 2006, which found only little change from its earlier study—the percentage of women on the *NewsHour* and that the news program ranked higher than other network news programs in gender and racial diversity.[54] Executive producer Linda Winslow said the study's methods were questionable: "FAIR seems to be accusing us of covering the people who make decisions that affect people's lives, many of whom work in government, the military, or corporate America...In that sense, this report simply proved that FAIR is quite incapable of rendering selective judgments about who, and what, is important and worth listening to."[55]

Soon after, FAIR responded,

[Wilson's] argument that the *NewsHour* simply covers the people "who make news" pretends that news outlets have no role in determining what is newsworthy and what is not. The idea that "newsmakers" are overwhelmingly government officials ignores the fact that public interest advocates—representing civil rights, labor, consumer, environmental and other advocacy groups—have a direct relationship to "developments and policy decisions that affect large numbers of Americans." These voices are outnumbered on the *NewsHour* by official sources by more than 10-to-1.[56]

FAIR, however, received a more positive response from PBS ombudsman Getler, formerly with the *Washington Post*, when it criticized a January 8, 2007, *NewsHour* panel discussion of Iraq policy as presenting a limited range of political views by failing to include anyone who was critical of the Bush administration.[57] Getler noted, "[T]his was a poorly constructed panel, in my view, and its imbalance stood out dramatically, not only because it seemed lopsided at the beginning, which startled me and I'm sure others, but because it was a debate over a crucial subject on the eve of one of the president's most crucial and controversial decisions."[58] The PBS ombudsman even provided a link to FAIR's online Action Alert Debating the Iraq "Surge" on PBS in his column.[59]

NPR ombudsman Jeffrey A. Dvorkin also found merit in FAIR's 2004 study of its guest list that showed the radio service relied on the same elite and influential sources that dominate mainstream commercial news, even though NPR is widely believed to be liberal and an alternative to commercial news. The group examined the think tanks NPR relied on and on-air sources quoted—2,334 quoted sources, featured in 804 stories—in June 2003 on NPR's news shows: *All Things Considered, Morning Edition, Weekend Edition Saturday,* and *Weekend Edition Sunday,* finding that "government officials, professional experts and corporate representatives—accounted for 64 percent of all sources."[60] Dvorkin, noting that he had commissioned a similar study, said, "The FAIR study seems about right to me with a couple of exceptions."[61] Those exceptions, Dvorkin contended, were the designation of some individuals and think tanks as conservative instead of centrist or liberal, the failure to count guests who were academics, and the timing of the study, June 2003, when high-profile Republicans dominated the news and Democrats were keeping a low profile:

> FAIR is concerned whether the pendulum has swung too far. That's my concern as well. I think it may have and NPR needs to do a better job in general and especially in an election year—to make sure that the range is both wide and deep. At the same time, FAIR's study seems to reinforce the notion that what constitutes the center in American journalism is rapidly becoming an endangered species. For the left, NPR is never quite left enough. For the right of course, NPR remains a paragon of liberal bias. NPR sees itself as a bastion of fair-minded journalism. But fewer media critics are able to agree with that.[62]

Then there was the rare occasion when a target agreed unequivocally with FAIR's assessment. An August 9, 2001, FAIR "Action Alert" sent to its subscribers noted, among other findings, that Yahoo! News Opinion/Editorial columnists are 67 percent male, 90 percent white, and only 24 percent liberal.[63] According to FAIR, Yahoo! News senior producer Kourosh Karimkhany responded with thanks: "To state it succinctly, we agree with you 100 percent. We have been trying to achieve exactly what you suggested."[64]

Media watchdog as think tank is a recent phenomenon. But the idea traces back in part to Nelson Antrim Crawford's *The Ethics of Journalism*,[65] originally published in 1924. In *The Ethics of Journalism*, Crawford, a journalism professor at Kansas State Agricultural College, called for "an analysis of representative examples of the American press by a committee of whose objective-mindedness, fairness and familiarity with journalistic practice there could be no doubt... The mere publication of the findings of the investigation would put the indubitable concrete facts about American journalism into the arena of public discussion, and this of itself would result in a speedy improvement."[66] The Hutchins Commission 1947 report, *A Free and Responsive Press*, called for "centers of intelligence" or "media think tanks," according to Everette E. Dennis and David L. Stebenne.[67]

It is unlikely that Crawford had a media watchdog group such as FAIR in mind. Avowedly progressive, FAIR might not fit Crawford's definition of "objective-mindedness," though that was the organization's intent behind bringing in social scientists Hoynes and Croteau. Arguably, FAIR's analysts do not have the "familiarity with journalistic practice" of which "there can be no doubt."[68] Still, FAIR incorporates the essence of a research center by expanding its analysis of news media beyond subjective analysis, presenting it as empirical and verifiable statistical findings.

The Media Research Center (MRC) is FAIR's right-wing counterpart in that it conducts studies seeking to show liberal bias in the news media. Founded in 1987 by L. Brent Bozell III, MRC has a news analysis division, which according to the center, "has worked to bring political balance to the nation's news media by documenting and countering liberal bias from television network news shows and major print publications."[69] According to a compilation of its research, "The Liberal Media Exposed," between 1964 and 2004, MSM journalists vote for Democratic presidential candidates more than Republican candidates; journalists are far more likely to say they are liberal than conservative; and they offer "reflexively liberal answers to practically every question a pollster can imagine."[70]

The Gannett Center for Media Studies (1984–1996), subsequently named the Freedom Forum Media Studies Center, was probably more what Crawford and the Hutchins Commission had in mind, as is the Pew Research Center's Project for Excellence in Journalism. The Gannett Foundation created the Media Studies Center at Columbia University in 1984.[71] According to Everette E. Dennis, the Media Studies Center's executive director, and David L. Stebenne, the research officer at the Center, the research projects and internal staff research yielded "scores of books and monographs, hundreds of scholarly and professional articles, reports, empirical studies, as well as the founding of the *Gannett Center Journal* (subsequently the *Media Studies Journal*).[72] The Gannett Foundation eventually scrapped the Center because "by the mid-1990s the center no longer served the foundation's purposes."[73]

The Project for Excellence in Journalism's best-known work is *The Elements of Journalism: What Newspeople Should Know and the Public Should Expect.*[74] Its authors, Bill Kovach, the project's senior counsel, and Tom Rosenstiel, its director, are widely quoted authorities on journalism ethics.[75] The project, founded in 1996, joined the Pew Research Center in Washington, D.C., in 2006.[76] The Center "conducts public opinion polling and social science research; reports news and analyzes news coverage; and holds forums and briefings."[77] "The State of the News Media" report typifies the project's use of social scientific methods to evaluate and study the performance of the press. Initiated in 2003, the reports track the status and health of the news industry. The reports rely on original research and aggregated data from other studies "to identify trends, mark key indicators, note areas for further inquiry and provide a resource for citizens, journalists, and researchers"[78] on digital journalism, newspapers, network television, cable television, local television, magazines, radio, and ethnic media.

CONCLUSION

A diverse and robust marketplace of ideas is the foundation of our democracy. According to Yale Law School professor Robert C. Post's First Amendment–derived public discourse theory, the First Amendment is "committed to diversity."[79] More specifically, the U.S. Supreme Court has said that the "widest possible dissemination of information from diverse and antagonistic sources is essential to the welfare of the public."[80] It would follow then, that the press—the institution that the First Amendment specifically identifies as deserving protection[81]—embraces viewpoint diversity as part of its core values. And most MSM news outlets do, too, including the ones whose guest lists and sources were deemed overwhelmingly white, male, conservative, and centrist by FAIR. ABC News is a member of the Radio-Television News Directors Association and Foundation. The foundation's code of ethics and professional conduct says electronic journalists should "[p]resent a diversity of expressions, opinions, and ideas in context."[82] Similarly, PBS "Editorial Standards and Policy" states, "The goal of diversity also requires continuing efforts to assure that PBS content fully reflects the pluralism of our society, including, for example, appropriate representation of women and minorities."[83] The NPR News Code of Ethics and Practices makes clear that "[t]reating the people we cover and our listeners with respect means we recognize the diversity of the country and world on which we report, and the diversity of interests, attitudes and experiences of our audience."[84] Yahoo! News[85] subscribes to Society of Professional Journalists' Code of Ethics. One key aspect of the Society's diversity committee's mission is to "expand the depth and quality of news reports through better sourcing."[86]

These public declarations make ABC, PBS, NPR, and Yahoo! News accountable to their audiences and the public on questions about the inclusiveness of their guest and sources lists. The outlets have struck a compact with the public that they will present a wide range of views, a range as diverse as the range of views held by the American public in some cases. Consequently, FAIR's studies showing a pattern of exclusiveness practiced by the four news outlets serve as evidence of breach: the news outlets failed to live up to their promises to their audiences and public.[87] The varied responses by the outlets—inviting FAIR to a meeting, engaging in public debate with the organization about the merits of its claims, or acknowledgement of the validity of the claims in part or in full— are implicit acknowledgment by those outlets of their promises to provide diversity of opinions and views. Likewise, the news outlets that ran reports on the studies' findings have acknowledged that FAIR critiques are credible.

From its start, FAIR professed to advocate for "greater diversity"[88] of the experts and sources quoted and interviewed by corporate media, and the evidence shows that it has consistently asked its news outlets to add left-of-center views and those from women and people of color. But it has never asked news media outlets to exclude its ideological opponents or content that represents such beliefs. It is widely believed that the widespread exchange of diverse views and ideas undergird democracy. By that gauge, FAIR's call for the inclusion of new and diverse voices to be heard in the mass media places it squarely in the mainstream of democratic and First Amendment theory and practice.

Though it has a progressive political agenda that its detractors argue undermines its credibility, for the most part, its research stands up to scrutiny. For example, Danielle Gorash, manager of media relations for Fox News, which promotes itself as fair and balanced, responded to FAIR's breakdown of guests interviewed on Fox News Channel's *Special Report With Brit Hume*, during the first five months of 2001 by saying FAIR is known to be biased and therefore lacks credibility.[89] But the *Minneapolis Star Tribune* reported, "She was unable to point to any inaccuracy in FAIR's numbers or its methodology."[90]

FAIR, the evidence shows, plays that way. It is transparent in its goals, methods, and methodology and temperate in its language. Though it remains highly critical of corporate media, it seeks to engage executives, editors, and journalists in discussions. Listen to FAIR media analyst Hart: "The irony of being a media criticism group is that you try to make a series of arguments about mainstream media, and at the same time, you hope that people from the mainstream media will want to write about that or have you on their TV programs."[91]

.

Brill's Content: "An Inside-the-Sausage-Factory Look at Media for People Who Eat Sausages, Not Those Who Make Them"[1]

More than a year before Steven Brill would coin the phrase "Pressgate," New York's media elite buzzed with rumors of his next big idea. It was late February 1997 and Brill announced that he was getting out of the legal journalism business. He had not invented the genre of legal journalism, but he certainly revolutionized it. A best-selling author at 27, Brill founded *The American Lawyer* magazine in August 1978.[2] He parlayed the unique magazine into a mini-empire, American Lawyer Media, L.P., and by 1991 he reigned as chairman and CEO over nine regional legal and business publications, an online service for lawyers, and the Courtroom Television Network, or Court TV.[3] The idea of Court TV, a 24-hour cable network, struck him when he heard a news item promoting a televised trial blaring from a taxicab radio. He sold the idea and a majority interest in his company to Steve Ross, then-chairman of Warner Communications.[4] Court TV won him a national audience, a nationally known name and face, and the backing of the media conglomerate Time Warner Inc.

The partnership ended tumultuously, however, when Time Warner's Ted Turner bought Brill's interest in the venture for an estimated $20 million to $40 million.[5] According to *Mother Jones* magazine, "Time Warner pressured [Brill] not to air a profile of a Federal Trade Commission official, for fear that it might jeopardize Time Warner's then-pending merger with Turner Broadcasting."[6] So by the first week of March 1997, Brill, a master at creating buzz, talked about one of his new ideas to the *New York Times*: a journalism review targeting news consumers because "journalists are probably the only people on the planet who make lawyers look good."[7]

Never has a press-media criticism magazine stirred such unease and fanfare among the media so many months before its subscribers would thumb through its pages. By late July 1997, the public learned the name of the proposed magazine: *Content*.[8] Later that month, the *Washington Post* noted that Clinton White House communications director and strategic planning chief Donald A. Baer joined Brill to launch a national media review magazine.[9] That September, Brill described the proposal to the *American Journalism Review*, a future rival, as a monthly magazine that would investigate "anything that purports to be non-fiction" because "[t]here's no magazine telling people what's true, what's real, what's reliable—whether it's on the Web, a magazine, advertising, newspapers, television."[10] Some 500,000 prototype copies of the magazine had been tested in two national direct mail campaigns, Brill said, noting that he needed to attract "between 300,000 and 400,000 subscribers in the first four years" to make the publication successful.[11] A November *MediaWeek* article found him working to meet a May 1998 launch date, although the publication that would eventually be called *Brill's Content* did not reach the public until late June of that year.[12]

When Brill started *The American Lawyer*, he hired largely untested talent. But for the magazine that was to become *Brill's Content*, Brill hired veterans— *Time* magazine's chief political correspondent Michael Kramer, *Time* contributor Calvin Trillin, *U.S. News & World Report* assistant managing editor Amy Bernstein, and former *Entertainment Weekly* vice president of marketing and business development Deana Brown was named associate publisher—attracting more press coverage and sustaining the buzz.[13] When it was clear that his proposed magazine would not be ready for a March launch, the *New York Times* devoted 907 words to the delay.[14] Even in an article about *Fortune* magazine, the *New York Times* quoted Brill, adding that he was "starting *Content* magazine in June, which is expected to be tough on the media."[15] He made the pages of *Variety* when Home Shopping Network (HSN) Inc. media mogul Barry Diller and financier George Soros invested in the project.[16] Prototype covers appeared in surprisingly opportune places, providing him with publicity that could not be bought. Then-President Bill Clinton, for instance, waved a copy at an audience attending the White House Correspondents' Dinner that April.[17]

Perhaps *New York Times* columnist Maureen Dowd best sized up the effect of the promotion and marketing campaign that preceded the magazine's arrival.

> Reporters are cowering at the imminent arrival of their very own Godzilla, Steven Brill....The famously abrasive, smart and successful Mr. Brill, who made a fortune on *The American Lawyer* magazine and Court TV, is starting a splashy new media criticism magazine, *Content*...He has plastered posters on the sides of New York

City buses with the grinning faces of Brokaw, Rather and Jennings, promising "This June, the Media's Free Ride Comes to a Screeching Halt." *Content* wooed subscribers by vowing that "legendary journalist" Steven Brill will guard the guards, "unmask the charlatans" and hold journalists' feet to the fire.[18]

The premiere issue of *Brill's Content: The Independent Voice of the Information Age,* dated August 1998, reached most subscribers and newsstands by June 29, though the media had copies by early June. Public relations experts estimated that Brill spent about $1 million to promote the first issue, about one-fifth of his estimated first-year marketing budget.[19] It was 9×11, 152 pages, and its cover was a graphic design faux pas. It featured Independent Counsel Kenneth Starr surrounded by a torrent of journalists, microphones, and four different typefaces in black, white, yellow, and red.[20] The inaugural issue, however, was not to be judged solely by its cover, but rather by its content. And the strongest story was "Pressgate," penned by Brill.

The 25,000-word, 29-page cover story indicted the media's coverage of the first three weeks of the Monica Lewinsky–Bill Clinton sex scandal, which broke that January 19,[21] as a "true example of an institution being corrupted to its core."[22] Their sins, Brill documented, were publishing accusations supplied by one source, Starr's office, labeling them as anonymous or mischaracterizing them as multiple anonymous sources, and failing to verify the truth of the accusations.[23] Others had opined and speculated on Starr's leaks to the media. Brill, however, relied on his immense reporting and interviewing skills to get scoops: Starr's admission to leaking information about prospective grand jury witnesses and expected testimony to reporters, reporters revealing the identities of their sources, and, for example, "acknowledgments from the likes of Tom Brokaw that journalists had their feet on the gas pedal, and at times seemed to be careening out of control."[24] Days before the premiere issue reached the public, Brill gave the *New York Times* advanced copies of "Pressgate," priming the engine for a new round of free publicity, particularly exposure on TV and radio talk shows.[25] No press-media review before had promoted its launch so effectively. By September 2000, the magazine reached a paid circulation of 286,124.[26] Brill had planned to reach a circulation of 500,000 subscribers by mid-2003,[27] so he seemed on pace toward meeting his self-imposed goal. Yet, by October 2001, the magazine ceased publication.

Brill believed he could defy history. As this chapter documents, no press review magazine has ever been profitable, and, among this genre, no such magazine targeting the general public and relying on advertising has survived more than seven years. Only George Seldes's *In Fact,* which like *Brill's* targeted news consumers, made money for a time and published for 19 years. But it was a newsletter, far less ambitious and expensive to run than a magazine. History shows that devoting a magazine to press-media criticism is a money-losing proposition and that long-term survival is linked to affiliation with universities or securing nonprofit funding.

Brill had some knowledge of the press-media review market and its history; he had discussions about buying *Columbia Journalism Review*, for instance. According to Brill, his *American Lawyer* magazine served as the model for *Brill's* and not the commentaries of A. J. Liebling in *The New Yorker*'s "Wayward Press" column or other journalism reviews.[28] *The American Lawyer* and Court TV served as Brill's laboratories for applied journalism ethics. For instance, he devised a hypertransparent corrections policy after the magazine published "*Ariel Sharon v. Time.*" (A February 21, 1983, *Time* news report implied that the then-Israeli general was responsible for the massacres during the 1982 Lebanon War. Sharon sued the magazine for libel.) Years later, he described announcing his correction policy—apparently unique in the industry—to his staff.

> *Time* had performed terribly. It had really done an awful job. Basically, the reporter had made up a story. Their arrogance was just breathtaking, and it turned out that the more I went through all of the legal papers in this article, the more I found, for example, that *Time* and *Newsweek* had a policy at the time that they never, ever made a correction...Our corrections policy was going to be that if we made a mistake, we'd correct it in our own voice and the correction would always be as prominent as the mistake. So that if one of our legal newspapers, by then we had a bunch of these papers, ran a mistake on the front page, that's where the correction would go. Then I said this really terrible thing: "We're going to put a byline on the correction. We're going to say who made the mistake."[29]

Similarly, he proposed "A New Code for Journalists" in 1994 that *The Open Mind* host Richard Heffner called "quite an extraordinary proposal."[30] Among the innovations were "a journalist should always be candid about the quality and certainty of his or her information. "[A journalist's] first priority...is not to entertain or otherwise attract an audience or please advertisers but to give people information that they think is important for them to know."[31]

He was as certain about the prospects of *Brill's Content* as he was about the viability of the innovative *American Lawyer* and *Court TV*. Had not those outlets succeeded despite the carping of a host of naysayers? And, unlike his predecessors in press-review magazines, Brill had years of experience as a media outlet owner and manager, and substantial capital. He believed that his timing was perfect. The advent of the Web had ushered in a new information age, and polls showed that the public was largely dissatisfied with the press performance.

He was right in one respect. His publication attracted more than 300,000 subscribers,[32] a number few but Brill thought a press-media review could attain.[33] On that account, *Brill's*[34] was a unique publication and, accordingly, merits recognition as an effective press critic because its 300,000 subscribers quantify the publication's success in spurring debate mostly among nonjournalists about news-media performance. Brill engaged information consumers, as he was fond of calling them, in a discussion about news performance, including the operation of his own magazine. And unlike almost all previous press-review magazines,

Brill's Content empathized with many news consumers, giving a voice to their displeasure with mainstream media. More specifically, the publication engaged its readers in conversation. It surveyed them and set up focus groups and a media complaint board to mine their opinions about press performance. According to Jonah Goldberg, a contributing editor, the magazine was a "sort of *Consumer Reports* dedicated to making sure the ingredients of other journalistic fare checked out in their independent tests."[35]

Media critic James Boylan argued that the magazine reduced "criticism of journalism to consumer choice," confronting "us with the question of whether journalism criticism is becoming useless in a public context."[36] Though the magazine offered advice about preferred news outlets and rated television pundits, on the whole it did not as Boylan contend "acutely" strip "from media criticism most public values."[37] On the contrary, in philosophy and in execution the magazine sought to hold the news media accountable to the public for a grander purpose than saving news consumers' money and time: "I want to tip the balance of power away from the increasingly arrogant and defensive media and put it back with those who use information, not those who manufacture it. If we fail—if the media goes unchecked, unquestioned, and unscrutinized—our very freedoms are at risk."[38]

The magazine's reports often made an immediate impression on its targets, not because it persuaded news media outlets to change—there is little evidence of such an impact—but because the strength of its fact-based assertions compelled their targets to defend themselves, often in the pages of *Brill's Content*. No doubt that is largely due to the demographics of the magazine's readers. They were largely sophisticated readers, listeners, and watchers of news content and nonfiction publications. They consumed the content that *Brill's* targeted. Consequently, a hard-hitting critique from *Brill's* could mean a loss in sales or audience. Of course, its targets must have felt a greater need to respond when Brill penned the criticism, given his track record as a news-media executive and outstanding journalist. For instance, when the magazine criticized Bob Woodward's *Shadow: Five Presidents and the Legacy of Watergate* in 1999, the renowned journalist sparred with Brill in the publication.[39] And, at least by Pulitzer Prize winning editorial writer Michael Gartner's standards, who praised the magazine in a *Columbia Journalism Review* article, the magazine "really pissed off Kenneth Starr and Norman Pearlstine [*Time* magazine] and *New York Times* reporters and Bob Woodward, among others, and that means that it takes on important issues and that big-time people read it and take it seriously and think it is important and try to spin it."[40]

Perhaps *Brill's* greatest value lay in its ability to stimulate discussion among the public and the news media about media accountability in new and provocative ways because Brill made original concrete proposals for reform—a credibility environment rating to assess the outlet's reliability, full disclosure corrections, voluntary self-restraint policies when covering grieving families and children, media dispute forums, and a quality-control procedure that a news outlet might use to check up on its journalists. Again, the industry discussed them at the time, did not adopt them, but it has not fully rejected all of them as some of the proposals resurface from time to time when a news scandal erupts. Finally, during the magazine's short life span and beyond the MSM and scholars recognized Brill as an authority on journalism ethics.

When the magazine closed in October 2001 observers offered a number of theories to explain why the publication failed: Brill's media business deals raised conflicts of interests that eroded his publication's integrity as a fair arbiter of media performance, the failure of a partnership with Primedia Inc., the dot.com collapse made advertising dollars scarce, or readers' interest in press-media criticism was wide but not deep. Claude-Jean Bertrand, for example, concluded, "But *Content* came under fire for a merchandising alliance with big firms (such as CBS and NBC) to sell media products on-line. Nevertheless, it found it impossible to survive the 2001 economic downturn."[41] But based on interviews with Brill, media critics, and an examination of the publication and contemporary commentary, this chapter argues that the magazine failed because press reviews are inherently unattractive to advertisers of high-end products, particularly makers of luxury media technology products.

Critics, including social commentators, book authors, civic leaders and organizations, and members of the press, have leveled complaints against news outlets' newsgathering, editorial, and business policies and practices since the early 1600s in England.[42] This chapter's scope, however, is limited to nonacademic periodicals—magazines and Web sites and, to a lesser degree, newsletters—devoted to press-media criticism.

Wisely, several press-media criticism publications never tried to turn a profit. *Quill*, the Society of Professional Journalists' national magazine, has published for more than 90 years.[43] The *Bulletin of the American Society of Newspaper Editors* started in 1922 as a mimeographed sheet for its organization's daily newspaper editors.[44] Starting in 1925, the American Society of Newspaper Editors published it on a monthly and occasionally semimonthly basis for members, journalism schools, and others.[45] By 1944, the *Bulletin* had "become a major forum for receiving complaints as well as being the object of complaints" that it too often was little more than a house organ.[46] By 1995, the monthly was renamed *The American Editor*.[47]

George Seldes, one of America's most prominent press critics in the first half of the twentieth century, sought a lay audience for his commentary. He created the fortnightly newsletter *In Fact: An Antidote for Falsehood in the News* in 1940 to "supply news for that part of the American people, estimated at 30 million, which has in several public-opinion polls expressed its doubt as to the honesty of the American press."[48] Seldes deemed the May 20, 1940, inaugural issue a success because "we had 6,000 subscribers and money in the bank." The newsletter contained reportage and commentary but seldom advertising, which Seldes considered a corrupting influence.[49]

It remained a newsletter throughout its 19 years of publication and perhaps that explains its longevity compared to the short-lived press-media journalism reviews such as *Brill's* that also targeted the general reader. *In Fact* has been described as "the nation's first successful journalism review"[50] and claimed 176,000 subscribers at its peak in 1947, a figure media executive, editor, and author Harold Evans years later characterized as "amazing."[51] It left its mark. Seldes's publication of a suppressed 1939 study, "Tobacco Smoking and Longevity" led to the U.S. Surgeon General's report on smoking and health 30 years later.[52] Seldes ceased publication because he concluded there were not enough liberals to reach his goal of a million subscribers during the Red Scare years.[53]

From the launch of the *Bulletin* in 1922 to 1968, *In Fact* was the exception among press-media reviews because Seldes engaged in a conversation about the media with media consumers and *In Fact* was not affiliated with a university or nonprofit. In contrast, Harvard University's *Nieman Reports*, a quarterly founded in 1947, has never been pitched to the general news consumer, carving out "a unique role in the community of journalism publications" allowing journalists to talk to other journalists about their craft.[54] Its editor, Melissa Ludtke, says it does not belong in the genre of press-media criticism: "It's press education."[55] "The result is a blend of critical and utilitarian coverage mostly devoid of scolding," *Columbia Journalism Review* observed. "Although the how-I-got-the-story pieces sometimes border on the self-congratulatory, they also allow NR to include the social ramifications of what journalists do."[56]

Since *Nieman Reports* does not hold itself out as a press-media criticism publication, former University of Montana School of Journalism Dean Nathaniel Blumberg's claim that the *Montana Journalism Review* is "the first journalism review published by a university...and the first periodical to critically analyze press performance on a regular basis aside from George Seldes' marvelous *In Fact*," rings true.[57] According to Blumberg, about 2,000 copies have been distributed each year to the school's journalism graduates and to publishers, editors, and editorial writers of daily and weekly publications. "All expenses were paid by the school and university until recent years when advertisers were solicited, a decision I oppose," Blumberg said. From 1991 to 1999, Blumberg published 20 issues of the *Treasure State Review*, a 12-page almost-quarterly and a *Treasure State Review* Web site that has not been updated for some time.[58]

Grassroots Editor has a university and organization affiliation. Howard Rusk Long of Southern Illinois University and co-founder of the International Society of Weekly Newspaper Editors (ISWNE) launched the quarterly in 1960 to be the society's publication. It has a mission similar to *Nieman Reports*, though "many of its contributors have proved themselves critics."[59] Now it is affiliated with Missouri Southern State University. The magazine, which still comes with ISWNE membership, is also available by subscription.[60]

None of the university-affiliated press-media reviews has gained the distinction and longevity of *Columbia Journalism Review* (*CJR*).[61] In 1971, it went from quarterly to bimonthly, added advertising in 1975 and editors, and according to founding editor James Boylan, "plans were also made to expand *CJR* into a kind of *Atlantic Monthly* of media criticism, with emphasis on consumer rather than professional appeal—somewhat the same experiment that the magazine *Brill's Content* attempted, without lasting success, in the 1990s."[62] Yet, since its inaugural issue October 1961, *CJR*'s paid circulation has never exceeded 40,000, and the majority of its subscribers are journalists.[63] In 1994, for example, 70 percent of its readers were media professionals.[64]

In the tradition of Seldes's *In Fact*, several journalists turned press-media critics launched a new breed of reviews seeking to engage news consumers and members of the news media, starting with the *Chicago Journalism Review* in October 1968. What some local reporters saw as the deliberate rewriting by the mainstream press of the Chicago municipal administration's handling of the riots that broke out during the Democratic Party convention that year spurred *Chicago American* reporter Ron Dorfman to create the "first watchdog publication focused on a single city's news media."[65] The review lasted seven years, but spawned 19 other, mostly short-lived press-media reviews focused on one city's news media, and typically operated and written by so-called dissident journalists, striving to empower other journalists.[66] For example, in Denver, *The Unsatisfied Man: A Review of Colorado Journalism* published from 1971 to winter 1975. It was the offspring of the Colorado Media Project and during its last two years was edited by Sue O'Brien, a former associate dean of the University of Colorado–Boulder School of Journalism and Mass Communication.[67] Other local press-media reviews included *Buncombe* in Baltimore, *Hawaii Journalism Review* in Honolulu, the *Houston Journalism Review*, the *Southern California Journalism Review* in Long Beach, *More* in New York, the *Philadelphia Journalism Review* in Philadelphia, the *Oregon Journalism Review* in Portland, the *San Francisco Bay Journalism Review* in San Francisco, and the *Twin Cities Journalism Review* in St. Paul.[68]

In New York, journalists Richard Pollak, William Woodward, and J. Anthony Lukas published *More* from June 1971 to July 1978.[69] It was created as an alternative to the *Columbia Journalism Review*, but its publisher, James Adler, sold it to Columbia University as a tax write-off with its 10,600 subscribers, and its circulation, at 15,000, never having cracked 23,000.[70] According to its co-founder Pollak: "We survived for the years we did on the generosity of donors, primarily Bill Woodward; we were never even close to being advertising dependent, and were naïve to think that we ever could be."[71] Another *More*'s editor, Michael Kramer, who later served a short stint as *Brill's* first editorial director, recalled that "[*More*] never made a dime, although our *More* conference turned a slight profit. But obviously not enough to make up the deficit."[72]

The *St. Louis Journalism Review: A Critique of Metropolitan News Media and Events* is the only survivor of the generation of local press-media reviews. By February 2006, however, its future was in doubt.[73] Charles and Rose Klotzer founded the publication in 1970, and today it comes out ten times annually and has a Web presence. According to Charles Klotzer, who financed the publication from money from his graphics company, the journal has never made money and Webster University in St. Louis took over the publication in 1995, though it does not have editorial control. Its circulation has never exceeded 4,000.[74]

The *Washington Journalism Review* (*WJR*) got off to a rocky start in October 1977 and never gained its footing. Roger Kranz launched the review, and it suffered during its first two years from an erratic publishing schedule—only four issues—and mounting debt, between $30,000 and $40,000.[75] In May 1979, Kranz sold it and its $50,000 debt to Henry and Jessica Catto. The couple published its first issue in January 1980.

Like the *St. Louis Journalism Review*, *WJR* is now university owned. In May 1987, the Cattos unburdened themselves of the magazine by donating it to the University of Maryland College of Journalism.[76] The university, however, changed the review's name to the *American Journalism Review*.

Unlike *WJR*, the *American Journalism Review* now covers media nationwide and publishes six times each year. Its editor and senior vice president Rem Rieder stresses that it relies on "heavily reported analysis of coverage as opposed to top-of-the-head, reporting-free commentary."[77] In 2003, its subscription circulation was merely 4,769,[78] and in 2004 the publication received a $500,000 five-year grant from the Knight Foundation.[79]

Accuracy in Media, a nonprofit founded in 1969—first producing a newsletter and now with a Web site and other publications—was not founded by a liberal, progressive, or a centrist journalist as is the tradition in press-media criticism. Its founder, Reed Irvine, was a former economist with the Federal Reserve. Like the *Chicago Journalism Review*'s Dorfman, Irvine also was spurred to correct what he saw as the bias in the media's coverage of the 1968 Democratic Party convention. He, however, believed the bias favored liberals and the Left.[80]

What accounted for the poor survival rate of the local press-media? Generally, the founders of these publications conducted little or no market research, direct mailing, promotion, or marketing. They did not test with mock-up issues to gauge reader responses. Though it is true that some magazines have conducted such studies and failed and some that have relied mostly on their founders' instincts have succeeded. Still, all of the owners seemed to have overestimated the costs in running such publications and the appetite of journalists, policy makers, or the general public to read about press-media bias, foibles, and scandals. Nevertheless, reform-minded media professionals cannot seem to part with the idea that there is a substantial readership beyond those who subscribe to trade publications willing to spend money to read about how the sausage gets made in the news media business or to read critiques of press performance.

In 1981, Les Brown, a former television critic of the *New York Times* and *Variety*, believed he had found the right editorial approach with *Channels of Communications: The Critical Review of the Electronic Media*. It was a "magazine of serious thought about television, for people who read," Brown said.[81] The John and Mary R. Markle Foundation funded Brown's venture until 1985. Then with a circulation of 30,000 (half paid), Brown formed a company, C.C. Publishing, with television producer Norman Lear as an investor. They set goals: make a profit, attract advertisers, and reach a paid circulation of 44,000.[82] The publication, however, closed in 1990.[83]

Meanwhile, the self-proclaimed progressive national media watch group and self-styled anticensorship organization, Fairness & Accuracy in Reporting (FAIR), started *Extra!*, a magazine of press criticism, in 1986. By 2005, *Extra!*, which receives money only from subscribers and is a creature of a nonprofit group, claimed "25,000 subscribers or so."[84] It targets nonjournalists and the magazine has a weekly radio program counterpart.[85]

In the early 1990s harsh marketplace realities halted two projects in their embryonic stages. In July 1990, accomplished journalists such as J. Anthony Lukas, Ken Auletta, Francis FitzGerald, David Halberstam, Bill Kovach, and Jonathan Alter believed there was a market to do something similar to *More*. They called their proposal *Mercury*. It was primarily the vision of *Newsweek* press critic Alter.[86] In Alter's view the university-owned reviews looked at the press too narrowly, so there was a need for an alternative: "But we were sailing into the recession of the early 1990s and could not raise the necessary money to launch."[87] Adam Moss, editor of the defunct *7 Days* magazine, was poised to launch *The Industry* in 1992 as its founder and editor in chief. *The Industry* was supposed to have been "both a trade magazine for media executives and a good gossipy read for the general reader," and a direct mail test provided favorable results by May 1992.[88] It, however, was never launched.

Success with the genre eluded the market savvy Forbes family. The publishing empire and self-proclaimed "capitalist tool" failed to make *Forbes MediaCritic* work. It went silent in November 1996, never gaining more than 10,000 in paid subscriptions in its three years.[89] Oxymoronically, Brill insisted that his publication was "a completely different iteration" of the *Mercury*, *The Industry*, and *Forbes MediaCritic*.[90]

Like his predecessors, Brill did not test the viability of his proposal through market research methods such as focus groups or surveys. Rather, he relied on favorable returns from two direct-mail tests that sampled 200,000 people. Each time more than 4 percent of the respondents subscribed, a success because he sought no higher than a 3½ percent sign-up rate as evidence that the proposed magazine had an audience that could reach 500,000 paid circulation within four years.[91] Former *More* and *Brill's* editor Kramer recalled, "The plan (such as it was) that I discussed with Brill highlighted [*More's*] lack of advertising and the general inability to attract an audience beyond journalists."[92] And *Newsweek's* Alter sent his proposal for the stillborn *Mercury* to Brill "and he adapted a few of my ideas."[93] Nevertheless, Brill's success with *The American Lawyer* remained his key model for *Brill's*.[94]

Brill's approach was different than his predecessor's in several notable ways. None of the heads of previous press-media reviews hired an ombudsman to critique their publication's performance. Brill, however, hired first Bill Kovach and then Michael Gatner as ombudsmen and gave them guaranteed contracts to shield them from possible pressure—perceived or real—from management to mute their criticism of their boss. None of *Brill's* predecessors had the financial backing of the likes of media magnate Diller, financier Soros, real estate tycoon

Howard P. Milstein, and financier Lester Pollack and a recently minted multi-millionaire, Brill, as its principal owner and editor, putting up a total of $27 million in seed money.[95] Perhaps, *Brill's* predecessors did not need ombudsmen as much as *Brill's* because their owners avoided business entanglements that raised conflicts of interests. Investor Diller owned USA Networks, Inc. and later Brill's online venture, *Contentville,* included CBS, NBC, *TheStreet.com* founder James Cramer, Primedia, EBSCO, and Ingram Book Group.[96] Earlier, Brill cut his ties with *Dateline NBC* and later dropped tobacco advertising after press critics took him to task for affiliations that they said eroded his credibility as an impartial arbiter of media.[97] Even the widely praised "Pressgate" exposé was tainted in the eyes of some because of Brill's failure to disclose his campaign contributions to Clinton and other Democrats.[98]

At best, there are a handful of reports or essays on press performance that have provoked public self-examination among journalists and widespread public discussion of press performance. In the second half of the 1800s, magazines of commentary and literary criticism—*Nation, Arena, Century, Dial, Forum, Atlantic Monthly*—combined published hundreds of articles of press criticism.[99] But no single article alone in their pages rattled the Yellow Press to self-examination. Will Irwin's "The American Newspaper" raised public awareness of the "concern over the corruption and moral decay of newspapers," press criticism historian Marion Tuttle Marzolf notes.[100] But it was not a single article; it was a series that ran in *Colliers* magazine from January–July 1911. However, Ben Bagdikian's 1968 *Esquire* magazine article, "The American Newspaper Is Neither Record, Mirror, Journal, Ledger, Bulletin, Telegram, Examiner, Register, Chronicle, Gazette, Observer, Monitor, Transcript, nor Herald of the Day's Events,"[101] inspired efforts to create ombudsmen and news councils. A June 11, 1967, *New York Times Magazine* article by A.H. Raskin, "What's Wrong with American Newspapers?" also is considered to have stimulated discussion about creating ombudsmen positions at newspapers.[102]

Measured by those precedents, "Pressgate" ranks as a historically significant piece of press criticism. (Years later, Brill said the highly controversial "Pressgate" "didn't help us in advertising" because "[a]dvertisers don't like controversy. That didn't bother me because I knew the first order of business was to get subscribers."[103]) Of course, the larger controversy over President Bill Clinton's affair with Monica Lewinsky and special prosecutor Kenneth Starr's performance boosted the article's public profile. But had it not stood on its own merits, those bigger controversies would have swamped it. According to the trade publication *Quill:*

> For a week in mid-June, Brill and his new monthly seemed to dominate the headlines and airwaves with his coup—an on-the-record interview with Starr in which the special prosecutor acknowledged that he and his office regularly leaked and spun to reporters. Brill pounded individual reporters and news organizations as a frenzied pack of "lapdogs" and prosecutor's "stenographers." He singled out *Newsweek's*

Michael Isikoff, ABC's Jackie Judd, NBC's David Bloom, Don Hewitt and Ed Bradley of CBS's 60 *Minutes* and *The Washington Post*'s Susan Schmidt. The howls of protest from them about accuracy and context sounded an awful lot like complaints routinely brushed off by news executives. To the average reader or viewer, it may have been a perfect example of being able to dish it out, but not take it.[104]

New York Times's Francis X. Clines noted some of the media's reaction: "Treacheries were decried. Lawsuits were threatened by bloodied reporters. Headlines were tinged with shock, shock! as Mr. Starr openly confirmed that, for all the anti-leak strictures, he most certainly did dispatch agents to operate amid the jostling, murmuring crowds of anonymous sources who work the mean media streets of Washington."[105]

Soon after, Brill appeared on several television shows to discuss his charges such as CNN's *Reliable Sources*, NBC's *Meet the Press*, CNN's *Larry King Live*, and PBS's *Newshour*. On July 30, 1998, Brill entered the lion's den, a National Press Club luncheon in Washington, D.C. He did not back down from the core point of "Pressgate." Rather, he iterated his concern that in its rush to compete, journalists at the top-level news outlets abandoned skepticism of official power.

> My view of the coverage of the first weeks of the Lewinsky saga is that it really was the product of new and old media competing in a way that we really hadn't seen before. And it produced some strange results; you know, *The Wall Street Journal* rushing to get on-line with a story that it then has to take back; MSNBC deciding that this story was going to do for them what the Iranian hostage crisis did for Ted Koppel and *Nightline*, the difference being Ted Koppel and *Nightline* was a half-hour and MSNBC is 24 hours a day. That puts a different kind of burden on you to fill air.[106]

From the start, Brill promised a nonideological approach: "Readers who expect us to favor victims of inaccuracy on the left or on the right, or who expect that we'll always find that large media companies are doing something 'good' or something 'bad,' will be sorely disappointed."[107] Perhaps the most important distinction about *Brill's* is that it appears to be the only one among its genre to view press-media criticism in consumer protection terms. Brill reasoned that "consumers of news and information in this Information Age should know how what they watch, read, or log on to is produced, and how much they can rely on it," and the media should be held accountable.[108] He also attempted to connect with news consumers in a way that had not been done before. The online version of his magazine, for example, provided a Media Complaint Board that invited individuals, businesses, and institutions to report offending media to the magazine.[109]

The strength of the ten-times-a-year press-media review was its emphasis on in-depth reporting; its meat-and-potatoes was advocacy journalism or muckraking. Such an approach tended to blunt the criticism from the Left—who grumbled that a press-media review that took advertising compromised its ability to buck big advertisers—by producing reports that examined media conglomerates' effects on news reporting such as the December 1998–January 1999 cover story, "Mouse-ke-fear" and the January 2000 cover story, "Is This What's Ahead? Why Media Mergers Matter." Before he took over as *Brill's* second ombudsman, Pulitzer Prize winning editorial writer Michael Gartner called Elizabeth Lesly Stevens's "Mouse-ke-fear—a report on how ABC News damaged its credibility by killing a tough story about its corporate parent, Disney—"wonderful."[110] Dan Kennedy, media critic for the alternative newspaper, the *Boston Phoenix*, made note of the January 2000 cover story on the perils of media concentration. He muted his praise, however, by asserting that the "story inside is decidedly measured—as befits a magazine whose owner, Steven Brill, counts a smattering of media moguls among his softball buddies."[111] *Brill's* also frequently singled out individual journalists for reproach and quantified its case against them.[112]

Among Brill's many assets are his vision and the self-assurance to articulate his vision boldly and without seeking approval from others. Often, as was in the case of his "A New Code for Journalists," he drew the ideas from his experience in magazine and cable television. At a meeting of magazine publishers and media buyers in New York in October 1998, he proposed, "a cross-media 'Credibility Environment Rating,' which would assess which print, TV and web sources are most reliable."[113]

Brill's took on an activist role in an effort to persuade news media heavyweights to agree to rein in their news gathering to protect the privacy of children, in particular, children of celebrities. In late July 1999, Brill mailed a letter to hundreds of news organizations that read in part: "To protect the privacy of grieving families, our news organizations will not publish current photographs or show video images of family members, who have lost a loved one within one week following the death of that loved one, nor will we post reporters or photographers outside their homes, at the funeral, or in other places where we can accost them for interviews or photographs without their permission."[114] The public overwhelmingly favored the proposed self-regulation, according to the findings of the magazine's poll of registered voters nationwide.[115] "Overwhelmingly, the press did not," *CJR* noted.[116] The *Times* reported that *Time* magazine managing editor Walter Isaacson responded: "I'm opposed to the concept of industry-adopted rules and guidelines."[117]

About four years later, Brill described the survey and response this way:

> So we were doing this kind of survey of what news organizations did about privacy. It came right after the death of John F. Kennedy Jr. and what I thought were the horrible, terrible television coverage of Caroline Kennedy's little kids...just photographers hounding them wherever they went in the week or two or three right after the event. We had our reporters calling Sam Donaldson and Tom Brokaw and all of those people and saying, "What do you think about the fact that your organization's cameras are hounding these little kids?" And they hung up on of our reporters. And we'd write down everyone who hung up on our reporters. But a lot of them supported us but I remember getting one call from one seven-figure anchor woman at

one of the networks whispering in her special cloying way, that she really supported what we were doing and what her organization and the other network organizations were doing in this regard was outrageous, and I said, "Well, why don't you speak up," and she said, "Well, I couldn't possibly do that." Now if you knew who this person was, you'd know that the notion that anyone was going to retaliate against her was just absurd. But that to me was sort of a depressing example of why you can't depend on people to regulate themselves.[118]

Overall, the magazine received mixed reviews from critics and its readers, mainly male, middle-aged college graduates who earned a minimum of $80,000.[119] For example, in a 2001 *CJR* column, Margaret Sullivan praised as solid and groundbreaking the July/August 1998 "pressgate," a November 1999 story on the *New York Times'* handling of the Wen Ho Lee spy case, "The Hatchet Meter," a February 2001 examination of whether the news media were too hard or too soft on presidential candidates, and a June 2001 cover story about Rupert Murdoch, "Is This the Face of World Domination?"[120] *Boston Globe* media critic Mark Jurkowitz believed the magazine "was a breathtakingly ambitious, and an occasionally brilliant, effort to transform media criticism from an esoteric, academic pursuit into a subject with mass appeal."[121]

Bad reviews were often harsh and personal. *Brill's* often self-righteous tone and self-promotion seemed to generate vitriol and satire. Ticking off a list of the sharpest media critics in 2000, media heavyweight Evans described Brill and his staff as critics "who come cheerfully along to dispose of the bodies." *Online Journalism Review* critic Matt Welch accused Brill of becoming "the embodiment of the 'increasingly arrogant and defensive media' he was supposed to skewer."[122] Though *Epinions.com* does not offer scientifically gathered findings, 13 evaluations from *Brill's* subscribers during November 25, 1999, to October 3, 2000, echo the general sentiment about the magazine—"refreshingly written, multifarious viewpoints, informative" and "insightful, convenient, entertaining" to "not worth the high price and shiny paper it is printed on" and "[a]s exciting as the differences between the Republicans and the Democrats."[123] Several critics echoed the droll putdown, and Brill promised that the February 2000 issue would have "a much better mix so that the magazine doesn't have the feel of homework that it has had."[124] Despite a "barrage of naysaying," *Folio* magazine noted in 1999 that the magazine managed to have "commanded widespread media interest."[125]

To the end, it seemed as though Brill had a retort, qualification, or rationalization to deflect each critic and naysayer: It was just the press griping, he said, because "people don't like to be held accountable."[126] "Getting the pitch just right is a high art," he said in response to the criticism that the magazine's prose was ponderous.[127] When he announced the launch of *Contentville.com*—a venture widely criticized for the conflicts of interests it created for *Brill's*[128]—the entrepreneur-journalist said he required his new partners to sign an agreement that they could not take action to compromise the independence of the magazine.[129] Many observers believed the magazine struggled through 2000 to survive. But Brill told the *New York Daily News* in November 2000 the circulation and advertising numbers looked promising and *Contentville* was raking in subscriptions: "We project a break-even point of June–July of next year...I don't want to promise anything because stuff happens, but it's looking good."[130]

In May 2000, Kurt Andersen, Michael Hirschorn, and Deanna Brown launched *Inside.com*, "a digital information service about entertainment industry news" aimed primarily at industry professionals and secondarily at "people who have an interest in the creation and business of culture."[131] That spring, however, was a bad time to start a business as the air seeped out of the dot.com bubble. Six months later, *Inside.com* looked for a partner or buyer to keep it afloat. It found Brill.

On April 2, 2001, Brill Media Venture, L.P. announced that *Inside.com* and *Brill's* were to be merged as *Inside Content*. He fired half his staff.[132] A month later, there was a reversal: *Inside Content* reverted to *Brill's Content*, but with a new and ominous twist; it would be published quarterly. Its circulation had dropped to 290,000.[133] By the week ending October 20, 2001, *Brill's* was no more.[134]

There was no unanimous opinion about the value of *Brill's* when it existed. Likewise, several years after the publication's demise, observers give mixed reviews to its lasting impact. Nevertheless, based on interviews with press critics and other sources, its impact seems indisputable. Six respondents said *Brill's* has had little or no lasting impact. *More's* Pollak says the publication has had "very little" impact on ombudsmen or press critics."[135] *The Nation's* Eric Alterman said its impact was felt only when it published because "[y]ou had to be more careful because it was there."[136] *AJR* editor and senior vice president Rem Rieder says the publication did what *AJR* had been doing, "albeit with a far bigger budget and a more crowded masthead."[137] According to FAIR's founder Jeff Cohen, also a columnist for *Brill's*: "Occasionally, there were some powerful pieces in the magazine...But I can't think of much impact."[138] According to *Slate's* Jack Shafer, "I don't think it thought of itself as a press-media review. It was like *George*, a magazine based on an affinity for a subject."[139]

Online Journalism Review's Welch singled out *Content's* 1999 "Pundit Scorecard" series that rated the accuracy of television public affairs pundits—created by Nicholas Varchaver[140]—as a "clever" innovation that possibly might have had an impact on making the public "more skeptical of Sunday talks show types." His overall evaluation: "The magazine was really boring to read...I think more than anything it reflected, for a while, the fact that media criticism was growing even faster than media itself."[141]

Today we are engulfed in a flood of press-critic bloggers.[142] Did *Brill's* help to spur this phenomenon? Only 1 of the 11 former or current press-media critics who responded to a questionnaire believed that the magazine influenced the online Fifth Estate. *USA Today's* Peter Johnson said that it is possible that *Brill's* had "the most effect on the online websites that now do media criticism or compile it…"[143] Additionally, Linda J. Lumsden, writing in *American Journalism: History, Principles, Practices*, maintained that "*Brill's* demonstrated the Internet's potential to expand media criticism with its online, interactive media complaint board that the magazine touted as the first national 'media dispute forum.'"[144]

Four respondents said the magazine left a mark on press-media criticism in other ways. *Newsweek*'s Alter said, "Steve's largest impact—on ombudsmen, press critics, etc.—is his push for more transparency in news organizations… That has not happened, but his relentlessness about accountability has had a big effect."[145] (By 2005, news organization such as CBS had adopted transparency forums.) University of Missouri–Columbia professor Geneva Overholser, a former *Washington Post* ombudsman, identified "Pressgate" as "the first and strongest critique of the excesses and irresponsibility of journalism on that scandal and, as such, had an important impact."[146] *CJR*'s executive editor Mike Hoyt said because Brill "thought big" and "took on big issues…we began to look harder at ourselves. We wanted to get a little more hipper…more energy and voice in our writing."[147]

Ex-*Village Voice* press critic Cynthia Cotts, now a legal reporter at Bloomberg News, wrote columns that spurred Brill to drop cigarette advertising from his magazine.[148] Now she says Brill "is a businessman who seemed to be always in search of a new vehicle for profit and self-promotion." Still, his magazine "dignified press criticism as a genre…and created a place for young journalists to land and network and jump off from."[149] Thomas Kunkel, dean of the University of Maryland's Philip Merrill College of Journalism, says he believes the magazine had an impact and may have helped to create that climate that allowed online media critics to flourish: "[*Brill's*] was a noble effort."[150]

Perhaps the highest praise for Brill's legacy came indirectly and from an unlikely source, Time Inc. editor in chief Norman Pearlstine. In the fall of 1999, Pearlstine and *Brill's* reporter Abigail Pogrebin engaged in an acrimonious debate in the magazine and on the Web about the merits of "Time on Big Sugar: A Not-So-Sweet Deal," Pogrebin's article that raised questions about a *Time* article on Flo-Sun Incorporated and its owners, Florida's Fanjul family.[151] As noted earlier, Gartner said *Brill's* had "really pissed off" Pearlstine.[152] Yet, in the aftermath of the fabrication and plagiarism scandals that arose from the misconduct of *New York Times*' Jason Blair and *USA Today*'s Jack Kelly in 2004, Pearlstine publicly mused about adopting Brill's technique of randomly calling sources his reporters had quoted to check on his staff's fairness and accuracy: "[Brill] found that a very effective tool. I've been thinking of how we could do it."[153] About that same time, Brill told an audience at Washington and Lee University in Lexington, Virginia,

> Don't tell me the *New York Times* couldn't have caught Jayson Blair if they did these simple, routine quality controls that any consumer products company in this country does or should do. When General Electric sells you a refrigerator, you get a

questionnaire once in a while that says, "What do you think about the service people who are coming to take care of your refrigerator," don't you? Why shouldn't a newspaper company do that? What's wrong with that? Sure, there'll be complaints that are wacky and people will be bitter about stuff that is written about them, but you know, you're supposed to be smart. You can figure that out. You need to get that input.[154]

When a uproar ensued after *Newsweek*'s May 9, 2005, "Periscope" item reported that a U.S. military report would include an account of Guantanamo Bay interrogators trying to flush a Qur'an down a toilet and the sole source, an anonymous senior government official, backtracked, *Newsweek*'s Alter turned to Brill as one of its authorities on anonymous sourcing. Returning to one of the key ethical lapses he identified in "Pressgate," Brill told him, "Reporters habitually and loosely use 'sources' when they mean one source."[155] Alter agreed, "He's right, and it's simply wrong ethically to let sources personally attack anyone else in print from under a rock (e.g. 'Tom DeLay's a menace,' says one Democratic operative), as happens nearly every day in Washington."

Finally, some five years and nearly four months after *Brill's* demise, a magazine called *Good* listed it No. 41 of "The 51 Best* Magazines Ever: *Smartest, Prettiest, Coolest, Funniest, Most Influential, Most Necessary, Most Essential, etc." *Vanity Fair* editor Graydon Carter wrote the introduction to the list. Here is *Good*'s evaluation in its February 15, 2007 issue: "Brill's Content was an inside-the-sausage-factory look at media for people who eat sausages, not those who make them. From 1998 to 2001, watchdog-in-chief Steven Brill demanded more from the press through accountability, transparency, and shame. *Content*'s lasting gift was the awkwardly revolutionary premise that journalism is for consumers, and serving them should be a priority."[156]

CONCLUSION

Brill served as chairman and CEO of Media Central until January 2002, wrote *After: How America Confronted The September 12 Era* (2003) and a *Newsweek* column, and formed a company in 2003 to sell identity cards to speed screening at security checkpoints.[157] He says there was one reason the publication failed: "The problem with *Brill's* was that we never were able to articulate persuasively the category of advertising which I thought should have been...connoisseurs of media, people who buy a lot of media. They buy a lot of magazines, or they buy Direct TV or flat screen televisions."[158] He reasoned that had his publication been a ski magazine with 300,000 to 400,000 paid subscribers as he had at *Brill's*, it would have attracted "hundreds of manufacturers of ski equipment and people at ski resorts who sell all kinds of services and products related to skiing you can sell advertising to."[159]

Brill's reasoning is flawed. Consequently, so was his business plan. He banked on attracting an audience that, because it consumed a great deal of mass media content, would also buy a great deal of media technology products. He believed he could deliver such an audience to makers of content such as book publishers and television networks and, more critical, to makers of computer software, word processors, television sets, magazines, and books. With more than 300,000 in paid circulation, Brill believed he had the audience. But from the view of most advertisers of luxury media technology consumer goods and computer-related products, *Brill's* failed to deliver the right audience in the optimum environment. A magazine about press-media content is not the same thing as a magazine about media consumer technology, and news junkies are not necessarily media technology buyers.

Brill's mixed genres. It was a special interest magazine akin to *Consumers Digest* or *Consumer Reports*, yet it spoke in a stern—many called it self-righteous—often combative, voice more often heard in a magazine of political and social commentary or in a press-media review adhering to a political ideology. For the most part, it did not function as a *Consumers Digest* of media technology products. Besides, advertisers could turn to *Wired,* for example, that told "its readers, in great and explicit detail, how to spend their money on consumer luxuries (some expensive, some cheap, all hip)."[160] With the exception of its regular "Tools" column, *Brill's* mostly evaluated media content and its producers, not television sets, computers, software, or cell phones. Are news junkies and connoisseurs of nonfiction media necessarily buyers of media technology products? Apparently, many advertisers of such products did not share Brill's view that the audiences overlapped.

Brill's editorial concept was the wrong one to deliver consumers to makers of media technology luxury items, which leads to the inescapable conclusion that an advertising-dependent magazine of media and press criticism—without support from a nonprofit—cannot succeed. The issue is not the size of the audience. By attracting more than 300,000 subscribers within three years, *Brill's* proved a broad consumer audience exists for press-media reviews, even though many of *Brill's* subscriptions were heavily discounted.[161] The for-profit press-media review's challenge is to attract a critical mass of high-end advertisers. But press-media reviews primarily draw advertisers of media content, and when they do, it is far too little to keep even nonprofit trade books such as the *Columbia Journalism Review* and *American Journalism Review* afloat.[162]

Viewed from the perspective of the history of more than 90 years of press-media reviews, a study of the short-lived *Brill's* should serve as a cautionary tale for anyone contemplating yet another such publication. Brill, however, remains convinced that he is capable of creating a successful version of *Brill's*. He believes that the combination of the boom in press-media criticism blogs and sales in media technology products in the first years of the twenty-first century "only speaks to the viability of a magazine like this and not the contrary." And by a "magazine like this" he means one supported by advertising. Seconds later, however, he offers that "I may organize it just with my own money or a foundation. Do it that way so I don't have to worry about advertisers."[163]

CHAPTER 8

Public Journalism: Press Criticism as an Ongoing Experiment

At about 10 A.M., it looked as though Wednesday, August 22, 2007, was going to be a slow news day in Spokane, Washington. That view would change slightly in about two hours as the Spokane Valley police detained a teenager suspected of shooting someone in the foot and the results of the mayoral primary race trickled in. But at the *Spokane (WA) Spokesman-Review*'s 10 A.M. editorial meeting, there were no signs of urgency.

Seven editors sat around a rectangular, reddish-tan topped table, about 12-feet long. The man in charge, editor Steven Smith, occasionally sipped from a large travel mug. City editor Andy Hatch and senior editor for local news Carla Savalli sat at his immediate left. Managing editor Gary Graham sat immediately to Smith's right.[1] For most of the 20-minute meeting, the editors leaned back in their chairs. Few notes were taken. There was laughter and banter about the Washington State University Cougars football team. It was post-mortem time for the Wednesday edition. Smith was not thrilled about the front-page photograph of the two pieces of meat cooking on a grill. "It's sometimes difficult to photograph food and make it look appealing every time," he said. Photo editor Larry Reisnouer gave kudos for election night photos. "If there was no election, who knows what we'd have in the paper today," Smith remarked.

Anyone anywhere in the world with access to a computer, the broadband Internet, and the right software could peer inside of this inner sanctum of news gatekeeping, traditionally closed off to even a news outlet's own reporters. Now everyone is invited to view. It might not be as riveting as watching 20-somethings on a reality television show. But live steaming video Web casts, Monday through Friday, of twice-a-day news meetings, are key elements of the *Spokesman-Review*'s transparent newsroom.[2] Readers also can request to attend the meetings. Other components on the transparency Web site include Smith's blog, "News is a Conversation," where he engages in a give-and-take with readers about the paper's editorial decisions; "Daily Briefing" about 300 words of often playful notes about the daily meetings; an "Ask the Editors" blog where Smith, Savalli, Graham, and Doug Floyd reply to readers' questions; a "News Diary" penned by Graham and one written by interns; an editorial page; and a report by the Washington News Council on the daily's much debated coverage of its owner's, the Cowles family, involvement in River Park Square, a real estate development.

The transparent newsroom is Smith's experiment, engineered by then-interactive-editor Ken Sands.[3] The *Spokesman-Review* started webcasting June 13, 2006.[4] Even though transparency was the buzzword of newsroom innovation as early as 2004, the *Spokesman-Review* was still a unique ratcheting up of the approach in 2007. But its uniqueness is not its most surprising aspect. Smith is a leading advocate of public journalism, or civic journalism. The transparent newsroom was the movement's most recent effort targeting the traditional news industry. Smith explains that "with our Transparent Newsroom initiative, we've cut out the middleman, so to speak, and opened our doors (metaphorically) to anyone who wants to come in and criticize us for one thing or another. That is civic journalism in action."[5]

Yet Smith's webcasting initiative should not exist, considering that in 2003 many of public journalism's detractors were "ready to dance on its grave," as Don Corrigan[6] gleefully wrote after the Pew Charitable Trusts stopped bankrolling the movement. But it does. And in the same year that public journalism was supposed to have died, many of the movement's leaders, discouraged by many of professional journalism's applications of public journalism or its resistance to the movement, turned to the technology of the Internet and the emerging citizen or participatory journalism movement to carry on their cause.[7]

Public journalism is an activistic news media critique. Generally, its proponents seek to redefine journalism's core purpose and change how most of the mainstream news media in the United States has practiced the craft since the 1880s. When public journalism emerged in 1988,[8] the overwhelming majority of electronic, cable, and more that 1,650 dailies[9] defined themselves as information providers. In 1923, the American Society of Newspaper Editors' 107 members agreed that "[t]he primary function of newspapers is to communicate to the human race what its members do, feel and think."[10] The most current version of the Society of Professional Journalists (SPJ) Code of Ethics links journalism's duty as a provider of information to help democracy prosperity: "Members of the Society of Professional Journalists believe that public enlightenment is the forerunner of justice and the foundation of democracy. The duty of the journalist is to further those ends by seeking truth and providing a fair and comprehensive account of events and issues."[11] Both codes acknowledge obligations to readers or the public welfare. The SPJ, for instance, advises its members to "[c]larify and explain news coverage and invite dialogue with the public over journalistic conduct."[12]

It is also widely accepted that journalists employed by the mainstream media (MSM) should avoid involvement in civic and political activities. This notion of detachment from civic activities is so highly valued by some that the *Tacoma (WA) News Tribune* fought a court battle with one of its employees over the principle and won.[13] The *New York Times* goes so far as to warn that its journalists "must be sensitive that perfectly proper political activity by their spouses, family or companions may nevertheless create conflicts of interest or the appearance of conflict."[14]

The MSM's concern about maintaining distance from the people and institutions they cover stems from their adherence to the discipline of objectivity.[15] Objectivity demands that reporters and editors strive to keep their biases, prejudices, emotions, and opinions from affecting the presentation of news. An objective news report relies on verifiable assertions and observations. It is a method journalists use to test information and provide their audiences with an ability to judge the agendas and biases of information sources, for example, elected officials, officials documents, and experts. It is almost universal in dailies in the United States that editorial pages and columns are the appropriate place for opinion. Some MSM publications, however, allow a reporter to draw conclusions from assertions and evidence presented in a news account. Deviations from that practice are often labeled "analysis." The sports and entertainment pages, however, are more relaxed about separating opinion and interpretation from news accounts. Watchdogging, investigative reporting, also is a departure from a narrow type of objectivity in that it allows a reporter to take a position—a government official is guilty of malfeasance, for example—based on verifiable facts. Even within the industry, rigid objectivity came under attack as early as the 1930s, as Marion Tuttle Marzolf observed, "Objective reporting, however, when shorn of its implied moral responsibility and devotion to truth and Jeffersonian democratic ideals, can degenerate into the mindless stringing together of facts by skilled practitioners."[16] Typically, news magazines and alternative and ethic periodicals do not adhere to a rigid objectivity requiring writers and editors to keep themselves out of the story.

Public journalism and MSM journalism recognize that journalism is a mainstay of democracy. But they diverge sharply on the methods news outlets should use to cultivate it. Public journalism advocates contend it is not enough for journalists to provide information about the decisions and conduct of politicians, government officials, and powerful private citizens. They argue that journalists "would need to change the ways in which they traditionally have conceived of the public and of their own role in public life."[17] According to its adherents, a news outlet's primary function is to engage the public in a conversation. Quoting Cole Campbell of the *Norfolk Virginian-Pilot*, New York University professor Jay Rosen, "one of the godfathers of the civic journalism movement,"[18] put it this way: "Here, 'the journalist works to give readers a way to talk about the news—among family, friends and associates, and among members of the larger community.' The audience is regarded not as clients receiving a professional service, or spectators to a compelling public drama, but as actors, 'people who have a stake in the news, who want to see the possibilities behind often troubling developments, who want to participate in solving shared problems.'"[19]

"News is a conversation" is something of a mantra for public journalists. And the emergence of blogging in the mid-1990s provided the movement with a vital tool to allow editors and staffers to talk to the public in an informal and spontaneous way that letters-to-the-editors columns cannot. The title of *Spokesman-Review's* Smith's blog, "News is a Conversation," underscores that assertion.[20] Why do journalists need to adopt the conversational model? Because, public journalism advocates argue, the informational model makes the majority of citizens see themselves as mere passive spectators of democracy, disengaging them from civic problem solving.[21]

Public journalism rejects the principle of neutrality of detachment, though it does not advocate partisanship. According to Tanni Haas's analysis, "journalists should be concerned with the processes, but not with the outcomes, of citizen deliberation; refrain from endorsing particular politicians, candidates for office, and political proposals; and avoid partnering with special interests groups that seek to further particular political interests."[22] In other words, a news outlet should provide a forum in its pages, online, by broadcast, or in public forums where citizens meet to discuss, share, and resolve issues and problems.

In its early years, the movement's advocates had a polarizing effect among news professionals. "Its most ardent supporters have taken on the trappings of evangelists," wrote Tom Goldstein in a review of Rosen's book about the movement, *What Are Journalists For?* "Its detractors have denounced it as a fad, a gimmick, a commercial ploy or an idea that was not new at all."[23] But Haas, who has written extensively about the movement, concluded that based on the findings of 13 studies, a majority of editors and reporters, mostly employed at small news organizations, "approve of many of the practices associated with public journalism."[24] Haas cautioned, however, that studies show that journalists—even at newsrooms practicing public journalism—are still most comfortable with traditional mainstream news practices and are less likely to agree that "it is their responsibility to sponsor forums where citizens can deliberate about and formulate possible solutions to problems, try to help citizens reach consensus on how given problems should be resolved, and work directly with local civic organizations to help implement actual solutions to problems."[25] Even the movement's "godfather," Jay Rosen, says the crusade fell short of fulfilling its mission:

Part of the reason you push an idea at an institution like big journalism is to force it to react, and in reacting it will reveal itself. One of the things that happens, for instance, is that the troops—in this case the journalists—ask themselves "Who do I actually believe: the people spouting these ideas, or the people defending our old way of doing things." The upshot in the case of public journalism was that it failed to change the press, or even to change common thinking in the press. At the same time it said something very, very important: it confirmed that there is this disconnect out there.[26]

This work offers a more vigorous defense for public journalism's effectiveness as a press critique than apparently even Rosen is prepared to muster. A press critic's value, I contend, must take into account how infrequently the tonnage of press criticism over the years has yielded results. From such a perspective, public journalism has enjoyed meteoric success. Never has one press reform movement persuaded so many newsrooms to reexamine how they practiced news gathering, reporting, and editorial decision making in so short a span of time.

Public journalism's activism and critique has prompted news outlets to expand their definition of news to include the audience's direct input and has persuaded mostly newspapers to experiment in civic involvement beyond their pages. The movement won converts among many professionals and scholars. It engaged its targets in public discussions about journalism ethics and practices at forums, online, on radio, and in MSM newspapers. MSM recognizes Rosen as an authority on news media performance. All that occurred between 1988 and 2003.

Lewis A. Friedland and Sandy Nichols's comprehensive study found that by 2002, "Civic journalism of some kind has been practiced in at least 322 newspapers, one fifth of all newspapers in the U.S."[27] As Goldstein and others have noted, public journalism is vaguely defined and can mean "vastly different things to different people"[28] and includes a wide range of ways to incorporate "new voices of citizens that simply would not have been otherwise heard."[29] Consequently, the movement counts an outlet's use of explanatory framing in a news account, the use of surveys and focus group studies of readers to gauge the public's concerns, and roundtable discussions, town hall meetings, task force groups, specific-action groups, and informal neighborhood discussion groups. Nearly 33 percent of the 617 projects studied merely employed some form of public opinion data survey that counted as public journalism initiatives.

Many of the experiments were soon dropped; "we found that 193 organizations, or 65% of all 322 organizations practiced civic journalism for two years or less."[30] Nevertheless, the movement's ability to persuade hundreds of news editors to broaden their criteria for news, even if only temporarily, is historically significant. It is undeniable that the movement's critique and activism led to content changes and a reform of news organizations practices and missions. It managed to persuade editors at small and midsize papers to try new ways to include the audience in shaping news coverage and engaging it in discussions about civic matters. "In sum, a larger number of news organizations than expected had a medium to high level of involvement with civic journalism, about 7% of all U.S. newspapers over our investigation period," Friedland and Nichols concluded. "A large proportion of the civic journalism published, 45%, came from these papers."[31]

For example, Rosemary Armao, managing editor of the *Sarasota (FL) Herald-Tribune*, was a vocal opponent of the movement's efforts, but by 2000 had moved "more toward the middle (in acceptance of public journalism)" by having the *Herald-Tribune* get in touch with its readers at regular sessions where she and the executive editor "discuss community issues and newspaper coverage; stints requiring news-editorial employees to talk directly to readers who call the paper with criticisms about everything from coverage to newspaper delivery."[32]

Of course, public journalism's claim that its approach would bring readers back to newspapers had a strong allure. Apparently, that promise remains unfulfilled. Nationwide, newspaper circulation continues to decline. At the *Wichita (KS) Eagle* where Knight Ridder chairman James Batten, *Eagle* publisher Reid Ashe, and editor Davis "Buzz" Merritt, Jr., oversaw major public journalism strategies in 1990 and 1992, the efforts failed to stave off circulation losses that led to the first layoffs in the paper's history in 1994.[33]

The movement's critique did not merely spur public debate in the news media about news media performance; rather, it ignited fiery disputes. For a press critic, such a reaction is not necessarily a bad development. The worst reaction is indifference from the targets of your assessments. Rosen, it seems, was the movement's most aggressive flame thrower. From 1993 to 1997, he directed the public journalism advocacy effort, Project on Public Life and the Press, funded by the Knight Foundation. As he notes in *What Are Journalists For?*, "I was termed 'an evangelist of public journalism' who 'travels the country warning journalists that traditional news organizations are in peril.'"[34] He got the *New York Times* to air his views in its own pages, an interview Rosen reprinted in his book.[35] Ultimately, "The *Times* rebuff of public journalism helped shove the movement into eclipse," news historian W. Joseph Campbell contends.[36] Meanwhile, Rosen developed into a leading press critic, frequently quoted by the MSM and penning his own blog, PressThink,[37] launched in September 2003, and he also blogs at The Huffington Post. As a proponent of citizen journalism, he experiments with open-source reporting projects.[38]

Finally, by the late 1990s the movement gained credibility overseas and here among nonprofit foundations and scholars. Haas lists Malawi, Senegal, Swaziland, Australia, Japan, New Zealand, Denmark, Finland, Sweden, Argentina, Colombia, and Mexico as countries where news organizations inspired by the experiments in the United States launched their own projects.[39] Over the years, the Kettering Foundation, Knight Ridder, and the Pew Charitable Trusts supplied financial support for the movement's projects, yet another measure of the movement's impact.[40] The debate over the merits of the movement's claims has generated more than 90 peer-review and scholarly articles with public or civic journalism in the title[41] and 37 books and reports on the subject.[42]

There is more evidence of impact. Three years after many had written its epitaph, the movement still helped shape news industry projects. For instance, the Associated Press Managing Editors continued until 2006 to hold sessions with newspapers and their communities to talk about journalism, the main component of its National Credibility Roundtables project.[43] The project was co-founded in 2001 by Chris Peck, one of the early newsroom proponents of public journalism.[44] The project's goal was "to encounter the public's big questions about news credibility" and to listen to the public "to build better journalism"; it ultimately involved 200 news organizations.[45]

Three years after public journalism's supposed expiration, the *Memphis (TN) Commercial Appeal*, under the leadership of Peck, assigned two editors to become citizen editors. "What we are really trying to do is engage the public about shaping of content, Peck explained.[46] And back at his former newspaper, the *Spokesman-Review*, Smith oversaw the launching of that daily's transparent newsroom.[47]

That same year, 2006, Rosen proclaimed a new revolution was under way: "The people formerly known as the audience wish to inform media people of our existence, and of a shift in power that goes with the platform shift you've all heard about...You were once (exclusively) the editors of the news, choosing what ran on the front page. Now we can edit the news, and our choices send items to our own front pages."[48] Public journalism had become citizen journalism; the movement had evolved into its "second phase."[49] Like Rosen, many in the public journalism movement had come to realize that multimedia digital technology allowed the most assertive form of citizen-directed news media to be created and disseminated.

According to Mark Glaser, a leading advocate of citizen journalism, the idea behind the movement is "that people without professional journalism training can use the tools of modern technology and the global distribution of the Internet to create, augment or fact-check media on their own or in collaboration with others."[50] And cybertechnology has allowed so-called amateur journalists and those formerly employed by mass commercial media to create Web sites allowing users to contribute neighborhood-centric news in the form of "calendar announcements, eyewitness accounts and audio and video of breaking events and public meetings, musings, testimonials, discussion threads and photos," leading to the coining of the term "hyperlocal citizen journalism."[51]

Four years after public journalism's misdiagnosed demise, many of the movement's leaders assembled at George Washington University in Washington, D.C.[52] Allied with the citizen journalism movement, they had come to brainstorm ways to finance and structure citizen journalism alternatives to traditional news operations in early August 2007. The workshop was called "Journalism That Matters: The DC Sessions."[53] There was a great deal of discussion during the two-day conference about developing ways of financing citizen journalism efforts. Much of that focused on nonprofit funding. Some critics of journalism performance came to similar conclusions in the early 1900s; they advocated unsuccessfully for the creation of an endowed press: "Is it not sufficiently clear that sound, clean, and dignified journalism cannot hope to take root...without at least temporary endowment?"[54] History, though instructive, is not necessarily determinative.

In theory, citizen journalism's efforts are yet another way to critique the MSM by producing tangible alternatives of news coverage that draw consumers and break news stories before the traditional news media does. But Haas, a long-time public journalism scholar, doubts that the citizen journalism movement "signifies the dawn of a new public's journalism, capable of furthering the democratic ideals that have animated the public journalism movement."[55] He contends there is little evidence to show that the MSM pays attention to citizen-produced blogs, that such blogs produce much independent, original reporting, or challenge the MSM's range of topics and sources. "Rather than challenging the dominance of mainstream news media, either through their own reporting or by linking to and commenting on that of an ideologically diverse range of alternative news providers, weblog writers help strengthen their dominance by further circulating, if not amplifying, their discourse."[56]

Meanwhile in Spokane, a first-phase public journalism experiment, enhanced by Web 2.0[57] technology, continued. That August, about 14 months after launching the transparent newsroom, *Spokesman-Review* editor Smith believed that his initiative was achieving public journalism's goals. As a former managing editor at the *Wichita (KS) Eagle* and editor and vice president of the *Colorado Springs (CO) Gazette*, Smith had been involved in two major public journalism efforts in the 1990s.[58]

> The initial concept behind public journalism was to align the journalism of the newspaper to the public life needs of citizens—producing journalism relevant to the issues that really have meaning to citizens and that allows them to function as citizens with more knowledge and insight...We know our webcast meetings are watched by people because we'll get phone calls or emails from folks suggesting ways to develop a story, or learn that newsmakers have changed their approach to a story pitch because of what they heard in our conversation...In my view, the transparent newsroom initiative, tied to the interactivity of the Web, makes it possible to actually achieve public journalism goals consistently as opposed to the occasional project-driven means we had in the past.[59]

CHAPTER 9

Press Criticism as a Laughing Matter

So the Emperor went in procession under the rich canopy, and every one in the streets said, "How incomparable are the Emperor's new clothes! what a train he has to his mantle! how it fits him!" No one would let it be perceived that he could see nothing, for that would have shown that he was not fit for his office, or was very stupid. No clothes of the Emperor's had ever had such a success as these.

"But he has nothing on!" a little child cried out at last.

"Just hear what that innocent says!" said the father: and one whispered to another what the child had said.

"But he has nothing on!" said the whole people at length. That touched the Emperor, for it seemed to him that they were right; but the [sic] thought within himself, "I must go through with the procession." And so he held himself a little higher, and the chamberlains held on tighter than ever, and carried the train which did not exist at all.[1]

"Stop, stop, stop, stop hurting America." On October 15, 2004, almost at noon on a Friday, Jon Stewart, the host of *The Daily Show with Jon Stewart,* played the boy; Cable News Network (CNN)'s hosts collectively played the emperor; later, the blogosphere played the townsfolk.[2] But in this incarnation of "The Emperor's Clothes," Stewart was no innocent. He played the role of a cutting, sometimes crude, satirist. In the tradition of the satirist, he was not what he seemed to be;

he did not play by the convention. *Crossfire* had invited him to promote his humorous book, *America (The Book): A Citizen's Guide to Democracy Inaction*. And he was just supposed to be there for the laughs. There were laughs—at his hosts' expense, though. He was humorous, yet annoyed. He employed irony, sarcasm, ridicule—even an expletive—to level an attack against pundits Tucker Carlson and Paul Begala, calling them "partisan hacks" who "have a responsibility to the public discourse" but "fail miserably." During a particularly contentious portion, he called the bow-tie wearing conservative Carlson "a dick."[3]

Carlson and Begala were taken aback. They were there for glib, cocktail-hour repartee; Stewart brought his soapbox. They should not have been caught off guard. Did they think that Stewart saved his satire solely for politicians? The very book they thought they were helping Stewart promote devotes its Chapter 7 to excoriating the news media. Actually, there are two first pages to Chapter 7. The first opening is entitled, "The Media: Democracy's Guardian Angel." At first, the authors write in a typical sober textbook tone: "A free and independent press is essential to the health of a functioning democracy. It serves to inform the voting public on matters relevant to its well-being."[4] The tone abruptly changes: "Why they've stopped doing that is a mystery. I mean, 300 camera crews outside a courthouse to see what Kobe Bryant is wearing when the judge sets his hearing date, while false information used to send our country to war goes unchecked? What the fuck happened? These spineless cowards in the press have finally gone too far. They have violated a trust."[5]

Two pages later, still Chapter 7: "The Media: Democracy's Valiant Vulgarians," an apology is offered: "We sincerely apologize for the false start on the chapter concerning the press. The authors have assured us it was a momentary lapse in restraint caused by a deadline-induced Red Bull Binge. In no way was it meant to portray any sense of anger and/or disappointment in the behavior and standards of the modern media."[6] Even in the disingenuous apology, the authors get in another dig and critique of the media by footnoting: "Modern media" is a wholly owned subsidiary of Warner Books, a wholly owned subsidiary of Time Warner Inc."[7]

Often satire is a diatribe hidden in reverence that, once revealed, slips into a feigned apology—a monologue sodden with mimicry, irony, and sarcasm—"a mixture full of different things"[8] that judges harshly. Because it is the nature of satire to cloak its true intention in understatement and irony, it is often misunderstood. "Wait. I thought you were going to be funny," Carlson whined that day. "Come on. Be funny."[9] Carlson and Begala should have read the book. Apparently, they were not regular viewers of *The Daily Show* either. There is always someone—typically the butt of the joke—who does not get the point behind the satirist's jab. The "townsfolk," however, understood. Judging by their laughing responses to Stewart, the television studio audience seemed to, and within hours Stewart's *Crossfire* appearance became one of the most downloaded video clips in Internet history with about 260 people downloading the clip each hour.[10] A week later, the on-air dustup had become the "talk of Washington," according to *Newsweek* editor Fareed Zakaria.[11] Within two months, bloggers had linked to the show's transcript 1,880 times, making it the No. 1 blogged news item in 2004.[12] It was as though Stewart had channeled the ire of the blogosphere that day. For example, the anonymous author of abstractfactory .blogspot.com, who identifies himself only as a California programmer, a late-stage Ph.D. candidate in computer science employed by a large technology company—and apparently he is Asian American judging by his photograph—mused, "I think that people find Jon Stewart's *Crossfire* appearance satisfying partly because they understand it as an attack on shallow hackery in general, and not merely the particular shallow hackery of debate shows like *Crossfire*. Stewart's been declaiming from his little alcove on Comedy Central for years."[13] Partly in response to Stewart's critique and the din of the blogosphere rabble, Jonathan Klein, president of CNN/U.S., announced in early 2005 that the show would soon be canceled.[14]

Media giant Viacom's cable Comedy Central Network airs *The Daily Show with Jon Stewart* Monday through Thursdays.[15] First, ex-ESPN sportscaster Craig Kilborn anchored the show when it debuted in 1996. Stewart, a stand-up comedian, turned irregular late night show host, replaced Kilborn in December 1998, and the tone of the show changed. The show was renamed to highlight Stewart and now—with tongue in cheek, of course—beckons to viewers with the following pitch: "If you're tired of the stodginess of the evening newscasts, if you can't bear to sit through the spinmeisters and shills on the 24-hour cable news networks, don't miss *The Daily Show with Jon Stewart*, a nightly half-hour series unburdened by objectivity, journalistic integrity or even accuracy."[16] Now eight Emmys and two Peabody Awards later, there is a great deal of debate among journalists and media scholars over whether Stewart is a journalist. Repeatedly, Stewart insists he is not one. Still, among Americans under age 30, Stewart ranks as their most admired journalist. Among all ages, he tied with Dan Rather, Tom Brokaw, Brian Williams, and Anderson Cooper as the No. 4 most admired journalist.[17] The debate becomes tiresome, almost pointless. *The Daily Show* delivers meaningful information about current events in a timely and regular fashion, though that is not its raison d'être. Case in point: After the presidential debate in late September 2004, 2.4 million viewers "tuned to Comedy Central to hear *The Daily Show* host Jon Stewart's take on the action."[18]

Most of all, *The Daily Show* and its kid brother, *The Colbert Report* hosted by Stephen Colbert, traffic in satire; and the satirist's use of irony, hyperbole, wit, and the donning of a persona that conveys a message at odds with one's words befuddles some. For example, *San Francisco Chronicle* television critic Tim Goodman did not seem to appreciate the multilayered purpose of Stewart's comedy at first. Shortly after the faux anchorman/textbook writer castigated the *Crossfire* hosts, apparently ignorant of the role satirists have played for some 2,400 years, Goodman wondered whether it was not "a little disingenuous for Jon Stewart to be castigating the media for not doing its job when he is, in fact, making a living off its failure?"[19] But after the cancellation, Goodman declared Stewart "our nation's most powerful media critic…In the past week, media critics across the country have had to face the fact that inches upon inches of fine prose—filled with salient points and passion—were no match for Stewart telling Tucker Carlson that he and *Crossfire* were hurting America."[20]

Surely, Stewart's performance that Friday morning ranks as one of the most effective critical analyses—not merely a critical statement[21]—of news media in the history of press criticism because it spurred widespread public discussion about the news affairs debate program's civic obligations that led to news management's decision to end the program. Over the years it has been observed, as Lee Brown put it, "the press has generally dealt with criticism from outside its membership by discounting it, ignoring it, or by counterattacking with what has sometimes been described as paranoiac fever."[22] Few press critics can boast of such an accomplishment, even if the typically self-deprecating Stewart is correct in his assessment that the show already was on its "last legs"[23] before his comments and that CNN continues to use the same partisan hacks on its regular news coverage, which it does. Consider that CNN management exceeded Stewart's plea. Stewart did not call for the show's cancellation, only its reform. CNN's Klein explained, "I think Jon Stewart made a good point about the noise level of these types of shows, which does nothing to illuminate the issues of the day. A bunch of guys screaming at each other simply doesn't accomplish that."[24]

Why did Stewart's comments have an impact when as Goodman correctly noted, "inches upon inches of fine prose—filled with salient points and passion" from media reporters and scholars had failed? His celebrity helped. But it had more to do with credibility than fame. The fallout from Stewart's *Crossfire* appearance testifies to the widespread credibility the so-called fake news show host had earned previously on the subject of journalism performance among the public. Since he took the helm of the show in 1998, rarely has a program aired that has not targeted the excesses, hypocrisies, and absurdities of the 24-hour news cable channels. Still, Stewart could have earned credibility and clout using empty rhetoric or demagoguery, appealing to fellow travelers as Rush Limbaugh has done.[25] That is not Stewart's approach. Generally, Stewart takes a centrist, populist, and commonsense approach to his media criticism, and his benchmark for judging appears to be the public's good. For example, the basis of his complaint against *Crossfire* was rooted in the core obligation of journalism in a democracy: "the primary purpose of journalism is to provide citizens with the information they need to be free and self-governing."[26]

Generally, news media find it easy to ignore scrutiny fired from a distance—books, newspaper columns, or televised news criticism shows such as *Reliable Sources*. In contrast, Stewart's success can also be attributed in part to the point-blank vantage he gained as a guest on the show. He made a salient and passionate plea, and it was confrontational. Once directly confronted, neither Begala nor Carlson was capable of mustering a coherent retort. Other guests abide by the television pundit show/beltway game rule—they do not question the authority of the host so they can be invited back and continue to bask in prime-time celebrity. But this was Stewart's Joseph Welch-to-Senator Joseph McCarthy moment: "Have you no sense of decency, sir? At long last, have you left no sense of decency?"[27]

Just as important—essential, perhaps—the comments struck a responsive chord in the unmediated blogosphere where public opinion coalesced around the issue. Before the advent of a social networking site such as YouTube, a television show's repeat airing was controlled by a media organization. Consequently, few beyond the original viewers would have a chance to see an airing a day, weeks, or months after the initial broadcast. Controversies that network management could previously deflate by eliminating repeat airings now are more likely to inflate when millions more of the public can review the controversial actions and words repeatedly. Such was the case with the October 15, 2004, *Crossfire* episode. *Crossfire* averaged about 447,000 viewers each weekday.[28] It is estimated that about 550,000 viewed the October 15 episode when it first aired.[29] But several Web sites, including YouTube, posted the October 15 episode and within three days "more than a million people...downloaded video of the exchange."[30] By early November, the *Crossfire* clip had

> been viewed over 2-million times on online clip site *IFilm* alone...Thanks to interested folks who saw the clip, recorded it (or more likely, Tivo-ed it), and then injected the clip into the Internet bit-stream...The clip rapidly took on a life of its own, being mentioned on various blogs and in short order becoming available on all the major file-downloading services (especially the newly ascendant *Bittorrent*). The Stewart segment was almost certainly viewed more times in clip form in the five hours after the show was broadcast than it was seen live.[31]

Apparently, it will take much more than Colbert's monologue at the 2006 White House Correspondents' Association Dinner to shame the lapdogs of the White House press corps into being less deferential to the executive branch. Nevertheless, Colbert's speech triggered public debate about the propriety of the press corps rubbing elbows with the government officials it should keep at arm's length.[32]

Finally, the provocative nature of satire in a democracy must be appreciated to understand why *The Daily Show* and *The Colbert Report* resonate with the public and with many members of the news media. The art of satire can be traced to Aristophanes, the 5–4th century B.C. dramatist known as the Father of Comedy.[33] Satire is more than humor, of course; it is "pragmatic criticism" that seeks to improve political and social behavior.[34] "Seeking to justify the unpleasant task of dealing unpleasantly with the seamy or foolish side of life, [satirists] have tended to claim that they are only telling the truth, thereby redeeming their audience, punishing fools and sinners, and generally setting the world right. In short, satire reforms."[35] And it is hardly alien to the tradition of democratic

discourse in the United States. In "American Theory of Satire, 1790–1820,"
George L. Roth posits that early American satirists played an important role in
the workings of the new republic:

> Satire is the mode of literature best calculated to sway people's minds and change
> their beliefs. And so "whoever of the citizens sees a public evil" prints a satiric
> pamphlet, confident that in less favored realms citizens and authors have so spoken,
> and that in America he may speak to far greater effect than his predecessors in the
> satiric tradition had ever been able to do.[36]

Abandon news all ye who enter here.
                        —A faux scroll painted on the entrance to the studio
        on 11th Avenue in New York City where the *Daily Show* is taped.

> Wherein, although our title, sir, be News,
> We yet adventure here to tell you none,
> But show you common follies, and so known
> That though they are not truths, th'innocent Muse
> Hath made so like, as fant'sy could them state.
>   —*The Staple of News*[37]

Press criticism as satire is older than the Anglo press and flourished simultaneously with the first English news periodicals, or corantos and then newsbooks,
that published at irregular intervals in the early 1600s. As early as 1606, Ben
Jonson—yes, the towering literary figure and friend and rival of William Shake-
speare—satirized the Italian gazettes, weekly handwritten newssheets, in his
play *Volpone* (1606). (The oldest surviving coranto printed in English is dated
1620.[38]) The first numbered series of corantos were published in October
1622.[39] By the mid-1620s, other British satirists had joined Jonson in taking
aim at the nascent news business: John Fletcher's *The Fair Maid of the Inn*
(1626), James Shirley's *The Schoole of Complement* (1625), Donald Lupton's *London and the Countrey Carbonadoed* (1632), and Richard Brathwaite's *Whimzies:
Or, A New Cast of Characters* (1631).[40] None, however, produced "the full-
blown satire" of the press "that Jonson incorporated in *The Staple of News*."[41]
    Jonson's satire targeted several ethical problems of the news business that now
seem episodic, if not eternal, in the nearly 400 years that followed. In the play's
note "To the Readers," Jonson attacks the profit motive of newsmongers; he calls
news a "cheat to draw money" because the mongers manipulate the timing of
information or fabricate information.[42] He says through his fictitious newsroom
employees that newsmongers satisfy the public's gullibility and hunger for
novelty by peddling knowingly false information and unverified gossip. (Fame
means rumor.)

> 'Tis the house of fame, Sir,
> Where both the curious and negligent,
> The scrupulous and careless, wild and staid,

The idle and laborious, all do meet,
To taste the *cornu copiae* of her rumors,
Which she, the mother of sport, pleaseth to scatter
Among the vulgar. Baits, sir, for the people!
And they bite like fishes. (III.ii.115–122)[43]

He took aim at the business of news. The fictional news office of his comedy seeks to monopolize dissemination of news.

Here in the house, almost on the same floor,
Where all the news of all sorts shall be brought,
And there be examin'd, and then register'd,
And so be issu'd under the seal of the Office,
As staple News, no other news be current. (I.ii 32–36)[44]

With the advent of news periodicals, Jonson confronted a genre of public communication he believed inferior to his poetry and plays in conveying the truth. English literature scholar Marcus Nevitt observes "there is a distinct sense that Jonson regards news-writing as the depraved, diametric opposite to his own vocation as poet and author."[45] Now, some ask, as Rachel Smolkin did in the *American Journalism Review*: "Has our slavish devotion to journalism fundamentals—particularly our obsession with 'objectivity'—so restricted news organizations that a comedian can tell the public what's going on more effectively than a reporter?"[46]

Apparently, Jonson and his contemporaries were at once the earliest practitioners of a subgenre—satirical humor judging news performance—and the predecessors of current-day news critics.[47] By that measure, *The Daily Show* and *The Colbert Report* writers and performers of news satire follow in the tradition of the first citizen news critics. A distinction, however, must be made between journalism satire and fake news humor. "Fake news" is better understood as content that mimics the form and framework of a widely recognized news genre with the intent to give the content credibility, a least at first glance. For the most part, fake news does not seek to lampoon news presentation conventions with the aim of illuminating the follies of news gatherers' decisions. Rather, the subgenre used journalistic conventions to spoof famous people and events, or in the case of Orson Welles's 1938 *The War of the Worlds* radio broadcast, to create drama. Thus, the satire of the 1960s British and American versions of *That Was the Week That Was* and *Saturday Night Live*'s Weekend Update is not part of this satirical strand. Both shows used the television news on-air presentation format as a device to cast a satirical light on political events and newsmakers.

Rarely did they comment on the absurdities, dubious practices, and ethical lapses of news outlets and their reporters and editors.[48] At least one time when *Saturday Night Live* chose to make the news media the target of its barbs, a Pew Research Center study found that the NBC comedy program played a major role in spurring the news media to change their coverage of the Democratic presidential primary race and of candidate Barack Obama. *Saturday Night Live* aired a skit on February 23, 2008, that showed debate moderators interrogating Amy Poehler's Hillary Rodham Clinton while fawning over Fred Armisen's Obama. During a real Democratic debate in Cleveland three days later, Clinton referenced the parody. "If anybody saw *Saturday Night Live*, you know, maybe we should ask Barack if he's comfortable and needs another pillow."[49] According to the Pew Research Center, critical news coverage of Obama increased within a few days of the skit and Clinton's remark.

> With no primary contests to consume press attention, Clinton's charges of a pro-Obama tilt reverberated in the media echo chamber last week. Obama's life and record came under a heightened degree of scrutiny, with everything from his legislative career to his ties to Louis Farrakhan to his African attire getting a public airing. Obama was the top campaign newsmaker and a significant or dominant factor in 69% of the stories from Feb. 25–March 2, a period between the Feb. 19 Wisconsin primary and the March 4 tests in Texas and Ohio. That was the highest level of coverage for any candidate in 2008. And part of it was news outlets—from *Good Morning America* to *The New York Times*—engaged in introspective inquiry aimed at answering this headline atop one Feb. 29 newspaper story: "Are the media giving Obama a free ride?"[50]

The journalism satire of *The Daily Show* and *The Colbert Report* targets news media practices and personnel almost as much as politics and politicians. And although the sets of both shows parody their respective targets—prime time television news and pundit-hosted current affairs talk shows—little attempt is made to pass them off as authentic. (Arguably the parody newspaper, *The Onion*, walks in the footsteps of Ben Jonson; it sometimes pokes fun at newspaper formulaic writing and news choices.[51] And *The Onion* has ties to both shows. Former *The Daily Show* executive producer and one of three co-creators of *The Colbert Report*, Ben Karlin, wrote for *The Onion*. David Javerbaum, *Daily Show* head writer, also wrote for *The Onion*.)

Stephen Colbert describes the intent of his and Stewart's on-air personas: "Jon deconstructs the news and he is ironic and detached. I falsely construct the news, and am ironically attached. . . . Jon may point out the hypocrisy of a particular thing that has happened in a news story or behavior. . . I illustrate the hypocrisy as a character."[52]

A June 11, 2007, bit, "Paris Hilton Gets in a Car," typifies *The Daily Show*'s humorous deconstruction of television news performance. The bit ridiculed CNN for elevating an insignificant event into a major news story at the expense of a legitimate one, for its abuse of "the breaking news" standard, and for its disingenuous complaint that it is powerless to ignore the public's obsession with celebrities as though it plays no role in creating that hunger. Additionally, Stewart adds a zinger about the decadence of our culture.[53]

Cheers and applause greet "anchorman" Stewart as the show opens. He sets up a skewing of CNN's news judgment by telling his audience that "obviously" the big story to talk about during the weekend was Marine Gen. Peter Pace announcing that he declined to resign from his position as Joint Chiefs chairman and was forced to quit. Then, video from a Friday, June 8, CNN newscast is played. A sober-looking Barbara Starr delivers a report of a breaking news item titled "Joint Chiefs Chmn. Leaving." In mid-sentence, however, an anchorwoman interrupts, announcing that a more important breaking news story needs to be aired. Video of a police car appears. The "Happening Now" news that preempts the report about Pace's ouster is "Judge Orders L.A. Sheriff's Dept. to Bring Paris Hilton to Courthouse." The story is about Paris Hilton getting into a police car.[54]

Stewart, with one hand to his ear as though he were listening to an urgent report from Hollywood, plays the role of a CNN anchorman.

> Barbara. I'm sorry, I'm sorry. Wait. I'm sorry, We have to get back to you. Paris Hilton is getting into a car. I'm being told she's getting into a car....[Reverting to himself.] Seriously, I can understand if she were getting into a spaceship...If CNN hadn't cut away right there, there might have been no record of her getting into the car. Accept for the—oh, I don't know—10,000 photographers gathered outside her house.[55]

A comment on our culture. "You know I have actually seen footage of a frenzy like that." Cut away to footage of throngs of worshippers of the Black Nazarene in the Phillipines. "Either our culture is irreparably crippled or Paris Hilton is a virgin to be worshipped." Hoots and laughs from the studio audience follow.[56]

Later, he notes that the other networks had cut away to cover Hilton. But he says, sarcastically, CNN said it did not want to. Next, there is footage of CNN news people on different shows puzzling over why so many people are interested in Hilton. "Poor CNN." 'Why are they making us do this?' he moans with mock concern. How reluctant was CNN to cover Hilton? It covered Hilton all day long, including the hour of Larry King, he notes derisively.[57]

Colbert's satire is often more nuanced than Stewart's, largely because his character engages in antiphrasis, "the ironic or humorous uses of a word phrase in a sense contrary to its normal meaning," and sarcasm, "a cutting, often ironic remark intended to wound."[58] The rope-a-dope effect of his rhetorical techniques is enhanced by his ability to assume the appearance and tone of a self-assured, self-righteous, right-wing pundit, fashioned after Bill O'Reilly and Sean Hannity. Staying in character, Colbert illustrated the hypocrisy of the White House press corps by delivering a 16-minute speech and a 7-minute video performance when he appeared before the White House Correspondents' Association Dinner on April 29, 2006. It is a performance dripping in verbal irony, antiphrasis, and sarcasm.

> But, listen, let's review the rules. Here's how it works: the president makes decisions. He's the decider. The press secretary announces those decisions, and you people of

the press type those decisions down. Make, announce, type. Just put 'em through a
spell check and go home. Get to know your family again. Make love to your wife.
Write that novel you got kicking around in your head. You know, the one about
the intrepid Washington reporter with the courage to stand up to the administration.
You know—fiction![59]

Minutes later, a video of a mock press conference with Colbert presiding as
White House press secretary appears on a large screen. (Colbert described it as
his audition tape for the press secretary job.) Of the several well-known reporters
depicted in the video only Helen Thomas, actually playing herself, asked tough
questions. "She won't stop asking why we invaded Iraq!" Colbert complains.[60]

In essence, Colbert scolded the White House press corps for failing to fulfill its
widely acknowledged ethical principles: its Fourth Estate or the watchdog obligations and maintaining independence from those they cover. The Radio-
Television News Directors Association code of ethics provides the following:
"Professional electronic journalists should operate as trustees of the public, seek
the truth, report it fairly and with integrity and independence, and stand
accountable for their actions...Gather and report news without fear or favor,
and vigorously resist undue influence from any outside forces, including advertisers, sources, story subjects, powerful individuals, and special interest groups."[61]
Similarly, the Society of Professional Journalists advises the following: "Journalists should be free of obligation to any interest other than the public's right to
know....Avoid conflicts of interest, real or perceived....Remain free of associa-
tions and activities that may compromise integrity or damage credibility."[62] In
1999, then–Washington bureau chief of the *New York Times* Michael Oreskes
made a similar point about the morality of journalists partying with the powerful
people they are supposed to challenge on behalf of the public by having his staff
boycott the event: "I just think the whole thing has become unseemly. It's the
whole circus atmosphere. It's the whole sense of bacchanalia."[63] And soon after
Colbert's performance, the *American Journalism Review*, without mentioning
Colbert, offered the following: "The problem is that this black tie [affair] underscores the notion that journalists are part of a wealthy elite, completely out of
touch with ordinary Americans—their audience."[64]

Colbert's and Stewart's humorous, but often, cutting criticisms of the news
media seem to stem from a tacit belief that television news anchors, reporters,
and pundits have breached a social contract with the ultimate consumer of news,
the public; that they have a responsibility in a democracy to exercise news
judgment for more than high ratings and self-aggrandizement. They often cast
themselves as the public's representatives, attempting to ridicule, implore, or
shame the news media into living up to their obligation to give the public information it needs to be self-governing. It is not known whether the comedians
have read Bill Kovach and Tom Rosenstiel's *The Elements of Journalism: What
Newspeople Should Know and the Public Should Expect*, but Stewart's critique of
the news media seems to be grounded in the social responsibility concept of

journalism promoted by the two well-known media critics. First articulated by the Hutchins Commission (Commission on Freedom of the Press) report in 1947, the concept defines journalism's mission by society's needs. Society, the commission said, needs "a truthful, comprehensive account of the day's events in a context which gives them meaning...a forum for the exchange of comment and criticism...a means of projecting the opinions and attitudes of the groups in a society to one another...a method of presenting and clarifying the goals and values of the society...and a way of reaching every member of the society by the currents of information, thought, and feeling which the press supplies."[65]

Kovach and Rosenstiel's "sixth principle or duty of the press: Journalism must provide a forum for public criticism and comment" requires ethical journalists to conduct meaningful debates on public issues.[66] Kovach and Rosenstiel argue that the Internet, radio call-in shows, and 24-hour cable news create a public forum that allows partisans, spin doctors, and other special interests to flood the public forum with distortions, half-truths, and lies. Therefore, they argue, "it is more incumbent on those providing us with journalism that they decipher the spin and lies of commercialized argument, lobbying, and political propaganda."[67] Stewart invokes that imperative in his *Crossfire* plea: "See, the thing is, we need your help. Right now, you're helping the politicians and the corporations. And we're left out there to mow our lawns."[68]

Stewart got a chuckle from the studio audience when he told Carlson that then presidential candidate John Kerry appeared on *The Daily Show* because, "Well, we have civilized discourse," implying that *Crossfire's* discourse typically lacked civility..."You know, the interesting thing I have is, you have a responsibility to the public discourse, and you fail miserably."[69] Kovach and Rosenstiel put it this way: "There is a difference between a forum and a food fight, or between journalism that mediates debate and pseudo-journalism that stages artificial debates to titillate and provoke."[70]

At first, Begala did not accept Stewart's premise. By late spring 2007, he still had not changed his opinion: "Jon Stewart, whose show I love, gave *Crossfire* its epitaph when he said it was 'hurting America.' I thought then, and I still think, that was bullshit. Sure, we yelled a lot. But at least people like Carville and me yelled to try to stop George W. Bush from lying us into a war."[71]

In its June/July 2007 issue, the *American Journalism Review* (AJR) asked journalism ethicists and professionals what lessons the profession could learn from Stewart. The magazine's managing editor, Rachel Smolkin, acknowledged that the question was "perhaps, a strange premise for a journalism review to explore" because the magazine's "mission is to encourage rigorous ethical and professional standards."[72] Several of the scholars and professionals said *The Daily Show* succeeds because it is not encumbered by a narrow definition of balance and objectivity.

"So-called fake news makes fun of that concept of balance," Martin Kaplan, associate dean of the University of Southern California's Annenberg School for Communication, said. "It's not afraid to have a bullshit meter and to call people spinners or liars when they deserve it. I think as a consequence some viewers find that helpful and refreshing and hilarious."[73]

In 2005, *Washington Post* media critic Howard Kurtz noted that Stewart and Colbert used video to show contradictions in what politicians say, therefore "non-fake journalists ought to be doing the same thing—even though they wouldn't be as funny."[74] In the *AJR*, Brooks Jackson, director of FactCheck.org, a project of the Annenberg Public Policy Center of the University of Pennsylvania, added that the technique was "'great fact-checking,' and a great lesson for journalists."[75]

A number of those interviewed talked about traditional news adopting a more sardonic, detached, or casual tone. According to the *AJR*, Phil Rosenthal, the *Chicago Tribune* media columnist, "thinks perhaps the time has come to abandon the old formality of newscasting but says such a process will be evolutionary."[76] But Public Radio International news satirist Faith Salie warned, "Don't try too hard to be funny...I don't think real news shows should try the scripted, cutesy, pithy banter. It gives me the heebie-jeebies. It makes me feel sad for them, and it feels pathetic."[77] (It is too late. Forced banter has been the staple of American television news casts for about three decades.)

If the *AJR* article accurately reflects the lessons many in the MSM and academia draw from the two satire shows, then sadly many have not been paying close attention. Blogger and interactive journalism teacher Jeff Jarvis almost had it correct: "I think what Stewart et al do is remind us of what our mission and voice used to be and should be."[78] But Jarvis fails to identify that mission and voice. Yet the message has been rather consistent as articulated by Stewart on *Crossfire*, by Colbert at the Washington Correspondents' Dinner, by Stewart, Ben Karlin, and David Javerbaum in *America (The Book)*, and on the two television shows four nights weekly: journalists and pundits should fulfill their obligation as watchdogs and give the public information it needs to make sense of the world. They want the MSM to live up to their responsibilities as serious journalists. *The Daily Show*'s Javerbaum, however, does not believe the MSM is prepared to reform itself. He told the *Missouri Review*, a literary journal, that he is not sympathetic to journalists who tell him they wish they could say it the way he can:

> I think it's absolutely pathetic. Fuck them. They can do what we do. What we do doesn't depend on humor. Humor is our why of making the truth interesting. There are other ways to do that. There are other forms of journalism that can do it. But they don't because their institutions, big media, are absolutely entrenched with the government. To indict the government for lying about the buildups in Iraq is to indict the media for not investigating it.[79]

CHAPTER 10

It Takes a Watchdog and a Village: News Media Accountability in Seven Days

A century ago, the news industry's response to requests for corrections and calls for reform typically bordered on glacial.[1] By the start of the twenty-first century, however, it was not uncommon for news outlets to acknowledge complaints from outsiders within a few days, sometimes within hours, often by the use of public editors or ombudsmen. By 2004, however, there was quite a bit of evidence indicating a sea change in the industry's attitude to criticism from outsiders. News management's response exceeded mere public relations Band-Aids such as apologies: Fewer than four months passed from September 8, 2004, when bloggers questioned the CBS News 60 *Minutes* report on President George W. Bush's stint in the Texas Air National Guard to January 5, 2005, when CBS issued its report by an independent panel that resulted in the dismissal of four CBS employees. CNN canceled *Crossfire* nearly three months after Jon Stewart's appearance.[2] CNN chief news executive Eason Jordan resigned February 11, 2005, 14 days after a blogger posted the remarks he made at the January 27 World Economic Forum about U.S. soldiers killing journalists in Iraq.[3]

What had caused the mainstream media to become more responsive? Media watchdog organizations and citizen press critics' use of the digital technology of the World Wide Web had. With blogs, e-mail newsletters, posting of broadcast video, and transcripts, almost anyone, for example, can share a critique of a broadcast with the public during, soon after, and weeks after a broadcast airs.

Digitalized media have given media watchdog groups and individuals unprecedented ability to talk back to the mainstream media (MSM) and with the public.

Yet, it came as a surprise that a specific complaint against radio host Don Imus and his nationally syndicated *Imus in the Morning* show posted on the Media Matters for America (MMA) Web site on April 4, 2007—"Imus Called Women's Basketball Team 'Nappy-Headed Hos'"[4]—would lead NBC News President Steve Capus to drop the simulcast of the radio show and CBS President and CEO Leslie Moonves to fire the well-connected, popular, and profitable Imus by Wednesday, April 11.[5] Though he was often referred to as a "shock jock," the political and media elite embraced Imus. He, for example, shared the cover of *Time* magazine's "The Most Influential People in America 1997": "Pols and pundits get to [make fun of themselves without making a fool of themselves] for an audience three times as large as that of the Sunday TV talk shows."[6] *Dateline*'s NBC correspondent Dennis Murphy noted: "Imus was a $30-plus million a year brand for his employers: CBS and NBC."[7]

MMA was hardly the first left-of-center media watchdog organization to ask the public or journalists to contact management or a news outlet employee to complain about Imus's racial remarks. In January 2000, Fairness & Accuracy in Reporting (FAIR) urged the public to "[a]sk Tim Russert whether his appearances on the *Imus in the Morning* show give "affirmation" to the kind of obvious racism that is featured on the program."[8] About the same time, Philip Nobile, writing for *Tom Paine.com*, an online public affairs journal of progressive analysis and commentary, "tried to raise journalists' awareness of what transpires on The Imus Show" by showing journalists a list of Imus's slurs.[9] Eric Burns, MMA's chief communications strategist, was at a loss to explain why the April 4 Web posting and e-mailing caught traction when so many others did not: "We do these items every day...We have been covering Don Imus and his history of negative language and racial slurs for a number of years."[10]

Perhaps the stars were aligned perfectly during those seven days in April to create a unique confluence of social, business, and political dynamics leading to a public relations crisis for CBS, the owner of Westwood One, Inc., the syndicator of the *Imus in the Morning* program, and MSNBC, NBC's news division cable operation that simulcast it: Imus's history of race, gender, and ethnic jokes; the MSM's fixation with itself that led to almost five days of 24-hour cable television coverage of Imus's clumsy efforts to apologize and the testimonials of his apologists, many of course high-profile news media personalities; the roles of Reverends Al Sharpton and Jesse Jackson, typically lightning rods for media coverage and conservative media vitriol; the complaints of high-profile black journalists and businessmen, black radio's coverage of the controversy and, of course, the loss of advertisers; and the innocence of the targets of Imus's remarks, the apolitical Rutgers University women's basketball team. Nevertheless, the campaign shares some core dynamics with the efforts that led to Eason Jordan's resignation at CNN, the firing of news personnel at CBS and Rather's subsequent resignation at CBS, and CNN's decision to cancel *Crossfire:* citizen press critics, online video posting, and nonmediated discussion on the Web that set off a raging public discussion online and then on the airwaves, which spurred the public to inundate media executives with complaints. Unlike the other circumstances, MMA's campaign brought protesters, including Newark Mayor Cory Booker, to the streets.[11]

To some political theorists, the debates that took place on MMA's Web site, YouTube, black radio, the blogs of black news personalities and journalists such as NBC's Al Roker, and on cable television talk shows do not meet the ideal circumstances of democratic deliberation because radio and television do not provide citizens equal and free debate in a public forum. Furthermore, it is difficult to ascertain whether CBS's Moonves bowed to the consensus of the majority.[12] Nevertheless, during the initial phase of the Imus controversy, individuals who simply had an interest in the topic engaged in vigorous unmediated online debate. A handful of individuals, for example, took it upon themselves to help spread the debate by posting video clips of the offending remarks and Imus's subsequent public apologies on YouTube. For about the first 48 hours after the April 4 program, the "top news outlets didn't mention the incident," the *Wall Street Journal* noted.[13] On Friday, April 6, sportswriter Filip Bondy of the *New York Daily News* was among the first in MSM print journalists to write about Imus's remarks, calling for MSNBC and the WFAN radio station to fire him.[14] So when MSNBC "was getting swamped with outraged viewer complaints"[15] on the afternoon of Thursday, April 6, that outpouring was the result of an egalitarian and freewheeling online discussion. At that point, neither Jackson, Sharpton, Booker, any black interest group, or news pundit had played a role in shaping public opinion on the controversy.

We may never know for certain whether the loss of advertisers, public opinion, the collective public and private views of African-American NBC news employees, or a combination of all three factors moved CBS Moonves to remove the broadcaster as host of the morning radio program. NBC News' Capus, however, said he made the decision to have MSNBC drop its simulcast of *Imus in the Morning* "after reading thousands of e-mails and having countless discussions with NBC workers and the public, but he denied the potential loss of advertising dollars had anything to do with it."[16] If we take him at his word, the communicative process that led to Capus's decision to discontinue telecasting *Imus in the Morning* has the earmarks of deliberative democracy.

Political scientist John S. Brady notes that deliberative democracy theorists "have put much of their energy into identifying the *degree* and *kind* of agreement citizens can expect from the deliberative process," but they "all share one assumption: reasonable agreement is ultimately possible."[17] According to political sociologist and psychologist Shawn W. Rosenberg,

> Allowing for some variation among theorists, most [deliberative democracy theorists] argue that the result will be a collaborative consideration of a problem or issue

through the assertion of fact or value (as personal narratives or explicit claims) that are actually or potentially backed by reasons or clarified by elaborations which may be subject to challenge, defense and revision. The assumption is that this presentation and interrogation will involve the free and equal expression of personal views and a respectful consideration of others' perspectives, fairness and common good.[18]

Soon after Imus's firing, the findings of a study by the Pew Research Center for the People & the Press showed that the public debate about Imus's remarks led to a consensus: "Majorities of both whites (53%) and African Americans (61%) who have been following the Imus story say that the punishment he received was appropriate."[19] Here, though, no overt political decision resulted, and citizens reached agreement on a highly public figure and controversy and appeared to have influenced news executives' decision making. The process might not meet the idealized conception of democratic discourse in the public sphere demanded by some democratic theorists, but many of the essential components of democratic deliberation were evident: a free and equal public exchange of personal views—much of it taking place on the inclusive forums of blogs—leading to a public consensus.

MMA's actions led to the dismissal of a major news/entertainment program host and triggered a national debate among the public, media personalities, and politicians about the use of racist and sexist language on the airwaves and in music and movies. By that measure alone, the Washington, D.C.–based media critic stands out among the many media watchdog organizations, activist groups, and individual press critics.[20] But the national conversation that MMA's action generated also stirred public confession and introspection by some high-profile journalists—regular guests on the Imus show—about the morality of their presence on a program with a history of racist, sexist, and homophobic jokes. MMA's critique led to a change of conduct of some journalists—no small feat—notably *Newsweek* editors Jonathan Adler, Howard Fineman, Evan Thomas, and Jon Meacham. Days before MSNBC and CBS dropped Imus, the four *Newsweek* editors agreed that they would no longer appear on the show. Meacham, the magazine's chief editor, said, "Are we being hypocritical—feigning shock in the tradition of *Casablanca*, that racism and sexism were parts of Imus's program? Perhaps; for too long too many of us looked the other way when it suited our purposes. To continue to do the wrong thing because we have done the wrong thing in the past, however, is senseless, and if being charged with hypocrisy is the price of ending up in the right place, then it is a price worth paying."[21]

During those seven days of April, it was fashionable—if not convenient—for mostly conservatives and Imus apologists to blame civil rights activists Sharpton and Jackson for engineering the media personality's ouster. But the true linchpin in the campaign was Ryan Chiachiere. Had the 26-year-old not watched the program that day, it is likely that Don Imus and his executive producer Bernard McGuirk might still be heard and seen five times weekly on CBS radio and MSNBC cable network. It started with a citizen, someone assigned to watch the watchdogs. That citizen was Chiachiere. He was a researcher for MMA in Washington, D.C. That April the Web-based nonprofit, which calls itself a "progressive research and information center dedicated to comprehensively monitoring, analyzing, and correcting conservative misinformation in the U.S. media," was a month shy of three years old.[22] David Brock, who renounced his ties to the conservative movement in 1997, founded MMA in 2004 and serves as president and CEO of the organization.[23] *The Nation* media critic Eric Alterman, author of *What Liberal Media? The Truth About BIAS and the News,* and Eric Boehlert, author of *Lapdogs: How the Press Rolled Over for Bush* are senior fellows at Media Matters for America.[24]

According to MMA's Eric Burns, the organization has more than 50 researchers in the Washington, D.C., office "listening to their appointed programs...for conservative misinformation, for falsehoods, omissions of important facts, for racist and sexist language."[25] The researchers have a big job; MMA monitors hundreds of media outlets, including *The Rush Limbaugh Show, Hannity & Colmes, Wolf Blizer Reports,* media critic Howard Kurtz's *Reliable Sources* on CNN, and the *New York Times.*[26]

So Chiachiere, a former reporter with the *Jackson (WY) Hole Daily,*[27] was hard at work on the first Wednesday of April 2007, watching the MSNBC simulcast of the Imus show. When Chiachiere smiles he resembles a boyish, innocent Beaver Cleaver. He looks as though he can take a joke. But that day, the sometimes blogger and part-time electric guitarist was not amused. According to the *Baltimore Sun,* he "took the rare step of removing his headphones and repeating the slur to his co-workers in the room."[28] At MMA, once a researcher identifies an offending statement, a report is written and edited for accuracy and fairness.[29] So Chiarchiere put together a 779-word report, including a written transcript, and posted it with the video, a total of 1 minute 24 seconds, and 1 minute and 1 second of the supposedly funny banter between sports announcer Sid Rosenberg, the Imus show's executive producer McGuirk, and Imus at 6 P.M. At the same time, the organization e-mailed the package to journalists and interest groups.[30]

IMUS:
So, I watched the basketball game last night between—a little bit of Rutgers and Tennessee, the women's final.

ROSENBERG:
Yeah, Tennessee won last night—seventh championship for [Tennessee coach] Pat Summitt, I-Man. They beat Rutgers by 13 points.

IMUS:
That's some rough girls from Rutgers. Man, they got tattoos and—

McGUIRK:
Some hard-core hos.

IMUS:
That's some nappy-headed hos there. I'm gonna tell you that now, man, that's some—woo. And the girls from Tennessee, they all look cute, you know, so, like—kinda like—I don't know.

McGUIRK:
A Spike Lee thing.

IMUS:
Yeah.

McGUIRK:
The Jigaboos vs. the Wannabes—that movie that he had.

IMUS:
Yeah, it was a tough—

McCORD:
Do The Right Thing.[31]

McGUIRK:
Yeah, yeah, yeah.

IMUS:
I don't know if I'd have wanted to beat Rutgers or not, but they did, right?

ROSENBERG:
It was a tough watch. The more I look at Rutgers, they look exactly like the Toronto Raptors.

IMUS:
Well, I guess, yeah.

RUFFINO:
Only tougher.

McGUIRK:
The [Memphis] Grizzlies would be more appropriate.

Each MMA posting asks readers to be polite and professional when contacting the media and express "your specific concerns regarding that particular news report or commentary, and be sure to indicate exactly what you would like the media outlet to do differently in the future."[32] MMA acknowledges, however, that its call for mass e-mailing is not always well received:

Speaking at the June 6 installment of the "Journalism Under Fire" conference series, jointly sponsored by the Missouri School of Journalism and the New School, *New York Times* public editor Byron E. (Barney) Calame responded to *Media Matters for America* readers' criticism of recent *Times* reporting, stating that the *Times* puts email from *Media Matters* readers "straight into a folder" because it is "just repetition" and "trying to rack up numbers, which don't impress us." Calame further stated that "that form of feedback…will have to go away because they'll find that people aren't paying attention to it."[33]

Eleven readers responded within the first six hours of Chiachiere's posting, and a total of 80 by Saturday April 7, ranging from tongue-in-cheek, frustration, and anger with Imus and, sometimes, with others who offered comments:

> For all you who believe in prayer, you better start praying like hell for the I-man, I'm sure there are some uncles, grand fathers, cousins, boyfriends, fathers, mothers, sisters etc. who will take offense at "That's some nappy-headed hos there' when referring [sic] to some exceptionally [sic] dedicated, talented and smart student atheletes [sic].[34]
>
> Does anyone here realize what today is? This is the day that MLK was shot and killed. For these slimeballs to spew this overt racist garbage today is obviously a provocation. Colon-'el' Campbell: you have every right to be a racist, ungentlemanly oaf, and mankind has the right to regard you as such. I suggest you return to whatever cave you came from.[35]
>
> Before the only talk radio station in my area was changed to a country music station, I loved listening to the I-man. His comments were so outrageous that I knew that he couldn't be serious. And so I found them to be funny. And now it cracks me up to see so many people on this comment board getting their panties in a bunch over something that was said on the Imus show. But I guess it's hard these days to tell the difference between satire and serious, what with the likes of Limbaugh claiming what they're saying is just joking.[36]

On the same day, Nielsen Media Research reported that the *Imus in the Morning* show was tightening the race between CNN and MSNBC for second place behind Fox News Channel's *Fox & Friends* for morning news show viewers. The ratings of Imus's show grew by 62 percent in the first quarter of 2007, averaging 361,000 viewers.[37] That day Don Imus had no inkling that news of his ratings climb would be the last bit of good news about his program that he would hear for some time.

One is hard-pressed to find any news account of the controversy the following day. (A posting on WNBC.com, "Imus Apologizes for Controversial Comments about Rutgers Players," is dated 4:50 P.M., April 5, and refers to his Friday morning apology. But that Friday was April 6. The story does have an updated posting of 4:40 P.M. April 6.[38]) Meanwhile, the video clip that MMA had posted was having a big impact. *Dateline NBC*'s Dennis Murphy reported that on Thursday MSNBC "was getting swamped with outraged viewer complaints."[39] His account implies that many viewers saw a clip of the program on YouTube. But the first posting of such a clip on YouTube appears to have been on the following day.[40] (That posting drew 439,726 by July 10. Another posting of the same clip drew 1,064,427 viewers by July 10, 2007.[41]) Apparently, the outraged viewers had watched the clip on MMA's Web site, as reported by the *Wall Street Journal*, quoting MSNBC General Manager Dan Abrams as saying, "executives were fielding complaints from viewers and employees who had seen a video clip of Mr. Imus's remark on the Media Matters site."[42]

NBC News' Capus quickly set the crisis management effort in motion. As mentioned earlier, crisis management 101 requires the Band-Aid apology. And that is precisely what NBC news and Imus did. Imus apologized on the air on Friday, April 6, and again on Monday, April 9. But NBC and Capus soon suspected that Imus's remarks had cut too deeply. "Something sunk in over the weekend that this was more than a two-line written apology on Friday," Capus told *Dateline NBC*.[43]

A call for Imus's firing from the typically protest-averse, 4,000-member National Association of Black Journalists (NABJ) surely was part of that "something" that gave Capus reason to believe that the controversy would not die quickly because on Friday at 5:30 A.M., NABJ President Bryan Monroe had posted the organization's demand for "an immediate and sincere apology."[44] What spurred Monroe? The MMA's posting had struck again. According to the *Wall Street Journal*, an NABJ executive board member sent an e-mail regarding the posting at 5:06 P.M., Thursday, that advised, "FYI do we need to address."[45] Monroe read the e-mail, looked at the clip, and wondered whether Imus had "lost his mind."[46] Wayne Dawkins, a member of the organization's seven-member media monitoring committee, noted that the decision to take a public stand against Imus came after intense deliberation because the NABJ's "largest bloc of members is working journalists who have to show neutrality when they're on the job. Yet Imus's behavior was about unacceptable media practices, not racial advocacy. NABJ was on rock-solid ground to unequivocally shock the radio jock."[47]

A wise student of commercial mass media knows never to underestimate the power of advertisers in controlling the fate of mass media content. Here, too, evidence shows that advertisers played a pivotal role in the media executive decision to suspend and fire Imus and that advertising companies reached their decisions largely as a result of the public opinion generated by the online dialogue. *Advertising Age* reported that on April 6—a day before most of the MSM started to cover the story[48]—Procter & Gamble (P&G) dropped the show in response to clogged inboxes and switchboards. The industry trade publication quoted a P&G spokeswoman: "We think we're accountable first to our consumers. This particular venue where our ad appeared was offensive to our target audience. And so that's not acceptable to us."[49] Because there had been so little coverage of the controversy by television, radio, or newspapers by April 6, it is reasonable to link P&G's decision to complaints from a public mostly informed by MMA-generated public debate.

Next, American Express, General Motors Corporation, and GlaxoSmithKline pulled advertising from the Imus show and MSNBC.[50] GEICO and Staples, Inc. followed.[51] Sprint and 1800PetMeds got MSNBC to promise not to have their ads appear during the show, but allowed them to appear during other MSNBC programming.[52] *Advertising Age* called it "the most notable demonstration of audience and advertiser pressure bringing down a broadcaster who had offended."[53] On April 6, Imus apologized on his morning show, but the NABJ released its statement calling the apology "too little, too late."[54]

On Sunday, April 8, the public forum for the debate shifted to black radio. Rev. Jesse Jackson used "his WWPR (105.1 FM) show to call for disciplinary action and also ask rappers and other black public figures to re-examine their own use of terms like 'bitch,' 'ho' and the n-word," and Sharpton and the NABJ "were joined by many callers and guests in demanding Imus be fired."[55] That Easter Sunday, at least 14 major newspapers, including the *Ottawa Citizen* (Canada), published reports on the controversy. The next day, *USA Today* reported that the Imus controversy "sparked the most feedback from readers over the weekend."[56]

On Monday night, April 9, Capus announced that MSNBC was suspending Imus for two weeks, effective April 16.[57] NBC News senior vice president Phil Griffin remarked, "Sharpton kept on saying, 'What are the consequences? What are you going to do now? and Don said, 'I don't know.' Another time he used the unfortunate phrase, of 'you people.'"[58]

Two days later, MSNBC announced that it planned to drop its simulcast of the *Imus in the Morning* radio program. That same day, CBS, owner of *Imus in the Morning* and its syndicator, Westwood One, announced its "decision to cease broadcasting the Imus in the Morning radio program, effective immediately, on a permanent basis."[59]

Almost immediately and in the days and weeks that followed Imus's downfall, NBC and CBS management were roundly criticized for their decisions. Though the Pew Research Center for the People & the Press reported that a majority of whites and African Americans supported CBS's decision, it also noted that roughly twice as many whites as blacks believe his punishment was too tough (35 percent vs. 18 percent).[60] Michael Myers, president and executive director of the New York Civil Rights Coalition, and a frequent critic of Jackson and Sharpton, told *Dateline NBC*, "This is a mistake of the executives of MSNBC. This is a mistake of executives at CBS radio. They have empowered the demagogues. They have empowered the censors."[61] This frequently repeated critique —Imus's firing squelched free speech and empowered those who maintain power by irrational appeals to small-mindedness—is facile and erroneous.

The First Amendment does not protect broadcasters/employees from being removed from the airwaves by their employers. In *Columbia Broadcasting System v. Democratic National Committee*, the U.S. Supreme Court recognized the right of Federal Communications Commission licensees' editorial integrity, the right to make editorial decisions checked only by what they are required to do as public trustees.[62] Consequently, an employee such as Imus has no right under the First Amendment or employment law to a guaranteed spot on the airways. If by free speech Myers and others meant that Imus had no forum to voice his views, then they were simply ignoring reality. Imus had the ability to appear on numerous talk shows, start his own Web site and blog, or with his money launch a magazine or put together a documentary film to give voice to his brand of comedy. And within weeks after his firing, there were reports that Imus would resurface and on CBS.[63] After a nearly eight-month absence, Imus returned to radio in early December on WABC-AM.[64]

Sharpton and Jackson have long been accused of demagoguery. Yet the words and tactics they employed in the debate about Imus do not support an accusation that they appealed to prejudices and emotions. More significant is the indisputable role of Media Matters for America and the hundreds of individuals inspired by it to flood CBS and MSNBC with complaints before Sharpton and Jackson spoke publicly on the issue.

Conservatives also charged that MMA and other left-leaning media watchdog groups were engaged in a vast political correctness conspiracy. "This smacks of a Leftist witch hunt in many ways," conservative syndicated talk show host Glenn Beck told CNN.[65]

Yet MMA's targeting of racially offensive speech is consistent with the Radio-Television News Directors Association and Foundation Code of Ethics and Professional Conduct electronic journalists mandate to "[s]eek to understand the diversity of their community and inform the public without bias or stereotype" and "[p]resent a diversity of expressions, opinions, and ideas in context."[66] Arguably, such standards apply to *Imus in the Morning*. The offending statements were made during the sport news segment of the show. Furthermore, in determining what is a bona fide newscast, bona fide news interview, or bona fide news documentary for purposes of exemption from the equal opportunities requirements under Section 315 (a)(2) of the Communications Act of 1934, the FCC has ruled that Howard Stern's radio program, Bill Maher's *Politically Incorrect*, and talk shows *Donahue*, *Sally Jessy Raphael Show*, and *The Jerry Springer Show* qualified for exemption.[67] Under the rationale of the Section 315 (a)(2) exemptions, *Imus in the Morning* would qualify as a bona fide news program even though it is primarily an entertainment show. Consequently, radio and television hosts—and presumably those employed by cable outlets linked to news broadcasting outlets—who provide news content along with comedy have an ethical obligation to refrain from language exploiting bias and stereotypes.

Widely recognized principles of journalism ethics also should have restrained the journalists from appearing on his program, a concern that was raised by several media ethicists soon after the firings were announced. Ralph Barney, founder of *Journal of Mass Media Ethics*, argued that the four *Newsweek* editors and other journalists who were frequent guests—"In this procession one could even find Howard Kurtz, media ethics specialist for the *Washington Post*"—failed to abide by "their primary obligations: Service to audiences (combined with the

inevitable reference to First Amendment protections that create a moral obligation to be of service)."[68] Those journalists, Barney argued, made a morally indefensible trade-off. They wanted to sell their books, boost circulation or ratings, or
justified their appearances by pointing to the appearances of elected officials and
other public figures. By doing so, they gave Imus a "reflected respectability that
may have prolonged his acceptance, and enabled his long run of corrosive
insults."[69]

Jeffrey Dvorkin, executive director of the Committee of Concerned Journalists, said the Imus scandal should prompt journalists and their employers
to "think about their responsibility in this mess, too...Journalists who make a
living from serious and sober reportage, suddenly find themselves all a-twitter
when the junior producer from Imus or Bill O'Reilly calls to ask if they might
appear on the show to engage in politically incorrect banter and ribaldry. Too
often, the answer is automatically "yes."[70]

On April 4, 2007, Media Matters for America made an appeal to its Web site
readers and journalists and interests groups who received its e-mail package.
It provided a written transcript and a video posting of the short segment. It urged
its readers and e-mail recipients to contact MSNBC. It used no coercion. Exercising their free will, citizens contacted MSNBC and voiced their displeasure.
Interests groups such as NABJ, those headed by Sharpton and Jackson, and the
National Organization for Women joined in the protest, as did many bloggers,
including some employed by NBC. Journalists and pundits joined the debate
on the cable news and talk shows and in magazine and newspaper columns.
MMA triggered a campaign that galvanized the public and persuaded two news
outlets to make a major programming change. It performed the role of the Fifth
Estate. With public opinion largely on its side, the media watchdog organization
got the Fourth Estate to listen and make a major content change.

NBC's Capus put it this way:

Rather than portraying it as caving to pressure groups, I would say that we listened
to America. An advertiser represents Americans. Reverend Sharpton represents
certain viewpoints. The people who work within NBC have very strong opinions
about this. So, it wasn't that we caved to groups or this or that. We listened to the
people who worked for us and we listened to the country.[71]

CHAPTER 11

A Prescription for Effective Press Criticism in a Democracy

What immediately follows is a prescription for effective press criticism in a democracy:

Adopt an adversarial approach: An effective press critic needs to perceive itself not as a foe to a news outlet, but as an adversary to it. There is a distinction. Foes attempt to injure, impede, or vanquish their enemy. In this context, of course, the press critic's foe would be a news outlet or its reporting, writing, and editing employees. A press critic that sees its target as an enemy does not seek to engage the news outlet and its personnel in a discussion or debate because the enemy is to be eliminated, if possible. The foe and its enemy have little in common and much that separates them. They are at war. There is little incentive for a news organization to engage in a constructive dialogue with a press critic who attacks it as an enemy to vanquish.

Adversaries, however, share a common goal. For example, in an adversarial legal system, a criminal prosecutor and a defense attorney share common goals: truth and justice. They agree to conduct themselves by the same codes of conduct: rules of evidence and legal ethics. Yes, war combatants may agree to codes of conduct, for example, the Geneva Convention. But the intent of foes at war is elimination, conquest, and submission. Adversaries seek only to win a particular contest. They shake hands and compete again. Just as important, adversaries win only when a judge or jury passes judgment.

Such an adversarial relationship is analogous to a debate between two parties over whether one has abided by the terms of a contract. In such a relationship, the parties share the same goal—press performance that abides by an outlet's social contract. Both parties are in agreement on the rules of evidence—the news outlet's duty to its audience as prescribed in its social contract. The public is the judge and jury, voting by commenting on blogs and electronic bulletin boards, or by registering their opinions with the news organization via e-mail and telephone calls, or by other forms of public protest.

Present a fact-based argument: Sweeping generalizations accusing a MSM news outlet of systematically or intentionally slanting coverage to pursue political, economic, gender, ethnic, age, or other agendas tend to be ignored by the MSM adhering to objectivity. Such statements are conclusions, not arguments, because a well-formed argument needs a premise and propositions developed from analysis. More problematic is such critical statements are easily refuted, for example, "No, we are not biased. We report the war; we do not take a position on it." And because such critical statements are essentially little more than a sermon to the choir, the targeted news outlet has little reason to respond.

In contrast, the successes of several of the press criticism campaigns explored in these pages make a strong case that even an ideologically biased press critic can engage the public beyond their fellow travelers, the MSM generally, and the target of their critiques in discourse provided it offers specific, fact-based systematic analysis or alternative reporting to challenge the accuracy of a specific news report. This should not come as a surprise. When a critic speaks the language of a journalist, it is more likely that the journalist will respond. Yet, for more than 100 years, a line of public criticism has condemned some news outlets for corrupting public values, providing little evidence of causality.[1]

Offer critical analysis based on the news' organization's failure to comply with the implicit or explicit terms of its social contract: In *Criticizing the Media: Empirical Approaches,* James B. Lemert explains that critical analysis "is characterized by appeals to standards and values that can be understood and shared by everyone and uses methods that are at least revealed to everyone."[2] For that reason, a critical analysis appealing to the standards and values of the news organization's social contract provides criteria that are readily understood by critics, their targets, and the public. As pointed out in the introduction (Chapter 1), for the most part, the terms of the contracts can be identified in industry-wide ethical codes or a news organization's own ethical code and standards.

Galvanize public opinion: This is the linchpin component. The press critic who seeks public support for its position is likely to be successful. Accuracy in Media (AIM), Fairness & Accuracy in Reporting (FAIR), and Media Matters for America (MMA) tap their own subscribers' lists, imploring them to e-mail, write, or phone a media target. With the advent of e-mail, such media watchdog groups can accelerate the process and expand their reach. MMA's campaign against Don Imus (Chapter 10) illustrates the newfound capabilities. The organization sparked a national debate on Imus's fate by e-mailing a transcript and video of the offending statements to its subscribers and others, such as the National Association of Black Journalists members. And as we saw with Jon Stewart's *Crossfire* appearance, individuals can take it upon themselves to build public opinion around a controversy by posting a broadcast on a blog or social networking site without the critic's knowledge. A news organization is more likely to address a critic's concerns when it believes the critic echoes the opinions of a vocal segment of the public that is its most likely audience.

Without a public audience, a journalist is little more than a diarist, writing for a small and private readership, or a chronicler, writing for a future audience. Most journalists seek to reach a sizable, public and current audience with regularity. And because an audience's allegiance must be regularly maintained, particularly in an information market providing numerous choices of news suppliers, journalism organizations and individual practitioners are more likely to respond to critiques that unfavorably affect their public image. Of course, losses in newsstand sales, ratings, subscribers, and advertising are firm signs of an erosion of public image. But a news organization or individual journalist would be unwise to wait until adverse public opinion inflicts a level of possibly irreversible damage.

Consequently, a press critic's greatest leverage is the ability to turn public opinion against a news organization or journalist. But over the years, the overwhelming majority of press critics have failed to strike at this vulnerable spot, often it seems because they held the public in contempt, or because they were middlebrow or highbrow and believed their judgments superior to the masses. That is a description of the majority of critics who assailed the vulgarity and sensationalism of yellow journalism that flourished in the late 1800s, promoted by the publishing giants Joseph Pulitzer and William Randolph Hearst. Nearly two decades of pounding from editors and writers at leading literary and cultural journals had little effect. Eventually, the erosion of his audience and the high cost of trying to keep them compelled Pulitzer to question the value of yellow journalism. In *Civilizing Voices: American Press Criticism 1880–1950*, Marion Tuttle Marzolf notes that Pulitzer toned down the yellow journalism at his *New York World* in the early 1900s, once it was clear that after the Spanish-American War in 1898, yellow press "circulations had dropped...For example, Hearst's [*New York*] *Journal* was losing 10,000 to 15,000 subscribers a week, but he could still go on pouring family money into his newspaper ventures."[3]

One wonders whether the news media in 1947 would have had a more favorable response to the findings of the Hutchins Commission's *A Free and Responsible Press: A General Report on Mass Comunication: Newspapers, Radio, Motion Pictures, Magazines, and Books*[4] if representatives from, for example, labor unions and leading social and professional organizations had sat on the Commission, or if it had held forums to elicit the public's views of newspaper and radio performance. But the Commission's membership was drawn mostly from academia, and all its sessions were closed to the public and the press.[5] Having failed to include the public in its fact-finding or to make its case directly to it in public forums, the Commission had no leverage to counter a great deal of the negative coverage it received. Successful news outlets, on the other hand, merely needed to point to their newsstand sales, subscriptions, or ratings as evidence of public support. Accordingly, the *Chicago Tribune* could legitimately dismiss the Commission's findings because, though it claimed to be speaking for the public, the Commission had no support for such a claim: "The professors would have done better if they had studied the readers of the newspaper itself. Some of the newspapers which did not get an Oscar from the professors are of the largest circulation."[6]

The Commission's approach is a lesson in how a press critic undermines its own goals. Though it took an adversarial approach to the news media, its report presented inexcusably little data to support its assessment of the news industry or its recommendations to reform it. The forward to *A Free and Responsible Press* acknowledges that the Commission "did not conduct elaborate research. It sought facts to fill out gaps in its information or to answer questions which arose in the course of its discussions."[7] Rather than study the mission statements and standards of news outlets, it sought to impose its own definition of social responsibility. And as noted above, the Commission disregarded the public. It operated from a belief in democratic elitism; its members believed that they knew what was best for the public. As journalism historian and lawyer Stephen Bates noted in "Realigning Journalism with Democracy: The Hutchins Commission, Its Times, and Ours," "The press saw itself as exuberantly of the people and the professoriate as snootily above them. Consequently, the press felt entitled to a level of democratic legitimacy that academics could never match. No wonder journalists paid little heed to the criticisms of, in *Editor & Publisher*'s description, '11 professors, a banker-merchant and a poet-librarian.'"[8]

Since their inception, the two leading national press reviews, *Columbia Journalism Review* (CJR) and *American Journalism Review* (AJR), have been engaged in conversations almost entirely with the news media industry. The news consumer is an afterthought. As I concluded in Chapter 7, the print magazine format is too costly and unattractive to high-end advertisers to support the press review genre, though *Brill's Content* proved there was widespread public interest in reading about media performance. The Internet, it seems, would provide an affordable medium for reaching the general public. And from 2004 to mid-2006, *CJR* Daily.org, the magazine's blog on press criticism, received "nearly 500,000 page views a month" by mid-2006.[9] Presumably, a substantial number of the Web site's viewers were nonjournalists as the magazine circulation was 20,000 at the time. But Nicholas Lemann, dean of the Columbia University Graduate School of Journalism, said the free site could not sustain an eight-member staff.[10] By fall 2007, *CJR* Daily had been scaled back to a blog called "The Kicker." As 2007 came to a close, *AJR* had yet to experiment with a blog. Until either *CJR* or *AJR* finds ways to galvanize public opinion, it is unlikely that either one will provoke debate among the public and the news industry leading to reform.

Because public opinion plays a pivotal role in bolstering a press critic's ability to correct ethical lapses by news media, the above prescription should be applied

to the creation of an effort to increase citizens' understanding of journalism practices, standards, and press criticism. Such an effort should take the form of a
weekly television show, largely because the medium is still the most effective
in reaching a mass audience. As regularly scheduled programs examining journalism performance, CNN's *Reliable Sources* and Fox News Channel's *Fox News
Watch* ostensibly perform such a task. One rarely hears *Reliable Sources'* host or
guests or *Fox News Watch*'s panelists refer to objective standards or rationales—
an industry-wide or news organization's ethical codes or standards—in an effort
to help viewers understand whether a journalist or news organization conducted
itself properly. Occasionally, *Fox News Watch*'s Neal Gabler articulates standards
and rationales that explain news media decisions. For example, in an April 22,
2006, broadcast, Gabler explained why the publication of the names of the Duke
University athletes accused of rape was justified: "No, it's fair. Because as a
matter of public policy, we withhold the names of victims so that they will come
forward. There is no comparable public policy interest in withholding the names
of the accused. They are presumed innocent, they will have their day in court."[11]
Both programs tend to talk at citizens and not to them. Neither program takes
calls from viewers. *Reliable Sources'* guests are journalists and MSM-paid media
critics. Fox's panelists are MSM insiders.

In keeping with my prescription for effective press criticism, I propose a
weekly press criticism program with a call-in format that would include interviews with journalists, editors, media executives, and citizen press critics, as well
as discussions about specific journalism practices. The program would air on
C-SPAN, which has perfected such programming formats, particularly the call-
in format. The authors of *The C-SPAN Revolution* explain that "C-SPAN's
call-in format is different, and it has made a difference. Unlike other hosts of
such programs, C-SPAN hosts are not 'agent provocateur[s]'...They are not in
the business to make points; success is measured by the quality of dialogue and
by the amount of information provided."[12]

One of the program's key goals would be to increase citizens' awareness of press
criticism and to that end increase the public's awareness of recognized journalism
ethics and standards. The formats of *Reliable Sources* and *Fox News Watch* would
generally be avoided. *Reliable Sources* takes a scatter-shot approach to covering
news scandals and performance that generates highly superficial analysis. *Fox
News Watch* tends toward the shout-fest format in which speakers frequently
interrupt each other and thoughts are rarely fully expounded. Instead, the program I propose would use a range of formats. Sometimes, an interviewer would
elicit explanations and answers from a citizen press critic, such as FAIR's Jeff
Cohen or *Powerline.blog.com*'s John H. Hinderaker, who would also field questions from viewers. Rarely in public discussions about press performance do we
hear from media management, and when we do it too often is in the form of a
press release. The proposed show also would seek to make media executives more
directly accountable to the public through the interview and call-in format. But
unlike the neutrality that C-SPAN-originated programming maintains, the

proposed press critic program would occasionally engage in activism similar to *Brill's Content*'s letter campaign to news organizations to protect the privacy of grieving families.[13] The show would also provide a public forum for journalists to explain their reporting methods and concepts of social responsibility.

In this book, I have argued for the inclusion of press critics engaging in irrational, acid-tongue, outrageous—"undesirable because it is inconsistent with common canons of decency"[14]—public speech and activism in the dialogue about press performance in our democracy. I have argued that under a constitutional concept of public discourse, a wide range of speech that the status quo finds objectionable is permissible and desirable because of its inclusiveness; that it opens the public sphere to a wide variety of press critics, particularly citizen press critics—ideologues, satirists, partisans, and anonymous and pseudonymous speakers. As these varied critics engage in a process of debate and critical interaction with news organizations and journalists, a common understanding can be reached about a news entity's obligation to its audience and the people it covers. Because a free press is vital to a thriving democracy, citizens must exercise some influence over advertising-dependent news media beyond the commercial marketplace. They must participate in the marketplace of ideas as well. Otherwise, big money interests more than news consumers are likely to play a definitive role in shaping a news entity's social obligations. Democratic dialogue is distorted when advertisers exert excessive influence on news content much the way the democratic process is corrupted by big money lobbyists. The power of big money in the political system allows a wealthy minority superiority over the poorer majority, absent any legal or constitutional fiat. Thus, the political power of the elite is exercised over and at the expense of the majority. That is oligarchy, not democracy.

Nearly all news entities, even those run by undemocratic regimes, claim to be the voice of the people. The participation of an array of press critics having no former or current affiliation with the professional news media, however, is one important way to assure that news organizations and journalists live up to such claims without infringing on their editorial freedoms. Though I generally do not subscribe to the axiom that the ends justify the means, the overwhelming majority of the effective press critics examined here—the ones whose critiques drew meaningful responses from their targets, leading to reforms in news organizations' standards and practices—were citizen press critics. Thus, the inclusion of a wide range of citizen press critics enhances democratic deliberation and tends to lead to improved press performance.

Notes

CHAPTER 1

1. Corey Pein, "Blog Gate," *Columbia Journalism Review*, http://cjrarchives.org/issues/2005/1/pein-blog.asp (accessed May 23, 2007).

2. Glenn Reynolds, "Update: Matt Welch Defends the Press," May 16, 2007, http://instapundit.com/archives/023022.php (accessed September 26, 2007).

3. I derive the term "citizen press critic" from Rosa A. Eberly's *Citizen Critics: Literary Public Spheres* (Urbana & Chicago: University of Illinois Press, 2000).

4. Lee Brown, *The Reluctant Reformation: On Criticizing the Press in America* (New York: David McKay Co., 1974), 13–14.

5. Marion Tuttle Marzolf, "Honor Without Influence," *Media Studies Journal* 9, no. 2 (Spring 1995): 47.

6. Peter Bachrach, *The Theory of Democratic Elitism: A Critique* (Boston: Little Brown, 1967), 8.

7. Linda J. Lumsden, "Press Criticism," in *American Journalism: History, Principles, Practices*, ed. W. David Sloan and Lisa Mullikin Parcell (Jefferson, NC: McFarland & Co., Inc., 2002), 55–65.

8. See Wendy N. Wyatt, *Critical Conversations: A Theory of Press Criticism* (Cresskill, NJ: Hampton Press, 2007), 41–59.

9. Stephen J.A. Ward, *The Invention of Journalism Ethics: The Path to Objectivity and Beyond* (Montreal & Kingston: McGill-Queen's University Press, 2006), 120.

10. Clarence N. Olien, George A. Donohue, and Phillip J. Tichenor, "A Guard Dog Perspective on the Role of the Media," *Journal of Communication* 45, no. 2 (Spring 1995): 115–132.

11. Blogger.com, "The Story of Blogging," http://www.blogger.com/about (accessed September 28, 2007).

12. Jack Shafer, "The Church of Liebling: The Uncritical Worshippers of America's Best Press Critic," *Slate.com*, http://www.slate.com/id/2105627/ (accessed May 26, 2007).

13. Commission on Freedom of the Press, *A Free and Responsible Press: A General Report on Mass Communication: Newspapers, Radio, Motion Pictures, Magazine, and Books* (Chicago: University of Chicago Press, 1947), 20–25.

14. Stephen Bates, "Realigning Journalism with Democracy: The Hutchins Commission, Its Times, and Ours," The Annenberg Washington Program in Communications Policy Studies of Northwestern University (1995), http://www.annenberg.northwestern.edu/pubs/hutchins/hutch01.htm (accessed October 11, 2007).

15. Susanne Fengler, "Holding the News Media Accountable: A Study of Media Reporters and Media Critics in the United States," *Journalism & Mass Communication Quarterly* 80, no. 34 (Winter 2003): 825.

16. Robert W. Snyder, Jennifer Kelley and Dirk Smiller, "Critics with Clout—Nine Who Matter," *Media Studies Journal* 9, no. 2 (Spring 1995): 1–18.

17. James Carey, "Journalism and Criticism: The Case of an Undeveloped Professional," *The Review of Politics* 36 (1974): 227–249.

18. Ibid., 236.

19. Ibid., 244.

20. Myra Marx Ferree, William A. Gamson, Jurgen Gerhards, and Dieter Rucht, "Four Models of the Public Sphere in Modern Democracies," *Theory and Society* 31 (June 2002): 294.

21. Jon Stewart, interview by Paul Begala and Tucker Carlson, "Jon Stewart's America, *Crossfire*, October 15, 2004, http://transcripts.CNN.com/TRANSCRIPTS/0410/15/cf.01.html (accessed March 15, 2008).

22. *The Federalists Papers No. 55*, February 15, 1788, http://usgovinfo.about.com/library/fed/blfed55.htm (accessed May 26, 2007).

23. James F. Bohman, *Public Deliberation: Pluralism, Complexity, and Democracy* (Cambridge, MA: The MIT Press, 1996), 4–5.

24. Nick Crossley and John Michael Roberts, *After Habermas: New Perspectives on the Public Sphere* (Oxford, UK: Blackwell Publishing, 2004), 2.

25. Peter Dahlgren and Colin Sparks, eds., *Communication and Citizenship: Journalism and the Public Sphere in the New Media Age* (New York: Routledge, 1991), 1.

26. Ferree, et al., "Four Models of the Public Sphere in Modern Democracies," 294.

27. Ferree, et al., "Four Models of the Public Sphere in Modern Democracies," 300.

28. Jürgen Habermas, *The Theory of Communicative Action, Vol, 1: Reason and The Rationalization of Society* (Beacon Press, Boston, c1984–1987), 25.

29. Ferree, et al., "Four Models of the Public Sphere in Modern Democracies," 300.

30. Ibid., 298.

31. Ibid.

32. Iris Marion Young, *Inclusion and Democracy* (Oxford, UK: Oxford University Press, 2000), 50.

33. Ferree et al., "Four Models of the Public Sphere in Modern Democracies," 314.

34. Robert C. Post, *Constitutional Domains: Democracy, Community, Management* (Cambridge, MA: Harvard University Press, 1995), 188, citing *Boos v. Barry*, 485 U.S. 312, 322 (1988).

35. Robert C. Post, "The Constitutional Concept of Public Discourse: Outrageous Opinion, Democratic Deliberation, and *Hustler Magazine v Falwell*," *Harvard Law Review* 103 (January 1990): 601–686.

36. Post, *Constitutional Domains*, 141.

37. Ibid., 151.

38. Ibid., 148.

39. Frank I. Michelman, "Review: Must Constitutional Democracy Be 'Responsive'?" *Ethics* 107 (July 1997): 706–723.

40. Post, *Constitutional Domains*, 139.

41. Ibid., 138.

42. Michelle Malkin, "Fake News vs. Real News from Iraq," http://michellemalkin.com/2006/11/28/fake-news-vs-real-news-from-iraq/ November 28, 2006 (accessed May 30, 2007).

43. Post, *Constitutional Domains*, 186.

44. *Brandenburg v. Ohio*, 395 U.S. 444 (1969).

45. *NAACP v. Claiborne Hardware*, 458 U.S. 886 (1982).

46. Ibid.

47. *Watts v. United States*, 394 U.S. 705, 706 (1969).

48. C. Edwin Baker, *Human Liberty and Freedom of Speech* (New York: Oxford University Press, 1989), 57.

49. Martin F. Nolan, "Was Agnew Right About TV News?" *Boston Globe*, November 17, 1999, A 23. Available from ProQuest LLC, Ann Arbor, Michigan.

50. Alan Cowell, "In Parting Shot, Blair Calls Press a 'Feral Beast,'" *New York Times*, June 12, 2007, http://www.nytimes.com/2007/06/12/world/europe/12cnd-blair.html?_r=1&hp&oref=slogin (accessed October 1, 2007).

51. *Dan Rather v. CBS Corporation*, September 19, 2007, ¶60, http://www.nytimes.com/packages/pdf/business/20070920_cbs_complaint.pdf (accessed October 1, 2007).

52. Ibid., ¶ 38–40.

53. Commission on Freedom of the Press, *A Free and Responsible Press*, 80.

54. *New York Times v. Sullivan*, 376 U.S. 254 (1964).

55. Post, *Constitutional Domains*, 144.

56. Brian Cowan, *The Social Life of Coffee: The Emergence of the British Coffeehouse* (New Haven, CT: Yale University Press, 2005), 255.

57. Marzolf, "Honor Without Influence," 47.

58. Commission on Freedom of the Press, *A Free and Responsible Press*.

59. Ibid., 9.

60. Ibid., 20.

61. Ibid., 14.

62. Ward, *The Invention of Journalism Ethics*, 26.

63. Commission on Freedom of the Press, *A Free and Responsible Press*, 18.

64. Ibid.

65. Marion Tuttle Marzolf, *Civilizing Voices: American Press Criticism, 1800–1950* (New York: Longman, 1991), 18–19.

66. Erwin G. Krasnow, "The 'Public Interest' Standard: The Elusive Search for the Holy Grail" (Briefing paper prepared for the Advisory Committee on Public Interest Obligations of Digital Television Broadcasters, October 22, 1997), http://www.ntia.doc.gov/pubintadvcom/octmtg/krasnow.htm (accessed October 10, 2007).

67. The *New York Times*, *Ethical Journalism: A Handbook of Values and Practices for the News and Editorial Departments*, September 2004, 19–22, http://www.nytco.com/pdf/NYT_Ethical_Journalism_0904.pdf (accessed October 9, 2007).

68. Time Warner, Corporate Social Responsibility Report, 2006, http://www.timewarner.com/corp/citizenship/index.page/csr_report_060519.pdf (accessed October 9, 2007).

69. Opinion Journal from the *Wall Street Journal Editorial Page*, "The Jordan Kerfuffle," February 14, 2005, http://www.opinionjournal.com/editorial/feature.html?id=110006289 (accessed September 19, 2007).

CHAPTER 2

1. Steve Daley, "Vietnam Aside, AIM Critique Exposes Cowardly PBS," *Chicago Tribune*, June 26, 1985, 8. Available from Lexis-Nexis Group, Dayton, Ohio.

2. Ibid.

3. Richard Zoglin, "Taking Aim Again at Viet Nam Pbs Gives Airtime to a Controversial Rebuttal, *Time*, July 1, 1985, http://www.time.com/time/magazine/article/0,9171,959554,00.html (accessed September 3, 2007).

4. Patrick J. Furlong, untitled, review of *Vietnam: A Television History*, by Richard Ellison, *The Public Historian* (Summer 1984): 121–122.

5. UPI, "Peabody Awards Given," *New York Times*, April 2, 1984, 14. Available from Lexis-Nexis Group, Dayton, Ohio.

6. Associated Press, "PBS Gets 9 New Emmys," *New York Times*, September 1, 1984, 41. Available from Lexis-Nexis Group, Dayton, Ohio.

7. Hannah Gourey, "Vietnam: A Television History," http://www.museum.tv/archives/etv/V/htmlV/vietnamate/vietnamate.htm (accessed September 3, 2007).

8. Accuracy in Media, "Who We Are," http://www.aim.org/static/20_0 7_0_C (accessed September 5, 2007).

9. Laurence Jarvik, *PBS: Behind the Screen* (Rocklin, CA: Prima Publishing, 1997), 198.

10. "Biography," http://www.reedirvine.net/biography.html (accessed September 5, 2007).

11. Fox Butterfield, "A Critique on PBS of Vietnam Series Sets Off a Dispute," *New York Times*, June 13, 1985, A1. Available from Lexis-Nexis Group, Dayton, Ohio.

12. Ibid.

13. Reed Irvine, "Experts Demolish PBS Viet Film," *AIM Report*, August B, 1984, http://www.aim.org/publications/aim_report/1984/08b.html#6 (accessed September 9, 2007).

14. Jarvik, *PBS: Behind the Screen*, 198.

15. James Day, *The Vanishing Vision: The Inside Story of Public Television* (Berkeley: University of California Press), 282.

16. Michael Massing, "The Rise and Decline of Accuracy in Media," *The Nation*, 200–215; 200. Available from ProQuest LLC, Ann Arbor, Michigan.

17. Jack Thomas, "Conservatives on the Attack," *Boston Globe*, June 26, 1985, 69. Available from ProQuest LLC, Ann Arbor, Michigan.

18. Reed Irvine, "Grilling the Grillers," *AIM Report*, June A, 1985, http://www.aim.org/publications/aim_report/1985/06a.html (accessed September 3, 2007).

19. Ibid.

20. Daley, "Vietnam Aside, AIM Critique Exposes Cowardly PBS."

21. Clarke Taylor, "PBS Series on Vietnam Draws Fire," *Los Angeles Times*, June 22, 1985, 1. Available from ProQuest LLC, Ann Arbor, Michigan.

22. Zoglin, "Taking Aim Again at Viet Nam Pbs Gives Airtime to a Controversial Rebuttal."

23. Bruce Cumings, *War and Television* (London and New York: Verso, 1992), 95.

24. Gourey, "Vietnam: A Television History."

25. Dom Bonafede, "One Man's Accuracy," *The National Journal*, May 10, 1986, 1111. Available from Lexis-Nexis Group, Dayton, Ohio.

26. Jarvik, *PBS: Behind the Screen*, 200.

27. Bonafede, "One Man's Accuracy."

28. Reed Irving, "Perils of Journalism," Accuracy in Media, June 27, 2001, http://www.aim.org/aim_column/A2459_0_3_0_C/ (accessed September 5, 2007).

29. Richard C. Post, *Constitutional Domains: Democracy, Community, Management,* (Cambridge, MA: Harvard University Press, 1995), 186.

30. C. Edwin Baker, *Human Liberty and Freedom of Speech* (New York: Oxford University Press, 1989), 56.

31. Ibid.

32. Public Broadcasting Act of 1967, Sec. 496 [47 U.S.C. 396], http://www.cpb.org/aboutcpb (accessed September 4, 2007).

33. Ibid.

34. Zoglin, "Taking Aim Again at Viet Nam Pbs Gives Airtime to a Controversial Rebuttal."

35. Tribute to Reed Irvine. Senate Floor Statement of Senator Sessions, November 20, 2004, http://www.reedirvine.net/tributes_jeff_sessions.html (accessed September 8, 2007).

36. Christine D. Urban, *Examining Our Credibility: Perspectives of the Public and the Press* (Reston, VA: American Society of Newspaper Editors, 1999), http://www.asne.org/kiosk/reports/99reports/1999examiningourcredibility/ (accessed September 7, 2007).

37. Ibid.; "Perceived Bias," http://www.asne.org/kiosk/reports/99reports/1999examiningourcredibility/p27-32_Bias.html (accessed September 7, 2007).

38. Ibid., Table 15: Presumed Motive, http://www.asne.org/kiosk/reports/99reports/1999examiningourcredibility/tables/table15.html (accessed September 7, 2007).

39. "Biography," http://www.reedirvine.net/biography.html; Bonafede, "One Man's Accuracy."

40. Bonafede, "One Man's Accuracy."

41. "Biography," http://www.reedirvine.net/biography.html.

42. Bonafede, "One Man's Accuracy."

43. Martin F. Nolan, "Was Agnew Right About TV News?" *Boston Globe,* November 17, 1999, A 23. Available from ProQuest LLC, Ann Arbor, Michigan.

44. Pat Buchanan, "Richard Nixon's Revenge," *The American Conservative,* February 14, 2005, http://www.amconmag.com/2005_02_14/buchanan.html (accessed September 5, 2007).

45. Bonafede, "One Man's Accuracy."

46. Reed Irvine, "AIM to Seek Help of Network Shareholders," *AIM Report,* February A, 1976, http://www.aim.org/publications/aim_report/1976/02a.html (accessed September 5, 2007).

47. Ibid. (accessed September 6, 2007).

48. Scott R. Schmedel, *Wall Street Journal,* May 7, 1975, 6. Available from Lexis-Nexis Group, Dayton, Ohio.

49. William J. Jones, "'77 Should Set Records, Post Stockholders Told," May 12, 1997, C1. Available from Lexis-Nexis Group, Dayton, Ohio.

50. William J. Jones, "Another Good Year Seen for Post Co.; Another Good Year Predicted for Post Co.," *Washington Post,* May 11, 1978, F1. Available from Lexis-Nexis Group, Dayton, Ohio.

51. William Jones, "Post Sees Rebound; The Washington Post Co. Sees Stronger 2d Quarter," *Washington Post,* B1. Available from Lexis-Nexis Group, Dayton, Ohio.

52. Patricia Sullivan, "Media Watchdog Reed Irvine, 82," *Washington Post*, November 18, 2004, B08, http://www.washingtonpost.com/wp-dyn/articles/A58852-2004Nov17.html (accessed September 5, 2007).

53. Martin Arnold, *New York Times*, March 18, 1975, p. 17. Available from Lexis-Nexis Group, Dayton, Ohio.

54. "Fed. Reserve Bd. Investigation Clears Reed J. Irvine," *New York Times*, March 21, 1975, 35. Available from Lexis-Nexis Group, Dayton, Ohio.

55. Massing, "The Rise and Decline of Accuracy in Media," 202.

56. Stephen Goode, "Irvine Fights War of Words to Correct Media's First Draft," *Insight on the News*, March 17, 1997, http://findarticles.com/p/articles/mi_m1571/is_n10v13/ai_19201676 (accessed February 20, 2007).

57. Associated Press, "ABC Shareholders to Vote on 'Propaganda 'Resolution," April 3, 1984. Available from Lexis-Nexis Group, Dayton, Ohio.

58. Christopher Lindsay, "Olympics Will Be Profitable, With or Without Soviets, Says ABC, *Associated Press*, May 15, 1984. Available from Lexis-Nexis Group, Dayton, Ohio.

59. Reed Irvine and Cliff Kincaid, "*Washington Post* Promises Higher Standards," June 16, 2000, Accuracy in Media, http://www.aim.org/media_monitor/A3028_0_2_)_C/ (accessed September 5, 2007).

60. Sarah Schaerr Norton, e-mail message to author, September 6, 2007.

61. AIM Report, "The Role of the Communist Party," November 1, 2000, http://www.aim.org/aim_report/A3725_0_4_0_C/ (accessed September 6, 2007).

62. Cassandra Tate, "Who's Out to Lunch Here," *Columbia Journalism Review*, November/December 1992, http://backissues.cjrarchives.org/year/92/6/stone.asp (accessed September 6, 2007).

63. Tom Shales, "CBS's Lavish Apologia; And the Chill After the 'Vietnam Inquest,'" *Washington Post*, July 19, 1982, C1. Available from Lexis-Nexis Group, Dayton, Ohio.

64. Ibid.

65. Raymond Bonner, "Massacre of Hundreds Reported in Salvador Village," *New York Times*, January 27, 1982, 1. Available from Lexis-Nexis Group, Dayton, Ohio.

66. Ibid.

67. Ibid.

68. Review & Outlook (Editorial), "On Credulity," *Wall Street Journal*, March 19, 1993, A.1. Available from ProQuest LLC, Ann Arbor, Michigan. See also Mark Danner, "The Truth of El Mozote," *The New Yorker*, December 6, 1993, http://www.markdanner.com/articles/print/127 (accessed September 6, 2007).

69. Danner, "The Truth of El Mozote."

70. Sydney H. Schanberg, "New York; Shoot the Messenger," *New York Times*, March 2, 1982, A23. Available from Lexis-Nexis Group, Dayton, Ohio.

71. Reed Irvine, "Savaging El Salvador," *AIM Report*, February B, 1982, http://www.aim.org/publications/aim_report/1982/02b.html (accessed September 6, 2007).

72. Ibid.

73. Reed Irvine, "The Ray Bonner Division," *AIM Report*, July B, 1982, http://www.aim.org/publications/aim_report/1982/07b.html (accessed September 6, 2007).

74. Ibid.

75. Ibid.

76. Ibid.

77. Mike Hoyt, "The Mozote Massacre," *Columbia Journalism Review*, February 1993, http://backissues.cjrarchives.org/year/93/1/mozote.asp (accessed September 6, 2007).

78. Reed Irvine, "Journalistic Corruption," *AIM Report*, April B, 1984, http://www.aim.org/publications/aim_report/1984/04b.html (accessed September 8, 2007).

79. Ibid.

80. Jack Shafer, "A. M. Rosenthal (1922–2006)," http://www.slate.com/id/2141630/ (accessed September 10, 2007).

81. Stanley Meisler, "Teaching Notes: The Massacre in El Mozote," in *Thinking Clearly: Cases in Journalistic Decision-Making*, ed. Tom Rosenstiel and Amy S. Mitchell (New York: Columbia University Press, 2003), http://www.concernedjournalists.org/node/435 (accessed September 10, 2007).

82. "The Mozote Horror, Confirmed," *New York Times*, October 26, 1992, late edition, A16. Available from Lexis-Nexis Group, Dayton, Ohio; Danner, "The Truth of El Mozote;" Robin Andersen, *A Century of Media, A Century of War* (New York: Peter Lang, 2006), 83–102.

83. Meisler, "Teaching Notes: The Massacre in El Mozote."

84. Hoyt, "The Mozote Massacre."

85. Meisler, "Teaching Notes: The Massacre in El Mozote."

86. *Hustler Magazine, Inc. v. Falwell*, 485 U.S. 46, 53 (1998).

87. Post, *Constitutional Domains*, 151.

88. Ibid, 165.

89. Review & Outlook (Editorial), "On Credulity."

90. Meisler, "Teaching Notes," 122.

91. *Galloway v. FCC*, 778 F.2d 16, 20 (D.C. Cir. 1985). See also Richard Labunski, *Libel and the First Amendment: Legal History and Practice in Print and Broadcasting* (New Brunswick, NJ: Transaction Publishers, 1989), 186–187.

92. Labunski, *Libel and the First Amendment*, 186.

93. Sally Bedell Smith, "Decision's Effect on CBS, 60 Minutes, and Rather," *New York Times*, June 7, 1983, C11. Available from Lexis-Nexis Group, Dayton, Ohio.

94. Reed Irvine, "Libel Suit Help with No 'Ideological Ax to Grind,'" *New York Times*, June 21, 1983, Late City Final Edition, 28. Available from Lexis-Nexis Group, Dayton, Ohio.

95. Massing, "The Rise and Decline of Accuracy in Media," 201.

96. Rinker Buck, "Three Cheers for CNN," *Adweek*, February 25, 1991, 16. Available from Lexis-Nexis Group, Dayton, Ohio.

97. Howard Kurtz, "Fox News Boss Out after Thrashing Staff; The Biting Memo That Bit Back," *Washington Post*, September 10, 1993, G1. Available from Lexis-Nexis Group, Dayton, Ohio.

98. Michael T. Kaufman, "Reed Irvine, 82, the Founder of a Media Criticism Group," *New York Times*, November 19, 2004, late edition, 9. Available from Lexis-Nexis Group, Dayton, Ohio.

99. L. Brent Bozell III, "Reed Irvine, R.I.P.," http://www.mediaresearch.org/BozellColumns/newscolumn/2004/col20041124.asp (accessed September 10, 2007).

100. Cliff Kincaid, "AIM Report: 'Can Dan' Campaign on Verge of Success," October 21, 2004, http://www.aim.org/aim_report/A2055_0_4_0_C/ (accessed September 11, 2007).

101. Ibid.

102. Dick Thornburgh and Louis D. Boccardi, "Report of the Independent Review Panel on the September 8, 2004 *60 Minutes Wednesday* Segment 'For the Record,'" January

5, 2005, 18, http://www.cbsnews.com/htdocs/pdf/complete_report/CBS_Report.pdf (accessed September 11, 2007).

CHAPTER 3

1. Kristin Taylor, comment on "Report: D.C. Chapter and Accuracy in Media's RatherGate Freep at CBS," The Free Republic Blog, comment posted September 21, 2004, http://www.freerepublic.com/focus/f-news/1223070/posts (accessed September 12, 2007); Cliff Kincaid, "Dan Rather Must Go," September 21, 2004, http://www.aim.org/special_report/A1953_0_8_0_C/ (accessed September 12, 2007).

2. Ibid.

3. Tony Snow, "Talking Points: Are Bush Memos Authentic?" The O'Reilly Factor, September 10, 2004. Available from Lexis-Nexis Group, Dayton, Ohio.

4. Jim Geraghty, "A Communique to the Pajamahadeen," September 22, 2004, http://www.nationalreview.com/kerry/kerry200409221122.asp (accessed September 12, 2007).

5. Dick Thornburgh and Louis D. Boccardi, Exhibit 1B: "Report of the Independent Review Panel on the September 8, 2004 60 Minutes Wednesday Segment 'For the Record,'" January 5, 2005, http://www.cbsnews.com/stories/2005/01/10/national/main665818.shtml (accessed September 15, 2007).

6. Dick Thornburgh and Louis D. Boccardi, "Report of the Independent Review Panel on the September 8, 2004 60 Minutes Wednesday Segment 'For the Record,'" January 5, 2005, 18, http://www.cbsnews.com/htdocs/pdf/complete_report/CBS_Report.pdf (accessed September 11, 2007).

7. Ibid., 2.

8. Roderick Boyd, "How Four Blogs Dealt a Blow to CBS's Credibility," New York Sun, September 13, 2004, 1. Available from Lexis-Nexis Group, Dayton, Ohio.

9. Buckhead, comment on "Documents Suggest Special Treatment for Bush in Guard [post 47]," Free Republic Blog, comment posted September 8, 2004, 8: 8:59:43 P.M., http://www.freerepublic.com/focus/f-news/1210662/posts?#47 (accessed September 12, 2007).

10. Michael Dobbs, "Parallels Drawn between CBS Memos, Texan's Postings," Washington Post, September 18, 2004, A2, http://www.washingtonpost.com/ac2/wp-dyn/A30043-2004Sep17?language=printer (accessed September 12, 2007).

11. CBS/AP, "CBS: Bush Memo Story A 'Mistake'" September 20, 2004, http://www.cbsnews.com/stories/2004/09/21/politics/main644719.shtml (accessed September 13, 2007).

12. Reed Irvine, "CBS Head Lauds Blast at Rather," June A, 1988, http://www.aim.org/publications/aim_report/1988/06a.html (accessed September 12, 2007).

13. Taylor, "Report."

14. CBS, "CBS News Statement on Panel," September 22, 2004, http://www.cbsnews.com/stories/2004/09/22/politics/main644969.shtml (accessed September 14, 2007).

15. William Ardolino, comment on "Freepers Protest CBS (Update)," The INDC Journal Blog, comment posted September 28, 2004, http://www.indcjournal.com/archives/2004_09.php (accessed September 15, 2007).

16. Thornburgh and Boccardi, "Report of the Independent Review Panel on the September 8, 2004 60 Minutes Wednesday Segment," 28.

17. CBS, "CBS Ousts 4 for Bush Guard Story," January 10, 2007, http://www.cbsnews.com/stories/2005/01/10/national/main665727.shtml (accessed September 15, 2007).

18. Ibid.

19. *Dan Rather v. CBS Corporation* (September 19, 2007), http://www.nytimes.com/packages/pdf/business/20070920_cbs_complaint.pdf (accessed October 1, 2007).

20. Steve Bryant, comment on "Schlock and Awe," *Read Me Blog,* comment posted March 2, 2003, http://journalism.nyu.edu/pubzone/ReadMe/article.php%3Fid=156.html (accessed September 15, 2007).

21. Glenn Harlan Reynolds, "Godzilla vs. the 'Blogosphere,'" *Wall Street Journal,* Eastern edition, September 1, 2004, A.12. Available from ProQuest LLC, Ann Arbor, Michigan.

22. Stephen D. Cooper, *Watching the Watchdog: Bloggers as the Fifth Estate* (Spokane, WA: Marquette Books, 2006), 18.

23. Scott Maier, "Getting It Right? Not in 59 Percent of Stories," *Newspaper Research Journal* 23 (Winter 2002): 11.

24. Ibid., 10.

25. Thornburgh and Boccardi, "Exhibit Appendix 1: "Report of the Independent Review Panel on the September 8, 2004 *60 Minutes Wednesday,*" January 5, 2005, http://www.cbsnews.com/stories/2005/01/10/national/main665818.shtml (accessed September 15, 2007).

26. Thornburgh and Boccardi, "Report of the Independent Review Panel on the September 8, 2004 *60 Minutes Wednesday,*" 23.

27. Ibid., 44.

28. Ibid., 54.

29. Ibid., 54.

30. Buckhead, comment on "Documents Suggest Special Treatment for Bush in Guard [post 47]."

31. Thornburgh and Boccardi, "Report of the Independent Review Panel on the September 8, 2004 *60 Minutes Wednesday,*" 18.

32. Scott Johnson, comment on "The Sixty-First Minute," the Powerline Blog, comment posted September 9, 2004, http://www.powerlineblog.com/archives/007760.php (accessed September 15, 2007).

33. Johnathan V. Last, "What Blogs Have Wrought," *The Weekly Standard,* September 27, 2004, 27–31.

34. Boyd, "How Four Blogs Dealt a Blow to CBS's Credibility."

35. William Ardolino, comment on "Are the CBS National Guard Documents Fake?" the INDCJournal Blog, comment posted September 9, 2004, http://www.indc journal.com/archives/2004_09.php (accessed September 15, 2007).

36. Ibid.

37. Ibid.

38. Joseph M. Newcomer, comment on "The Bush 'Guard Memos' Are Forgeries," the Flounder Blog, comment posted September 12, 2004, http://www.flounder.com/bush2.htm (accessed September 16, 2007).

39. Hunter, comment on "TANG Typewriter Follies; Wingnuts Wrong," the Dailykos Blog, comment posted September 10, 2004, http://www.dailykos.com/story/2004/9/10/34914/1603 (accessed September 16, 2007).

40. Bill Sammon and Stephen Dinan, "McAuliffe Shifts the Blame to Rove and Republicans," *Washington Times,* September 11, 2004, 1. Available from Lexis-Nexis Group, Dayton, Ohio.

41. Thornburgh and Boccardi, "Report of the Independent Review Panel on the September 8, 2004 *60 Minutes Wednesday,*" 45.

42. Mary Mapes, *Truth and Duty: The Press, the President, and the Privilege of Power* (New York: St. Martin's Press, 2005), 200.

43. Kristinn, comment on "Buckhead Refutes Mary Mapes on Rathergate Docs," the FreeRepublic Blog, comment posted November 21, 2005, http://www.free republic.com/focus/f-news/1526303/posts (accessed September 12, 2007).

44. John H. Hinderaker, comment on "How Did Buckhead Know?" the Powerline Blog, comment posted November 21, 2005, http://www.powerlineblog.com/archives/2005/11/012147.php (accessed October 17, 2007).

45. Howard Kurtz, "Online Nude Photos Are Latest Chapter in Jeff Gannon Saga," *Washington Post*, February 16, 2005, C1, http://www.washingtonpost.com/wp-dyn/articles/A27730-2005Feb15.html (accessed September 16, 2007).

46. Daniel Lyons, "Attack of the Blogs," *Forbes*, November 14, 2005, 128. Available from ProQuest LLC, Ann Arbor, Michigan.

47. Ibid.

48. Tim O'Reilly, comment on "Call for a Blogger's Code of Conduct," the O'Reilly Radar Blog, comment posted March 31, 2007, http://radar.oreilly.com/archives/2007/03/call_for_a_blog_1.html (accessed October 17, 2007).

49. *McIntyre v. Ohio Elections Commission*, 514 U.S. 334 (1995), http://supreme.justia.com/us/514/334/case.html (accessed September 16, 2007).

50. Ibid., 334.

51. Ibid., 343.

52. Ibid., 357.

53. Ibid., 348.

54. *Dan Rather v. CBS Corporation*, September 19, 2007, ¶60, http://www.nytimes.com/packages/pdf/business/20070920_cbs_complaint.pdf (accessed May 5, 2008).

55. Thornburgh and Boccardi, "Report of the Independent Review Panel on the September 8, 2004 *60 Minutes Wednesday*," 29.

56. Ibid., 28.

57. *Galloway v. FCC*, 778 F.2d 16, 20 (D.C. Cir. 1985). See also Richard Labunski, *Libel and the First Amendment: Legal History and Practice in Print and Broadcasting* (New Brunswick, NJ: Transaction Publishers, 1989), 186–187.

58. Labunski, *Libel and the First Amendment*, 186.

59. Ibid.

60. Labunski, *Libel and the First Amendment*, 186–187; Tom Shales, "Jury Backs CBS and Rather in Physician's Slander Suit," *Washington Post*, June 7, 1983, Final Edition, A1.

61. CBS, "Independent Review Panel Examining CBS News '60 Minutes Wednesday' Broadcast of September 8 Issues Report of Its Findings; Leslie Moonves Issues Statement in Response to Panel Report," January 10, 2005, *PR Newswire*. Available from Lexis-Nexis Group, Dayton, Ohio.

62. Ibid.

63. Ibid.

64. Rony Abovitz, comment on "Thoughts on Being on O'Reilly—Power to the People," FixtheWorld Blog, comment posted February 15, 2005, http://fixtheworld.blogs.com/fixtheworld/2005/02/thoughts_on_bei.html (accessed October 17, 2007).

65. Rony Abovitz, telephone interview by author, September 21, 2007.

66. Neil Reisner, "The Accidental Blogger," *American Journalism Review* (April/May 2005), http://www.ajr.org/Article.asp?id=3841 (accessed September 18, 2007).

67. Ibid.

68. Abovitz, interview by author.

69. Howard Kurtz, "In the Blogosphere, Lightning Strikes Thrice," *Washington Post,* February 13, 2005, D1. Available from ProQuest LLC, Ann Arbor, Michigan.

70. World Economic Forum, "World Economic Forum Names Its 2005 Technology Pioneers," December 6, 2004, http://www.molecularimprints.com/NewsEvents/news _articles04/WEF2005TechPio.pdf (accessed September 18, 2007).

71. Reisner, "The Accidental Blogger"; Katherine Q. Seelye, "Resignation at CNN Shows the Growing Influence of Blogs," February 14, 2005, http://www .nytimes.com/2005/02/14/technology/14cnn.html?pagewanted=1&ei=5070&en=83292d fac1622496&ex=1190260800 (accessed September 18, 2007).

72. Society of Professional Journalists, "Minimize Harm," 1996–2007, http://www .spj.org/ethicscode.asp (accessed September 18, 2007).

73. Katherine Q. Seelye, "Bloggers as News Media Trophy Hunters," *New York Times,* February 14, 2005, http://urielw.com/refs/050214.htm (accessed October 22, 2007).

74. Abovitz, interview by author.

75. Rony Abovitz, comment on "Do U.S. Troops Target Journalists in Iraq?" the Forum Blog, comment posted January 28, 2007, http://www.forumblog.org/blog/2005/01/ do_us_troops_ta.html (accessed October 17, 2007).

76. Ibid.

77. Ibid.

78. Eason Jordan, "The News We Kept to Ourselves," *New York Times,* April 11, 2003, Late Edition—Final, A25, http://query.nytimes.com/gst/fullpage.html?res=9506E7DC 173BF932A25757C0A9659C8B63&sec=&spon=&pagewanted=print (accessed October 3, 2007).

79. Jennifer Harper, "CNN Chief Stands by Iraq Omissions; Ethics Debate Flares on withholding of Saddam Atrocities," *Washington Times,* April 12, 2003, A1. Available from Lexis-Nexis Group, Dayton, Ohio.

80. Jim Geraghty, "Just What Did Eason Jordan Say?" February 1, 2005, *National-ReviewOnline,* http://tks.nationalreview.com/post/?q=ZjExODhjMTdjYzcwMjU0Y WIzMjk1OWE2ODZhMTYyYTg= (accessed September 18, 2007).

81. James B. Murphy, Stephen J. A. Ward, and Aine Donovan, "Ethical Ideas in Journalism: Ethical Uplift or Telling the Truth?" *Journal of Media Ethics* 21 (2006): 323.

82. Jim Geraghty, "Ladies and Gentlemen, the Next Big Blogstorm Will Be…," February 2, 2005, *NationalReviewOnline,* http://tks.nationalreview.com/post/?q =OGM1YWViNmYzNzFlNTM5OTgxNjI3OTU2MmU2OTA1Zjk= (accessed September 18, 2007).

83. Roger L. Simon, comment on "Is This Treason," the Roger L. Simon Blog, comment posted February 1, 2005, http://www.rogerlsimon.com/mt-archives/2005/02/ is_this_treason.php (accessed October 17, 2007).

84. Glenn Reynolds, comment on "February 1, 2005." Instapundit Blog, comment posted February 1, 2005, http://instapundit.com/archives/020917.php (accessed October 17, 2007).

85. John H. Hinderaker, comment on "How Crazy Are They?" the Powerline Blog, comment posted February 1, 2005, http://powerlineblog.com/archives/009414.php (accessed October 17, 2007).

86. Michelle Malkin, comment on "Results for 'Davos.'" the Michelle Malkin Blog, comments posted from February 4, 2005–January 28, 2007, http://michellemalkin.com/?s=davos (accessed October 17, 2007).

87. Hugh Hewitt, "Media Notes; Two Incidents Highlight the Mainstream Media's Defects and Biases," *The Weekly Standard*, February 3, 2005, http://www.weeklystandard.com/Content/Public/Articles/000/000/005/208lbgat.asp (accessed October 10, 2007).

88. Abovitz, interview by author

89. Ibid.

90. Emiliya Mychasuk, "Messages from the Mount," January 20, 2006, *Financial Times.com*, http://www.ft.com/cms/s/1a1f30d0-88b1-11da-94a6-0000779e2340,_i_rss Page=daa36138-ce4f-11d7-81c6-0820abe49a01.html (accessed October 18, 2007).

91. Michelle Malkin, comment on "Easongate: Barney Frank Talks," the Michelle Malkin Blog, comment posted February 7, 2005, http://michellemalkin.com/2005/02/07/easongate-barney-frank-talks/ (accessed September 19, 2007).

92. CNN, "CNN Executive Resigns after Controversial Remarks," February 11, 2005, http://www.cnn.com/2005/SHOWBIZ/TV/02/11/easonjordan.cnn/index.html (accessed September 19, 2007).

93. Jack Shafer, "I Would Have Fired Eason Jordan," February 14, 2005 http://slate.com/id/2113493/ (accessed September 19, 2007).

94. Opinion Journal from *The Wall Street Journal Editorial Page*, "The Jordan Kerfuffle," February 14, 2005, http://www.opinionjournal.com/editorial/feature.html?id=110006289 (accessed September 19, 2007).

95. *IraqSlogger.com*, "About Us," http://www.iraqslogger.com/index.php/category/8/AboutUs (accessed September 19, 2007).

96. Michelle Malkin, comment on "Looking for Jamil Hussein: Accepting Eason Jordan's Invitation," the Michelle Malkin Blog, comment posted December 14, 2006, http://michellemalkin.com/2006/12/14/looking-for-jamil-hussein-accepting-eason-jordans-invitation/ (accessed September 19, 2007).

97. Thomas Wagner and Qais Al-Bashir (AP), "Insurgents Gun Down 21 Shiites in Iraq," http://www.washingtonpost.com/wp-dyn/content/article/2006/11/25/AR2006112500291.html (accessed September 19, 2007).

98. Michelle Malkin, comment on "The Media Fog of War," the Michelle Malkin Blog, comment posted November 27, 2006, http://michellemalkin.com/2006/11/27/the-media-fog-of-war/ (accessed September 19, 2007).

99. Michelle Malkin, comment on "Archive Jamil Hussein," the Michelle Malkin Blog, comment posted November 27, 2006–January 31, 2007, http://michellemalkin.com/category/media-bias/jamil-hussein/ (accessed September 19, 2007).

100. Steven R. Hurst, "Iraq Threatens Arrest of Police Captain Who Spoke to Media," January 4, 2007, http://www.ap.org/FOI/foi_010407a.html (accessed September 19, 2007).

101. Howard Kurtz, "A Hard Right Punch; Michele Malkin's Conservative Fight Has Others Coming Out Swinging," *Washington Post*, February 16, 2007, C1. Available from ProQuest LLC, Ann Arbor, Michigan. Also available at http://www.washingtonpost.com/wp-dyn/content/article/2007/02/15/AR2007021502065.html (accessed October 10, 2007).

102. Michelle Malkin, comment on "Jamil Hussein Development: 'Faces Arrest?'" the Michelle Malkin Blog, comment posted January 4, 2007, http://michellemalkin.com/2007/01/04/jamil-hussein-development-faces-arrest/ (accessed September 19, 2007).

103. Ibid.

104. Maria Aspan, "A Disputed A.P. Source Turns Up, But Bloggers Are Not Appeased," *New York Times*, January 8, 2007, C8. http://www.nytimes.com/2007/01/08/business/media/08jamil.html?_r=1&ref=business&oref=slogin (accessed October 10, 2007).

105. Cooper, *Watching the Watchdog: Bloggers as the Fifth Estate*, 18–19.

106. *McIntyre v. Ohio Elections Commission*, 348.

107. Opinion Journal from *The Wall Street Journal Editorial Page*, "The Jordan Kerfuffle."

CHAPTER 4

1. Edwin B. Parker, Untitled, review of *The Information Machines: Their Impact on Men and the Media*, Ben H. Bagdikian, *The Public Opinion Quarterly* 35, no. 3 (Autumn 1971), 504–505.

2. Ben H. Bagdikian, *Double Vision: Reflection on My Heritage, Life, and Profession* (Boston: Beacon Press, 1995), 7.

3. Ibid., 29; *New York Times Co. v. United States* (403 US 713).

4. Bagdikian, *Double Vision*, 1.

5. As part of a group at the *Providence Journal and Evening Bulletin* in Rhode Island, Bagdikian won a Pulitzer in 1953 for "Local Reporting, Edition Time." See The Pulitzer Board, "The Pulitzer Prize Winners, 1953, "Local Reporting, Edition Time," http://www.Pulitzer.org (accessed July 1, 2007).

6. Parker, Untitled, review of *The Information Machines*, 505.

7. Ibid.

8. Christopher H. Sterling, "Seeking Influence: The Dozen Most Important Electronic Media Books Since 1956, *Journal of Broadcasting & Electronic Media* 40 (Fall 1996): 597–600.

9. Bagdikian, *Double Vision*, xiii–xiv.

10. "ASJA Honors Ben Bagdikian as Journalism's 'Most Perceptive Critic,'" *Journalism Educator* 33 (October 1978): 6–39.

11. "Winners, 1950," Peabody Winners Book, http://www.peabody.uga.edu/winners/winners_book.php (accessed July 1, 2007).

12. Ibid.

13. Bagdikian, *Double Vision*, 229; James Boylan, "An Editor Reflects: 40 Years of CJR," *Columbia Journalism Review* (November/December 2001), http://backissues.cjrarchives.org/year/01/6/boylan.asp (accessed July 31, 2007). See also Ben H. Bagdikian, *The Effete Conspiracy and Other Crimes by the Press* (New York: Harper & Row, 1972) in which several of his *CJR* columns are republished. His byline does not appear in the pilot issue, fall 1961, or in the second issue, spring 1962. It first appears in the summer 1962 issue: "Television—the President's Medium?"*Columbia Journalism*.

14. "ASJA Honors," 7.

15. Bagdikian, *Double Vision*, 34.

16. Ibid., 194.

17. Ibid., 198.

18. John Simon Guggenheim Memorial Foundation, "1961 Fellows," http://www.gf.org/bfellow.html (accessed August 9, 2007).

19. Elden Rawlings, "Introduction," in *Bagdikian on Political Reporting, Newspaper Economics, Law and Ethics* (Fort Worth: The Texas Christian University Press, 1977), 1.

20. Ben H. Bagdikian, "What Makes a Newspaper Nearly Great?" *Columbia Journalism Review* (Fall 1967): 30–36.

21. Ibid., 30.

22. David Halberstam, *The Powers That Be* (New York: Knopf, 1979), 647.

23. Ben H. Bagdikian and Leon Dash, *The Shame of Prisons* (New York: Pocket Books, 1972).

24. Halberstam, 574.

25. Ben H. Bagdikian, "The American Newspaper Is Neither Record, Mirror, Journal, Ledger, Bulletin, Telegram, Examiner, Register, Chronicle, Gazette, Observer, Monitor, Transcript, Nor Herald of the Day's Events," *Esquire*, March 1967, 124, 138–142.

26. Bagdikian, *The Effete Conspiracy and Other Crimes by the Press*, 3–17.

27. Bagdikian, *Double Vision*, 233.

28. Ben Bagdikian, e-mail to author, August 24, 2007.

29. Bagdikian, *Double Vision*, 17.

30. William L. Rivers et al., *BackTalk: Press Councils in America* (San Francisco: Canfield Press, 1972).

31. Ibid., 12.

32. Ibid., 12; William L. Rivers, "More Thoughts on Chilton Bush: He Cut His Own Path," *Journalism Educator* 31 (October 1976): 22.

33. Donald E. Brignolo, "How Community Press Councils Work," in *Readings in Mass Communication*, ed. Michael E. Emery and Ted Curtis Smythe (Dubuque, Iowa: William C. Brown Co., 1972), 67.

34. Ben H. Bagdikian, "Introduction," in *BackTalk*.

35. Brignolo, "How Community Press Councils Work."

36. Rivers, "More Thoughts on Chilton Bush: He Cut His Own Path."

37. Bagdikian, "Introduction," in *BackTalk*, v.

38. Ibid.

39. Rivers, *BackTalk*, 13.

40. Ibid., 118–119.

41. Brignolo, 68.

42. Ibid., 76.

43. Norman E. Isaacs, *Untended Gates: The Mismanagement of the Press* (New York: Columbia University Press, 1986), 107.

44. Ibid., 108–109.

45. Washington News Council, "History," http://www.wanewscouncil.org/History.htm (accessed August 20, 2007).

46. Knight Foundation, "News Councils to Form in Southern California and New England," June 28, 2006, http://www.knightfdn.org/default.asp?story=news_at_knight/releases/2006/2006_06_28_newscouncils.html.

47. John Hamer, telephone interview by author, August 15, 2007.

48. Arthur C. Nauman, "News Ombudsmanship: Its History and Rationale," http://www.newsombudsmen.org/nauman2.html (accessed August 11, 2007); Alfred JaCoby, "The Newspaper Ombudsman: A Personal Memoir of the Early Days," http://www.newsombudsmen.org/jacoby.html (accessed August 2, 2007). In 1968, Bagdikian co-authored with Kathleen Archibald a RAND study calling for the creation of a television program on which people in poverty areas could voice complaints, "Televised

Ombudsman," https://rand.org/pubs/papers/index67.html (accessed August 10, 2007).

49. Ibid.; A.H. Raskin, "What's Wrong with American Newspapers?" *New York Times Magazine*, June 11, 1967, 28, 84. Available from Lexis-Nexis Group, Dayton, Ohio.

50. "Exit the Ombudsman," *Time*, August 28, 1972, http://www.time.com/time/magazine/article/0,9171,906281,00.html?iid=chix-sphere (accessed August 1, 2007).

51. Neil Nemeth, *News Ombudsmen in North America: Assessing an Experiment in Social Responsibility* (Westport, CT & London: Praeger, 2003), 21.

52. Takeshi Maezawa, "The Controversy over the Origins and Functions of Ombudsmanship"; Linda Raymond, "We Were Wrong: *The Courier-Journal* Thought It was Creating the First News Ombudsman in 1967. In fact, the Japanese Invented the Idea in 1922"; Arthur C. Nauman, "Is it Fair and Accurate to Call Japanese Watchdogs "Ombudsmen?" n.d., http://www.newsombudsmen.org/maezawa.html (accessed August 12, 2007).

53. Nemeth, *News Ombudsmen in North America*, 48–51.

54. Bagdikian, *Double Vision*, 232.

55. Ibid., 233.

56. Ibid., 234.

57. "Exit the Ombudsman," *Time*.

58. Nemeth, *News Ombudsmen in North America*, 63.

59. James Ledbetter, "Content's Providers," *New York Village Voice*, June 17–23, 1998, http://www.villagevoice.com/news/9825,ledbetter,421,6.html (accessed August 22, 2007).

60. Geneva Overholser, "Dear NYT: Give Your Ombudsman Some Heft!" August 28, 2003, http://www.poynter.org/column.asp?id=54&aid=46055 (accessed August 13, 2007).

61. See David Pritchard, "The Impact of Newspaper Ombudsmen on Journalists' Attitudes," *Journalism Quarterly* 70 (Spring 1993): 77–86; Kenneth Starck and Julie Eisele, "Newspaper Ombudsmanship as Viewed by Ombudsmen and Their Editors," *Newspaper Research Journal* 20 (Fall 1999): 37–49; Neil Nemeth and Craig Sanders, "Meaningful Discussion of Performance Missing," *Newspaper Research Journal* 22 (Winter 2001): 52–64; Nemeth, *News Ombudsman in North American*, 143–144.

62. Larry McShane, "*New York Times* to create Position after Internal Review," *Milwaukee Journal Sentinel*, July 31, 2003, http://findarticles.com/p/articles/mi_qn4196/is_20030731/ai_n10903272 (accessed August 13, 2007).

63. Dick Meyer, "A Short Pre-History of Public Eye, September 12, 2005, http://www.cbsnews.com/blogs/2005/09/08/publiceye/entry828825.shtml (accessed August 13, 2007).

64. Nancy Snow, *The Arrogance of American Power* (Lanham, MD: Rowman & Littlefield, 2006), 105.

65. Boylan, "An Editor Reflects."

66. Ben H. Bagdikian, "News as a Byproduct," *Columbia Journalism Review* 6 (Spring 1967), 5–10. Available from ProQuest LLC, Ann Arbor, Michigan.

67. Bagdikian, *The Effete Conspiracy*, 5.

68. "When Is a Failure?" *Time*, July 28, 1967, http://www.time.com/time/magazine/article/0,9171,837119,00.html (accessed August 13, 2007).

69. Ben H. Bagdikian, *The Information Machines: Their Impact on Men and the Media* (New York: Harper & Row, 1971), 131.

70. Project for Excellence and Rick Edmonds, "Economics," *The State of the News Media 2006*," http://www.stateofthenewsmedia.org/2006/narrative_newspapers _economics.asp?cat=4&media=3 (accessed August 14, 2007).

71. Bagdikain, *The Information Machines*, 128.

72. For example, Bagdikian had published "Conglomeration, Concentration, and the Media" in the *Journal of Communication* (1980): 30, 59–64, excerpted from a paper he delivered in 1978 at the Symposium on Media Concentration at the Federal Trade Commission, Bureau of Competition, Washington, D.C., December 14 and 15, 1978.

73. Ben H. Bagdikain, "The Lords of the Global Village," *The Nation* (June 12, 1989): 805.

74. Norman Solomon, "Coverage of Media Mergers," *Nieman Reports* 54 (Summer 2000): 57, http://www.nieman.harvard.edu/reports/00-2NRsummer/NRsummer00.pdf (accessed August 2, 2007).

75. David Croteau and William Hoynes, *Media/Society: Industries, Images, and Audiences* (Thousand Oaks, CA: Pine Forge Press, 2000), 52.

76. John Theobald, "The Intellectual Tradition of Radical Mass Media Criticism: A Framework," in *Radical Mass Media Criticism: A Cultural Geneology*, eds. David Berry and John Theobald (Montreal: Black Rose Books, 2006), 33.

77. Robert W. McChesney, "The Problem of Journalism: A Political Economic Contribution to an Explanation of the Crisis in Contemporary US Journalism," *Journalism Studies* 4 (2003): 324. In endnote no. 4, McChensey writes, "I am indebted to Ben Bagdikian for much of what follows."

78. Demetri Sevastopulo, "Media Groups Battle over Curbs on Ownership Television Cap," *Financial Times*, September 3, 2003, 12.

79. C. Edwin Baker, *Media Concentration and Democracy* (Boston: Cambridge University Press, 2007), 1.

80. Robert C. Byrd, "The Death of Independent Voices in the Media," September 15, 2003, http://byrd.senate.gov/speeches/byrd_speeches_2003september/byrd_spee ches_2003september_li/byrd_speeches_2003september_li_5.html (accessed August 14, 2007).

81. Ibid.

82. Snow, *The Arrogance of American Power*, 105.

83. Mark Fitzgerald, "Dean's List," *Editor & Publisher*, June 1, 2006. Available from Lexis-Nexis Group, Dayton, Ohio.

84. Joshua L. Weinstein, "Iraq Has Largely Eluded the Grasp of Hollywood," December 14, 2006, http://www.variety.com/awardcentral_article/VR1117955807.html?nav =bestpic07 (accessed August 14, 2007).

85. Frank Ahrens, "Murdoch Bids for *Wall Street Journal*," May 2, 2007, Met 2 Edition, A01.

86. Baker, *Media Concentration and Democracy*, 3.

87. Ibid., 54.

88. "SPJ Names Three Fellows of the Society," August 7, 2006, http://www.spj.org/ news.asp?ref=605 (accessed August 14, 2007).

89. Bagdikian, *The Effete Conspiracy*, 5.

90. Byrd, "The Death of Independent Voices in the Media."

CHAPTER 5

1. Claude-Jean Bertrand, "Press Councils," in *An Arsenal for Democracy: Media Accountability Systems,* ed. Claude-Jean Bertrand, 125 (Cresskill, NJ: Hampton Press, Inc., 2003), 125.

2. Ibid.

3. Bill Richards, *Reporting on Yourself: An Independent Analysis of* The Spokesman-Review's *Coverage of and Role in the Spokane River Park Square Redevelopment Project* (Seattle: Washington News Council, May 2007). See also http://wanewscouncil. org/spokane-final/title-page.html (accessed August 20, 2007).

4. Ted S. McGregor, Jr., "News Needed," *The Pacific Northwest Inlander Online,* July 21, 1995, http://www.inlander.com/parking/288752449724200.php (accessed August 20, 2007).

5. Eileen Davis Hudson, "Market Profile; Spokane, Wash.," *MediaWeek,* December 8, 2003. Available from Lexis-Nexis Group, Dayton, Ohio.

6. Richards, *Reporting on Yourself,* 12–13.

7. Ibid., 8.

8. Ibid., 41.

9. Associated Press Managing Editors National Credibility Roundtables, "Credibility in Actions," 2001, 9, http://www.apme-credibility.org/CredibilityReport.pdf (accessed August 22, 2007); The American Society of Newspaper Editors, "The Election," *American Editor,* March 2005, 26, http://www.asne.org/files/tae200503.pdf (accessed August 22, 2007).

10. Associated Press Managing Editors National Credibility Roundtables, "Credibility in Actions."

11. Ibid.

12. Ibid.

13. "About Us," *Camas Magazine,* n.d., http://www.camasmagazine.com/aboutus.asp (accessed August 20, 2007).

14. Jim Camden, "Garage Deal Leaves City in Tight Spot," *Spokesman-Review,* March 28, 2004, http://www.spokemanreview.com/news/live/body.asp?ID=library%5Crps%5Cday1_story1.

15. Steven Smith, "Editor Explains Report," *Spokesman-Review,* May 5, 2007, http:// www.spokesmanreview.com/news/live/body.asp?ID=library%5Crps%5Cday1_story1 (accessed August 20, 2007).

16. Steven Smith, telephone interview by author, August 15, 2007.

17. Floyd Abrams, "Report on CNN Broadcast," 2000, http://www.cnn.com/US/9807/ 02/tailwind.findings/index.html (accessed August 20, 2007).

18. Rachel Smolkin, "Salt Lake Blues," *American Journalism Review,* August/September 2003, http://www.ajr.org/Article.asp?id=3077 (accessed August 20, 2007).

19. Blake Morrison, "Ex-*USA Today* Reporter Faked Major Stories," *USA Today,* March 19, 2004, http://www.usatoday.com/news/2004-03-18-2004-03-18_kelleymain _x.htm (accessed August 31, 2007). See also Jennifer Dorrah, "Knocking Down the Stonewall," *American Journalism Review,* December/January 2005, http://www.ajr.org/ Article.asp?id=3787 (accessed August 31, 2007).

20. Dick Thornburgh and Louis D. Boccardi, "Report of the Independent Review Panel on the September 8, 2004 *60 Minutes Wednesday* Segment 'For the Record' Concerning President Bush's Texas Air National Guard Service," January 5, 2005, http:// wwwimage.cbsnews.com/htdocs/pdf/complete_report/CBS_Report.pdf (accessed August 20, 2007).

21. Susan Rasky, "Independent Investigation Findings," *Technology Review*, April 20, 2005, http://www.technologyreview.com/Infotech/14356/ (accessed August 20, 2007).

22. John Hamer, e-mail message to author, August 29, 2007.

23. Smith, interview.

24. Steven Smith, e-mail message to author, August 21, 2007.

25. Ibid.

26. Ibid.

27. Geneva Overholser, "Washington's News Council—Why It Should Survive," *Columbia Journalism Review*, January/February 2001, http://backissues.cjrarchives.org/year/01/1/overholser.asp (accessed August 21, 2007).

28. *Seattle Post-Intelligencer* Staff, "Panel: P-I Unfair to Sheriff's Office," *Seattlepi.Com*, October 23, 2006, http://seattlepi.nwsource.com/local/289609_newscouncil23.html (accessed August 21, 2007).

29. Washington News Council, "Complaint Upheld at Washington News Council Hearing in Case of King County Sheriff Sue Rahr's Office vs. Seattle Post-Intelligencer," http://www.wanewscouncil.org/index.html (accessed August 21, 2007).

30. *Seattle Post-Intelligencer Staff*, "Panel: P-I Unfair to Sheriff's Office."

31. Washington News Council, "History," n.d., http://www.wanewscouncil.org/History.htm (accessed August 21, 2007).

32. Mike Flynn, "News Council Idea Has Merit," *Puget Sound Business Journal*, September 18, 1998, http://seattle.bizjournals.com/seattle/stories/1998/09/21/editorial2.html?jst=cn_cn_lk (accessed August 21, 2007).

33. Overholser, "Washington's News Council—Why It Should Survive."

34. Ibid.

35. Washington News Council, "Complaint Process," n.d., http://www.wanewscouncil.org/Complaint%20Process.htm (accessed August 21, 2007).

36. Ibid.

37. Washington News Council, "Complaints," n.d. http://www.wanewscouncil.org/Accomplishments.htm (accessed August 21, 2007).

38. Shannon M. Heim, "The Role of Extra-Judicial Bodies in Vindicating Reputational Harm," *CommLaw Conspectus* 15 (2007): 401–429, http://commlaw.cua.edu/articles/v15/15_2/Heim.pdf (accessed October 17, 2007).

39. Smith, interview; John Irby, telephone interview with author, August 21, 2007.

40. Irby, interview.

41. John Hamer, telephone interview by author, August 15, 2007.

42. Ibid.

43. Hamer, e-mail message to author.

44. Ibid.

45. Richards, *Reporting on Yourself*, 33–34.

46. "Agreement with the Washington News Council to Audit the *Spokesman-Review*'s River Park Square Coverage," *Spokesman-Review*, August 24, 2006, http://www.spokesmanreview.com/blogs/conversation/rpsagreement.asp (assessed August 16, 2007).

47. Ibid.

48. Ted S. McGregor, Jr., "Turning the Page," The Pacific Northwest Inlander, May 16, 2007, http://www.inlander.com/localnews/327314132979471.php (accessed August 21, 2007).

49. Tim Connor, "That Wasn't So Bad, Was It?" *Camas Magazine*, 2007, 3, http://www.camasmagazine.com/media/2007/WNC/Comment.pdf (accessed August 21, 2007).

50. Hamer, e-mail message to author.

51. Richards, *Reporting on Yourself*, 30–32.

52. Ibid.

53. Chris Peck, "RPS Rehash Irrelevant and Unfair, Ex-Editor Says," *Spokesman-Review*, May 12, 2007, http://www.spokesmanreview.com/breaking/story.asp?ID=9869 (accessed August 21, 2007); Bill Richards, *Reporting on Yourself*, 41.

54. Chris Peck, e-mail message to author, August 29, 2007.

55. W. Stacey Cowles, "Publisher's Response to the Report," *Spokesman-Review*, May 5, 2007, http://www.spokesmanreview.com/breaking/story.asp?ID=9772 (accessed August 21, 2007); Richards, *Reporting on Yourself*, 40.

56. Steven A. Smith, "Editor Responds to Recommendations," May 13, 2007, *Spokesman-Review*, http://www.spokesmanreview.com/breaking/story.asp?ID=9870 (accessed August 21, 2007); Richards, *Reporting on Yourself*, 44.

57. Ibid.; Richards, *Reporting on Yourself*, 45.

58. Ibid.; Ibid.

59. Ibid.; Ibid., 44.

60. Smith, interview.

61. "News Is a Conversation," *Spokesman-Review*, http://www.spokesmanreview.com/blogs/conversation/ (accessed August 22, 2007).

62. Tanni Haas, *The Pursuit of Public Journalism* (New York & London: Routledge, 2007).

63. Media Matters for America, "Who We Are," 2007, http://mediamatters.org/about_us/ (accessed July 9, 2007).

64. Brian Montopoli, "Imus in the Morning," *CBS News's Public Eye*, April 12, 2007, http://www.cbsnews.com/blogs/2007/04/12/publiceye/entry2678036.shtml (accessed July 12, 2007).

65. Charles Johnson comments on "Bush Guard Documents Forged," the LittleGreen-Football Blog, comment posteed on September 9, 2004, http://littlegreen footballs.com/weblog/?entry=12526&only (accessed October 17, 2007).

66. Steven Smith, e-mail to author, August 21, 2007.

67. Commission on Freedom of the Press, *A Free and Responsible Press: A General Report on Mass Communication: Newspapers, Radio, Motion Pictures, Magazine, and Books* (Chicago: University of Chicago Press, 1947), 100–101.

CHAPTER 6

1. Martin A. Lee, "Of Facts and Fiction in the Papal Shooting," *New York Times*, December 12, 1986, Late City Edition, 34. Available from Lexis-Nexis Group, Dayton, Ohio.

2. Jeff Cohen, "'Special Interests' Turned Upside Down," *New York Times*, Late City Final Edition, 38. Available from Lexis-Nexis Group, Dayton, Ohio.

3. FAIR, "Questionnaire for the *New York Times* on Its Central America Coverage," *Extra!* January/February 1998, http://www.fair.org/index.php?page=1543 (accessed July 17, 2007).

4. Ibid.

5. Jeff Cohen, "Progressive Is as Legitimate as Conservative," *New York Times*, July 7, 1988, Late City Final Edition, 22. Available from Lexis-Nexis Group, Dayton, Ohio.

6. See "Media Outlet/Personality: *New York Times*, http://www.fair.org/index.php?page=19&media_outlet_id=1.

7. Jeff Cohen, "Propaganda from the Middle of the Road: The Centrist Ideology of the News Media," *Extra!* October/November 1989, http://www.fair.org/index.php?page=1492 (accessed July 19, 2007).

8. Tim Bogardus, "FAIR's Fair—Fairness & Accuracy in Reporting Journal *Extra!* Editor Jim Naureckas—Interview," *Folio: The Magazine for Magazine Management*, October 1, 1994, http://findarticles.com/p/articles/mi_m3065/is_n16_v23/ai_15741555 (accessed October 11, 2007).

9. Constance L. Hays, "Making It Work: FAIR or Not?" *New York Times*, May 19, 1996, Late Edition-Final, 3. Available from Lexis-Nexis Group, Dayton, Ohio.

10. Howard Rosenberg, "CROSSROADS: Looking at 1999 and Beyond with Influential Figures in the World of Art and Entertainment; A Watchdog's Bark and Bite," *Los Angeles Times*, December 27, 1999, 1. Available from Lexis-Nexis Group, Dayton, Ohio.

11. "Jeff Cohen Interview: A Watchdog's Bark and Bite," n.d., http://www.jeffcohen .org/docs/interviewwatchdog.html (accessed July 18, 2007).

12. Tim Graham, "Fair Play," *Los Angeles Times*, January 15, 2006, home edition, 6. Available from Lexis-Nexis Group, Dayton, Ohio.

13. Michael Getler, "FAIR or Unfair Game?" *Washington Post*, April 24, 2005, final edition, B06. Available from Lexis-Nexis Group, Dayton, Ohio.

14. Ibid.

15. Deborah Howell, "The Limits of E-Mails En Masse," *Washington Post*, November 13, 2005, final edition, B06. Available from Lexis-Nexis Group, Dayton, Ohio.

16. Peter Hart, "FAIR's Media Activism Successes; Fighting Back," *Extra!* January/Februrary, 2006, http://www.fair.org/index.php?page=2815 (accessed July 19, 2007).

17. Ibid.

18. "What's FAIR?" n.d., http://www.fair.org/index.php?page=100 (accessed July 18, 2007).

19. Martin Mittelstaedt, "Is It Really All the News That's Fit to Print?" *The Globe and Mail*, October 8, 1988. Available from Lexis-Nexis Group, Dayton, Ohio.

20. Rosenberg, "CROSSROADS."

21. "If there be time to expose through discussion the falsehood and fallacies, to avert the evil by the processes of education, the remedy to be applied is more speech, not enforced silence." *Whitney v. California*, 274 U.S. 357, 377 (1927) (Brandeis, J., concurring).

22. Hays, "Making It Work: FAIR or Not?"

23. "What's FAIR?"

24. Robert W. McChesney, "FAIR at 20; A Cornerstone of the Media Reform Movement," *Extra!* January 2006, http://www.fair.org/index.php?page=2812 (accessed July 18, 2007).

25. FAIR Authors List, n.d., http://www.fair.org/index.php?page=9 (accessed July 18, 2007).

26. FAIR on the Air!, n.d., http://www.fair.org/index.php?page=115 (accessed July 18, 2007).

27. "What's FAIR?"

28. "FAIR's Financial Overview," n.d., http://www.fair.org/index.php?page=3063 (accessed July 18, 2007).

29. Jeff Cohen, *Cable News Confidential: My Misadventures in Corporate Media* (Sausalito, CA: PoliPointPress, 2006).

30. Jeff Cohen, interview by Amy Goodman, Part 1, October 17, 2006, http://video.google.com/videoplay?docid=-879480694762523489&q=jeff+cohen&total=433&start=0&num=10&so=0&type=search&plindex=3 (accessed July 18, 2007).

31. Dan Gilgoff and Bret Schulte, "War over War Crimes," U.S. *News & World Report,* September 6, 2004, 38.

32. Ibid., 4.

33. John C. Boland, "An ACLU Unit Loosens Up to Prior Restraint," *Wall Street Journal,* June 26, 1984, Eastern edition, 1. Available from ProQuest LLC, Ann Arbor, Michigan.

34. Jeff Cohen, interview by Mirabai of Woodstock, "Watching the Media: A Talk with Jeff Cohen," 2007, http://www.mirabai.com/articles/cohen/ (accessed July 21, 2007); Jessica Wakeman, "How Police Spies and Media Moles Helped Launch a Movement; The Secret Origins of FAIR," *Extra!* January/February 2006, http://www.fair.org/index.php?page=2871 (accessed July 23, 2007).

35. Wakeman, "How Police Spies and Media Moles Helped Launch a Movement."

36. Harry F. Waters, "A Storm Over 'Amerika," *Newsweek,* November 10, 1986, 90.

37. James P. Forkan, "'Amerika' the Controversial Drawing Fire; ABC Miniseries Set for February," *Advertising Age,* November 17, 1986, 22. Available from Lexis-Nexis Group, Dayton, Ohio.

38. John Carmondy, "The TV Column," *Washington Post,* February 6, 1987, C8. Available from Lexis-Nexis Group, Dayton, Ohio.

39. William Hoynes, "Consider the Source: The *Nightline* Study and Media Research," *Extra!* January/February 2006, http://www.fair.org/index.php?page=2872 (accessed July 23, 2007.

40. Ibid.

41. Ibid.

42. "Are You on the Nightline Guest List?" February 6, 1989, http://www.fair.org/index.php?page=2008 (accessed July 23, 2007).

43. Matt Roush, "Study Questions Fairness of ABC's *Nightline,*" USA *Today,* February 6, 1989, 3D; *John Carman,* "Liberal Group Calls *Nightline* Biased," *San Francisco Chronicle,* February 6, 1989, F.4; Joseph Kahn, "*Nightline* Guest List Called Bias," *Boston Globe,* February 6, 1989, 28. Available from ProQuest LLC, Ann Arbor, Michigan.

44. Kenneth R. Clark, "How's *60 Minutes* to Replace Sawyer," *Chicago Tribune,* February 9, 1989, 14. Available from Lexis-Nexis Group, Dayton, Ohio.

45. Walter Goodman, "Critic's Notebook Watchdog Group Criticizes 2 News Programs," *New York Times,* May 28, 1990, Late Edition-Final, 40. Available from Lexis-Nexis Group, Dayton, Ohio.

46. David Nyhan, "Taking 3 TV Icons to the Woodshed," *Boston Globe,* June 24, 1990, city edition, A5. Available from Lexis-Nexis Group, Dayton, Ohio.

47. "All the Usual Suspects: MacNeil/Lehrer and Nightline," May 21, 1990, http://www.fair.org/index.php?page=2007 (accessed July 23, 2007).

48. Joanne Ostrow, "Jim Lehrer Seeks 'Journalist' Label, Not Social Reformer," *Denver Post,* September 12, 1990. 1E. Available from ProQuest LLC, Ann Arbor, Michigan.

49. Jim Naureckas, "Media on the March: Journalism in the Gulf," *Extra!* November/December 1990, http://www.fair.org/index.php?page=1196 (July 23, 2007).

50. "All the Usual Suspects: MacNeil/Lehrer and Nightline."

51. Ibid.

52. Carmody, "The TV Column."

53. Nyhan, "Taking 3 TV Icons to the Woodshed."

54. Steve Rendall and Julie Hollar, "Are You on the *NewsHour*'s Guestlist? PBS Flagship News Show Fails Public Mission," *Extra!* September/October 2006, http://www.fair.org/index.php?page=2967 (accessed July 23, 2007).

55. Anne Bell and Rob Flynn, "The NewsHour with Jim Lehrer Stands by Its Program and Its Reputation in the Face of Accusations by FAIR," October 5, 2006, http://www.pbs.org/newshour/aboutus/press_releases/2006/fair_response_10-06.html (accessed July 23, 2007).

56. PBS Responds to FAIR *Newshour* Study, Activism Update, October 18, 2006, http://www.fair.org/index.php?page=2977 (accessed July 23, 2007).

57. Michael Getler, "Ombudsman's Mailbag," PBS Ombudsman, January 11, 2007, http://www.pbs.org/ombudsman/2007/01/ombudsmans_mailbag_16.html (accessed July 23, 2007).

58. Ibid.

59. "Debating the Iraq 'Surge' on PBS: NewsHour Panel Skews against Public Opinion," Action Alert, January 10, 2007, http://www.fair.org/index.php?page=3029 (accessed July 23, 2007).

60. Steve Randall and Daniel Butterworth, "How Public Is Public Radio? A Study of NPR's Guest List," *Extra!* May/June 2004, http://www.fair.org/index.php?page=1180 (accessed July 24, 2007).

61. Jeffrey A. Dvorkin, "Is FAIR Being Fair about NPR?" May 26, 2004 http://www.npr.org/templates/story/story.php?storyId=1911200&columnId=2781901 (accessed July 24, 2007).

62. Ibid.

63. "Yahoo! News agrees with FAIR criticisms '100 Percent;' *Boston Globe* Ombudsman Apologizes—Sort Of," August 24, 2001, http://www.fair.org/index.php?page=1676 (accessed July 24, 2007).

64. Ibid.

65. Nelson Antrim Crawford, *The Ethics of Journalism* (New York: Greenwood Press, 1969).

66. Ibid., 163–164.

67. Everette E. Dennis and David L. Stebenne, "Requiem for a Think Tank: The Life and Death of the Gannett Center at Columbia, 1984–1996, *Harvard International Journal of Press/Politics* 8 (Spring 2003): 11–35.

68. Crawford, *The Ethics of Journalism,* 163.

69. Media Research Center, "Media Bias Basics," n.d., http://www.mrc.org/newsdivision/welcome.asp (accessed October 5, 2007).

70. Media Research Center, "The Liberal Media Exposed, (PDF Report)," n.d., http://www.mediaresearch.org/biasbasics/biasbasics1.asp (accessed October 5, 2007).

71. Dennis and Stebenne, "Requiem for a Think Tank," 15–16.

72. Ibid., 18.

73. Ibid., 30.

74. Bill Kovach and Tom Rosenstiel, *The Elements of Journalism: What Newspeople Should Know and the Public Should Expect* (New York: Crown Publishers, 2001).

75. Project for Excellence in Journalism, "The People of PEJ," 2006, http://www.journalism.org/about_pej/staff (accessed October 5, 2007).

76. Project for Excellence in Journalism, "About Us," 2006, http://www.journalism .org/about_pej/about_us (accessed October 5, 2007).

77. Ibid.

78. Project for Excellence in Journalism, "The State of the News Media: An Annual Report on American Journalism," 2007, http://www.stateofthemedia.org/2007/ (accessed October 5, 2007).

79. Robert C. Post, *Constitutional Domains: Democracy, Community, Management* (Cambridge, MA: Harvard University Press, 1995), 141.

80. *Associated Press v. United States*, 326 U.S. 1, 20 (1945).

81. Congress shall make no law respecting an establishment of religion, or prohibiting the free exercise thereof; or abridging the freedom of speech, or of the press; or the right of the people peaceably to assemble, and to petition the Government for a redress of grievances. U.S. Constitution: Amendment 1.

82. Radio-Television News Directors Association & Foundation, "Ethics," 1997–2007, http://www.rtnda.org/ethics/coe.shtml (accessed July 24, 2007).

83. About PBS Editorial Standards," June 14, 2005, http://www.pbs.org/aboutpbs/ aboutpbs_standards.html#II (accessed July 24, 2007).

84. National Public Radio, "NPR News Code of Ethics and Practices," 2007, http:// www.npr.org/about/ethics/#conduct (accessed July 24, 2007).

85. Yahoo!News "Our Mission," 2007, http://hotzone.yahoo.com/about (accessed July 24, 2007).

86. Society of Professional Journalists, "Diversity," 1996–2007, http://www.spj.org/ divws1.asp (accessed July 24, 2007).

87. Stephen J.A. Ward, *The Invention of Journalism Ethics* (Montreal & Kingston: McGill-Queen's University Press, 2004), 23–26.

88. "What's FAIR?"

89. Eric Black, "Media Watch: Bias on the Right and Left: You Decide; Study Pokes a Hole in Fox News' Boast of Fairness and Balance," *Star Tribune*, July 6, 2001, Metro Edition, 8A. Available from Lexis-Nexis Group, Dayton, Ohio.

90. Ibid.

91. Hamilton Nolan, "Organization Profile—Reactive Tactic Keeps FAIR Analysis Heard," *PR Week* (U.S.), May 28, 2007, 7.

CHAPTER 7

1. Graydon Carter, "The 51 Best* Magazines Ever," *Good*, February 15, 2007, http:// www.goodmagazine.com/section/Features/the_best_magazines_ever (accessed April 5, 2008).

2. The author worked as a staff writer for *The American Lawyer* from 1987 to 1989.

3. Steven Brill, *After: How America Confronted the September 12 Era* (New York: Simon & Schuster, 2003).

4. Howard Kurtz, "On Trial and on the Tube: Media Entrepreneur Steven Brill's 24-Hour Cable Courtroom Hookup," *Washington Post*, May 28, 1991, D1. Available from Lexis-Nexis Group, Dayton, Ohio.

5. Laura Mansnerus, "As Brash Publisher's Empire Ends, Quest Begins for Another," *New York Times*, March 3, 1997, http://query.nytimes.com/gst/fullpage.html

?res=9F00E4D81F31F930A35750C0A961958260&n=Top%2fNews%2fBusiness%
2fCompanies%2fTime%20Warner%20Inc%2e.

6. Steven Brill, interviewed by James Ledbetter, September/October 1998, http://
www.motherjones.com/news/qa/1998/09/ledbetter.html (accessed September 25, 2007).

7. Ibid.

8. See *MediaWeek,* "At Deadline," July 14, 1997. Available from Lexis-Nexis Group,
Dayton, Ohio.

9. Al Kamen, "Waiting to Exile," *Washington Post,* July 21, 1997, A19. Available from
Lexis-Nexis Group, Dayton, Ohio.

10. Lori Robertson, "Steven Brill's New Target: The News Media," *American Journalism Review,* September, 14, 1997, http://www.ajr.org/Article.asp?id=2315 (accessed September 25, 2007).

11. Ibid.

12. Jeff Gremillion, "Publishing's Top Lawman," *MediaWeek,* November 10, 1997,
Available from Lexis-Nexis Group, Dayton, Ohio.

13. MediaWeek, "54 Seinfeld at $400K Too Much For Comfort, Stations
Say," *MediaWeek,* January 12, 1999. Available from Lexis-Nexis Group, Dayton,
Ohio.

14. David Firestone, "Public Lives: Creating a Forum to Rake the Media's Muck,"
January 29, 1998, *New York Times,* p. B2. Available from Lexis-Nexis Group, Dayton,
Ohio.

15. Robin Pogrebin, "Fortune Bucks Critics and Covers Its Parent," *New York Times,*
March 23, 1998, p. D2. Available from Lexis-Nexis Group, Dayton, Ohio.

16. Ibid.

17. Lynn Rosellini, "The Scariest Journalist," *U.S. News & World Report,* June 27,
1998. Available from Lexis-Nexis Group, Dayton, Ohio.

18. Maureen Dowd, "Liberties; We're NOT Worse Than Lawyers," *New York Times,*
April 19, 1998, p. 17. Available from Lexis-Nexis Group, Dayton, Ohio.

19. Stefani Eads, *"Brill's* Makes Waves. Can It Make Money, Too?" *BusinessWeek
Online,* December 22,1998, http://www.businessweek.net/bwdaily/dnflash/dec1998/
nf81222a.htm (accessed September 25, 2007).

20. See Michael Bierut, "The Final Decline and Total Collapse of the American Magazine Cover, *Design Observer,* http://desktoppub.about.com/gi/dynamic/offsite.htm?zi=1/
XJ&sdn=desktoppub&zu=http%3A%2F%2Fwww.designobserver.com%2Farchives%2F0
00103.html (accessed February 14, 2006).

21. All Politics, "A Chronology: Key Moments In The Clinton-Lewinsky Saga 1998,"
1998, http://www.cnn.com/ALLPOLITICS/1998/resources/lewinsky/timeline/ (accessed
February 14, 2006).

22. Steven Brill, "Pressgate," *Brill's Content,* July/August 1998, 122.

23. Ibid., 122–151.

24. David Firestone, "Steven Brill Strikes a Nerve in the News Media," *New York
Times,* June 20, 1998, A7. Available from Lexis-Nexis Group, Dayton, Ohio.

25. Eads, *"Brill's* Makes Waves. Can It Make Money, Too?"

26. *Brill's Content,* "Statement of Ownership," December/January 2001, 154.

27. Eads, *"Brill's* Makes Waves. Can It Make Money, Too?"

28. Steven Brill, interview by author, tape recording, November 1, 2005.

29. Steven Brill, "Holding Media Accountable in the Age of Osama, Kobe, and Arnold," October 3, 2003, http://journalism.wlu.edu/knight/Institute/brill.html (accessed September 24, 2007).

30. Steven Brill, interviewed by Richard Heffner, January 13, 1995, the Open Mind Online Digital Archive, http://www.theopenmind.tv/tom/searcharchive_episode _output.asp?id=139 (accessed September 25, 2007).

31. Steven Brill, "A New Code for Journalists: A Challenge to the Press to Live by the Code," *The American Lawyer*, December 1994, 5–7, 85.

32. Paul D. Colford, "*Brill's* Lack Thrills as Consumer Mag," *New York Daily News*, October 29, 2001, 43.

33. Eads, "*Brill's* Makes Waves. Can It Make Money, Too?"

34. According to Steven Brill, "Dear Reader," *Brill's Content*, July/August 1998, 7, "*Brill's*" was added to the magazine's title "because 'content' is such a generic word that others have used and still others might want to use, it's a simple matter of securing our trademark and avoiding litigation in a litigious world."

35. Jonah Goldberg, "Bye-Bye *Brill's*," October 22, 2001, http://article.national review.com/?q=N2Q3ZGNkYTNiZTUxN2NkYjBkZTJlZGU3OTIxNjQ1NjI= (accessed September 24, 2007).

36. James Boylan, "Gnats Chasing an Elephant," in *What's Next?* ed. Robert Giles and Robert W. Snyder (New Brunswick, NJ: Transaction Publishers, 2001), 125.

37. Ibid.

38. Norris Carden's, "Brill's Big Plan: Using Media to Sell Media-Check Mag," June 5, 1998, http://www.drudgereportarchives.com/dsp/specialReports_pc_carden_detail.htm ?reportID=%7BCCAA7764-7EE6-428F-8168-91FF5BD45ACD%7D (accessed September 24, 2007).

39. Steven Brill and Bob Woodward, "Rewind: Steven Brill Raised Some Serious Questions about Bob Woodward's New Book. Woodward Has Some Serious Questions about Brill's Critique. Here, They Fight It Out," *Brill's Content*, November 1999, 22–126.

40. Michael Gartner, "The Critics: Magazines: Brill's Content," *Columbia Journalism Review*, March/April 2000, http://backissues.cjrarchives.org/year/00/2/brills.asp (accessed September 24, 2007).

41. See Claude-Jean Bertrand, ed., *An Arsenal for Democracy: Media Accountability Systems* (Cresskill, NJ: Hampton Press, Inc.), 216.

42. Lee Brown, *The Reluctant Reformation: On Criticizing the Press in America* (New York: David McKay Company, 1974), 48.

43. Society of Professional Journalists, "Quill Information," 1996–2005, http:// www.spj.org/spjhistory.asp (accessed February 22, 2006).

44. See Brown, *The Reluctant Reformation*, 57; Paul Alfred Pratte, *Gods within the Machine: A History of the American Society of Newspaper Editors, 1923–1993* (Westport, CT: Praeger Publishers, 1995), 80.

45. Brown, *The Reluctant Reformation*, 193.

46. Ibid., 80.

47. Robert U. Brown, "A Call to Arms," *Editor & Publisher*, July 22, 1995, 6. Available from Lexis-Nexis Group, Dayton, Ohio.

48. Randolph Holhut, "Tell the Truth and Shame the Devil: The Story of In Fact," August 1, 2002, adapted from George Seldes, *Never Tire Of Protesting* (New York: Lyle

Stuart Hardcover, 1968), http://www.brasscheck.com/seldes/infact1.html (accessed September 25, 2007).

49. Holhut, "Tell the Truth and Shame the Devil; according to Pamela Brown, "George Seldes and the Winter Soldier Brigade: The Press Criticism of In Fact (1940–1950)," *American Journalism* 6 (1989): 90, "Ads in *In Fact* were nearly always for the newsletter itself or for the editor's books."

50. William Dicke, "Georges Seldes is Dead at 104; An Early, Fervent Press Critic," *New York Times*, July 3, 1995, 46. Available from Lexis-Nexis Group, Dayton, Ohio.

51. Harold Evans, "What a Century!" *Columbia Journalism Review*, January 1999, 27. http://backissues.cjrarchives.org/year/99/1/century.asp (accessed September 25, 2007).

52. John Guttenplan, "Obituary: George Seldes, *The Independent*, July 14, 1995, 14.

53. Brown, *The Reluctant Reformation*, 100.

54. *Nieman Reports*, 2005, http://www.nieman.harvard.edu/ (accessed February 15, 2006).

55. Melissa Ludtke, telephone interview by author, November 4, 2004.

56. Tracy McNamara and Brent Cunningham, "The Critics: Magazines: Other Magazines," *Columbia Journalism Review*, March/April 2000, http://archives.cjr.org/year/00/2/othermags.asp (accessed February 15, 2006).

57. Nathaniel Blumberg, "Re: *Montana Journalism Review*," e-mail message to author, December 16, 2005.

58. Ibid.

59. Brown, *The Reluctant Reformation*, 58.

60. The International Society of Weekly Newspaper Editors, "ISWNE Publications," http://www.mssu.edu/iswne/pubs.htm (accessed February 15, 2006).

61. *Columbia University News*, "Opinion Leaders Rate *Columbia Journalism Review* Among Most Influential Media in the Nation," December 2, 1996, http://www.columbia.edu/cu/pr/96_99/19015.html (accessed February 15, 2006).

62. James Boylan, "An Editor Reflects: 40 Years of *CJR*," November–December 2001, http://archives.cjr.org/year/01/6/boylan.asp (accessed February 15, 2006).

63. Ibid.

64. *Columbia University Record*, "Konner: We Must Take Responsibility for Ourselves," November 3, 1994, http://www.columbia.edu/cu/record/archives/vol20/vol20_iss10/record2010.26.html (accessed February 15, 2006).

65. Robert Stanford, "Chicago was a Trial for Press, Too Uneven Coverage of the Trial Helped Spawn Journalism Reviews," *St. Louis Post-Dispatch*, February 13, 1990, 3D. Available from Lexis-Nexis Group, Dayton, Ohio.

66. See Brown, *Reluctant Reformation*, 60–62; Don Rose, "New Voices of Newsmen," *The Nation*, January 10, 1972, 43–46. Available from http://www.thenation.com/archive/detail/12312726.

67. See University of Colorado, "Obituaries," August 12, 2003, http://newmedia.colorado.edu/silverandgold/messages/2256.html (accessed February 15, 2006); Fred Brown, "The Unsatisfied Woman," *Denver Post*, August 10, 2003, E6. Available from Lexis-Nexis Group, Dayton, Ohio.

68. Brown, *Reluctant Reformation*, pp. 60–61; Bertrand, *An Arsenal for Democracy*, 201–218.

69. Richard Pollack, *Stop the Presses, I Want to Get Off* (New York: Random House, 1978); Larry Kramer, "More Journalism Review Donated to Publisher of Its Rival," *Washington Post*, July 22, 1978, A7.

70. Kramer, "*More* Journalism Review Donated to Publisher of its Rival."

71. Richard Pollak, e-mail message to author, November 28, 2005.

72. Michael Kramer, e-mail message to author, January 5, 2006.

73. Jonathan Kleino, "*SJR* Faces Shaky Future," The Journal: The News Source for Webster University," Februrary 16, 2006, http://www.webujournal.com/media/paper 245/news/2006/02/16/News/Sjr-Faces.Shaky.Future-1614185.shtml?norewrite&sourcedo main=www.webujournal.com (accessed February 18, 2006); *St. Louis Journalism Review*, 2005, http://www.sjreview.org (accessed February 18, 2006).

74. Kleino, "*SJR* Faces Shaky Future."

75. Jerry Knight, "Journalism Review Has Money Trouble," *Washington Post*, October 18, 1978, E1.

76. Tom McNichol, "We Came Out with Issues Whenever We Could Scare Up Enough Bucks," *Publishing Trade*, April 1988, 8.

77. Rem Rieder, e-mail message to author," November 28, 2005).

78. Magazine Publishers of America, "Subscription Circulation for Top 100 BPA International Magazines," November 2005, http://www.magazine.org/circulation/circula tion_trends_and_magazine_handbook/6379.cfm (accessed February 18, 2006).

79. John S. and James L. Knight Foundation, "Journalism Initiatives: Active Grants," January 14, 2005, http://www.knightfdn.org/default.asp?story=journalism/grants -publicinterest.asp (February 18, 2006).

80. Michael Kaufman, "Reed Irvine, 82, the Founder of a Media Criticism Group," *New York Times*, November 19, 2004, B9. Available from Lexis-Nexis Group, Dayton, Ohio.

81. Gail Pool, "A Magazine Devoted to the Dissection of TV," *Christian Science Monitor*, February 1, 1985, B6. Available from Lexis-Nexis Group, Dayton, Ohio; see also Les Brown and Savannah Waring Walker, *Fast Forward: The New Television and American Society: Essays from Channels of Communications* (Kansas City & New York: Andrews and McMeel, 1983).

82. Phillip Dougherty, "Channels Magazine Changing," *New York Times*, January 27, 1986, D10. Available from Lexis-Nexis Group, Dayton, Ohio.

83. The Museum of Broadcast Communications, "Trade Magazines," http://www.museum.tv/archives/etv/T/htmlT/trademagazin/trademagazin.htm (accessed February 18, 2006).

84. Jeff Cohen, e-mail message to author, November 13, 2005.

85. Fairness & Accuracy In Reporting, "Counterspin," http://www.fair.org/index.php ?page=5 (accessed February 18, 2006).

86. Alex S. Jones, "The Media Business," *New York Times*, July 2, 1990, 6.

87. Jonathan Alter, e-mail message to author, November 22, 2005.

88. Deirdre Carmody, "The Media Business: Magazines Notes; At Last, It's Springtime for Start-ups," *New York Times*, May 18, 1992, D11. See also prototype cover at Jessica Helfand and William Drenttel, "Homepage," http://www.jhwd.com/edothmag4.html (accessed February 18, 2006).

89. Howard Kurtz, "MediaCritic Folds; Forbes Scratches a Niche Publication," *Washington Post*, November 13, 1996, D2.

90. James Ledbetter, "Clipboard," *New York Village Voice*, June 24, 1997, 30. Available from Lexis-Nexis Group, Dayton, Ohio.

91. Stefani Eads, "A Talk with Steve Brill."

92. Kramer, e-mail.

93. Alter, e-mail.

94. Steven Brill, interview by author.

95. Peg Tyre, "Requiem for a Dream," *Newsweek* Web Exclusive, October 22, 2001. Available from Lexis-Nexis Group, Dayton, Ohio; Eads, *"Brill's* Makes Waves, Can It Make Money, Too?"

96. See Matt Welch, "After *Contentville:* Profit 1, Ethics 0," *Online Journalism Review,* March 9, 2000, http://www.mattwelch.com/OJRsave/OJRsave/BrillContentville.htm (February 18, 2006); Cynthia Cotts, "Business and Edit: A Perfect Fit in Which '*Brill's*' Loses Its Virginity," *New York Village Voice,* February 8, 2000, http://www.villagevoice .com/news/0006,cotts,12381,6.html (accessed February 18, 2006).

97. See Cynthia Cotts, "Steele Appeal," *New York Village Voice,* January 27–February 2, 1999, http://www.villagevoice.com/news/9904,cotts,3699,6.html (accessed February 18, 2006).

98. Wolf Blitzer, Bob Franken, and Associated Press, "Starr Attacks Brill Article, Again," *All Politics CNN,* June 16, 1998, http://www.cnn.com/ALLPOLITICS/1998/06/ 16/lewinsky/#brill (accessed February 18, 2006).

99. Marion Tuttle Marzolf, *Civilizing Voices: American Press Criticism, 1880–1950* (New York: Longman, 1991)

100. Ibid., 56; See also Will Irwin, *The American Newspaper* (Ames: Iowa State University Press, 1969): reprinted from *Collier's* (January–July 1911).

101. Ben H. Bagdikian, "The American Newspaper Is Neither Record, Mirror, Journal, Ledger, Bulletin, Telegram, Examiner, Register, Chronicle, Gazette, Observer, Monitor, Transcript Nor Herald of the Days Events," *Esquire,* March 1967, 124, 138–142.

102. A.H. Raskin, "What's Wrong with American Newspapers?" *New York Times Magazine,* June 11, 1967, 28, 84.

103. Ibid.

104. Mark I. Pinsky, "Content's Premiere Lively; *Brill's Content* Magazine," *Quill,* July 1, 1998, 12. Available from Lexis-Nexis Group, Dayton, Ohio.

105. Francis X. Clines, "The Nation: Watchdogs Watching Watchdogs," *New York Times,* June 21, 1998, Late Edition-Final, Section 4, 3. Available from Lexis-Nexis Group, Dayton, Ohio.

106. "National Press Club Luncheon with Steven Brill, *Brill's Content* Magazine," Moderator: John Aubuchon, *Federal News Service,* July 30, 1998. Available from Lexis-Nexis Group, Dayton, Ohio.

107. Brill, "Dear Reader."

108. Ibid.

109. Eads, *"Brill's Content* Makes Waves, Can It Make Money, Too?"

110. Michael Gartner, "The Critics: Magazines: *Brill's Content,*" *Columbia Journalism Review,* March/April 2000, http://archives.cjr.org/year/00/2/brills.asp (accessed February 18, 2006.

111. Dan Kennedy, "Ex Post Facto," *Boston Phoenix,* November 25–December 2 1999, http://www.bostonphoenix.com/archive/features/99/11/25/DON_T_QUOTE_ME.html (accessed February 18, 2006).

112. See, for example, Sheryl Fragin, "Flawed Science at the *Times,*" October 1998, *Brill's Content,* 105–115; Alan Taylor, "*Brill's Content* with Nothing But the Truth,

The Scotsman, October 2, 29, 1998. Available from Lexis-Nexis Group, Dayton, Ohio.

113. Judy Quinn, "Brill Says We Need Credibility Nielsens," *Variety*, November 2–8, 1998, 3. Available from Lexis-Nexis Group, Dayton, Ohio.

114. Alex Kuczynski, "Media Talk; A Privacy Proposal Gets Mixed Reaction," *New York Times*, August 9, 1999, Late Edition-Final, 11. Available from Lexis-Nexis Group, Dayton, Ohio.

115. Steven Brill, "Curiosity Vs. Privacy," *Brill's Content*, October 1999, 98–109.

116. *Columbia Journalism Review*, "Immodest Proposal," November/December 1999, 20. Available from Lexis-Nexis Group, Dayton, Ohio.

117. Alex Kuczynski, "Media Talk; A Privacy Proposal Gets Mixed Reaction."

118. Brill, "Holding Media Accountable in the Age of Osama, Kobe, and Arnold."

119. Eads, *Brill's* Makes Waves. Can It Make Money, Too?

120. Margaret Sullivan, "As *Brill's* Pauses, Questions Linger," *Columbia Journalism Review*, July/August 2001, http://backissues.cjrarchives.org/year/01/4/sullivan.asp (accessed September 25, 2007).

121. Mark Jurkowitz, "The Media: The Ambitious *Brill's Content* Shuts Down," *Boston Globe*, C12. Available from Lexis-Nexis Group, Dayton, Ohio.

122. Welch, "*Brill's Content* after *Contentville*: Profit 1, Ethics 0."

123. Epinions.com, "*Brill's* Magazine," 1996–2006, http://www.epinions.com/mags -Brill_s_Content/display_~reviews (accessed February 18, 2006).

124. Alex Kuczynski, "At Brill's, More Light, Less 'Homework,'" *New York Times*, December 14, 1998, C7. Available from Lexis-Nexis Group, Dayton, Ohio.

125. Folio Staff, "Steven Brill: Primedia Business Magazines & Media Inc," 1999 May, Available from Lexis-Nexis Group, Dayton, Ohio.

126. Ibid.

127. Sullivan, "As *Brill's* Pauses, Questions Linger."

128. See Welch, "*Brill's* After *Contentville*: Profit 1, Ethics 0"; Cotts, "Business and Edit: A Perfect Fit in Which *Brill's* Loses Its Virginity," *New York Village Voice*, February 9–15, 2000, http://www.villagevoice.com/news/0006,cotts,12381,6.html (accessed September 25, 2007).

129. Howard Kurtz, "Steve Brill Steps Down as Editor of Magazine," *Washington Post*, C2; the Web site, which presented commentary and sold an array of reading material, was a venture of Brill Media, Primedia, and other partners.

130. Paul Colford, "Brill's Content Grows on Readers," *New York Daily News*, November 14, 2000, 70. Available from Lexis-Nexis Group, Dayton, Ohio.

131. David Rakoff, "The Way We Live Now: 4-16-00: Questions for Michael Hirschorn and Kurt Andersen; Inside Job," *New York Times Magazine*, April 16, 2000, http://kurtandersen.com/mags_insd_intrvw.html (accessed February 18, 2006).

132. Cynthia Cotts, "Brill's Contempt," *New York Village Voice*, April 11–17, 2001, http://www.villagevoice.com/news/0115, cotts,23785,6.html (February 18, 2006).

133. Alex Kuczynski, "Brill's Content to Trim Publishing Schedule,"*New York Times*, May 5, 2001, 15. http://query.nytimes.com/gst/fullpage.html?res=950DE6DD1138 F936A35756C0A9679C8B63&n=Top/Reference/Times%20Topics/Subjects/M/Maga zines (accessed September 25, 2007).

134. Jurkowitz, "The Ambitious *Brill's Content* Shuts Down."

135. Pollak, e-mail.

136. Eric Alterman, interview by author, November 11, 2005.

137. Rem Rieder, e-mail message to author, November 28, 2005.

138. Jeff Cohen, e-mail message to author, November 13, 2005.

139. Jack Shafer, e-mail message to author, November 29, 2005.

140. TimeWarner, "*Fortune* Announces New Editorial Sections and Staff Changes," November 1, 1999, http://www.timewarner.com/corp/newsroom/pr/0,20812,6675 25,00.html (accessed February 18, 2006).

141. Matt Welch, e-mail message to author, November 13, 2005.

142. Barb Palser, "Journalism's Backseat Drivers," *American Journalism Review,* August/ September 2005, http://www.ajr.org/Article.asp?id=3931 (accessed February 18, 2006).

143. Peter Johnson, e-mail message to author, November 30, 2005).

144. Linda J. Lumsden, "Press Criticism," in *American Journalism: History, Principles, Practices,* ed. W. David Sloan and Lisa Mullikin Parcell (Jefferson, NC: McFarland & Co., Inc., 2002), 62.

145. Alter, e-mail.

146. Geneva Overholser, e-mail message to author, November 14, 2005.

147. Mike Hoyt, interview by author, November 4, 2005.

148. Cotts, "Steele Appeal."

149. Cynthia Cotts, e-mail message to author, November 14, 2005.

150. Thomas Kunkel, interview by author, October 18, 2005.

151. Bill Kovach, "Report from the Ombudsman," October 1999, *Brill's Content:* 24–25.

152. Gartner, "The Critics: Magazines: *Brill's Content."*

153. Stephanie Kirchgaessner, "Life, but Not as We Know It. Even a Giant Such as Time Inc Has Had to Rethink Its Plans for Launching Titles," *Financial Times,* July 6, 2004, 2.

154. Brill, "Holding Media Accountable in the Age of Osama, Kobe, and Arnold."

155. Jonathan Alter, "A Big Source of Frustration," *Newsweek,* May 30, 2005, 38. Available from Lexis-Nexis Group, Dayton, Ohio.

156. Carter, "The 51 Best* Magazines Ever."

157. Daniel Gross, "The End of the Line," *Slate.com,* December 22, 2005, http://www.slate.com/id/2133060/ (accessed September 25, 2007).

158. Brill, interview.

159. Ibid.

160. Keith White, "The Killer App: *Wired Magazine,* the Voice of the Corporate Revolution," http://www.zooid.org/%7Evid/txt/decon_wired.html (accessed February 18, 2006).

161. Sullivan, "As *Brill's* Pauses, Questions Linger."

162. Ford Foundation, "Ford Foundation Grants $2 Million to Major Journalism Magazines: Funding Aims to Strengthen Critical Examination Of U.S. News Media. Ford Foundation," June 5, 2000, http://www.fordfound.org/newsroom/pressreleases/41 (accessed February 18, 2006).

163. Brill, interview.

CHAPTER 8

1. The description of the news meeting is based on the author's observation, news accounts, and Steven Smith's e-mail of August 22, 2007.

2. "The Transparent Newsroom," *Spokesman-Review*, http://www.spokesman review.com (accessed August 22, 2007).

3. See Kimberly Metzinger, "Shifting Sands," *American Journalism Review*, August/September 2007, 10, http://www.ajr.org/Article.asp?id=4391 (accessed October 1, 2007).

4. Mark Jurkowitz, "Reality TV Meets the Newsroom," *The Phoenix*, June 21, 2006, http://thephoenix.com/article_ektid15702.aspx (accessed August 27, 2007).

5. Steven Smith, e-mail interview by author, August 21, 2007.

6. Don Corrigan, "Requiem for a Loser: Pew Pulls the Plug on Public Journalism," *St. Louis Review*, July 1, 2003, 20. Available from Lexis-Nexis Group, Dayton, Ohio.

7. Leonard Witt, "Is Public Journalism Morphing into the Public's Journalism?" *National Civic Review*, Fall 2004, 49–57, http://www.ncl.org/publications/ncr/93-3/Witt.pdf (accessed August 27, 2007).

8. Tanni Haas, *The Pursuit of Public Journalism* (New York & London: Routledge, 2007), 12.

9. Photius Coutsoukis and Information Technology Associates, "Daily Newspapers—Number and Circulation by Size of City," 2006, http://www.allcountries.org/uscensus/933_daily_newspapers_number_and_circulation_by.html (accessed October 3, 2007).

10. American Society of Newspaper Editors, "Code of Ethics or Canons of Journalism, 2007, Center for the Study of Ethics in the Professions at IIT, http://ethics.iit.edu/codes/coe/amer.soc.newspaper.editors.1923.html (accessed August 24, 2007).

11. Society of Professional Journalists, "Code of Ethics," 1996–2007, http://www.spj.org/ethicscode.asp (accessed August 24, 2007).

12. Ibid.

13. *Nelson v. McClatchy Newspapers, Inc.*, 931 P.2d 870 (Wash. Feb. 20, 1997).

14. *New York Times, Ethical Journalism: A Handbook of Values and Practices for the News and Editorial Departments*, September 2004, 20, http://www.nytco.com/pdf/NYT_Ethical_Journalism_0904.pdf.

15. Marion Tuttle Marzolf, *Civilizing Voices: American Press Criticism 1880–1950* (New York and London: Longman, 1991), 119–130.

16. Ibid., 129.

17. Haas, *The Pursuit of Public Journalism*, 4.

18. Steven Smith, "Interesting Piece on Blogging," August 23, 2007, News is a Conversation, http://www.spokesmanreview.com/blogs/conversation/ (accessed August 27, 2007).

19. Jay Rosen, *What Are Journalists For?* (New Haven and London: Yale University Press, 1999), 135.

20. Steven Smith, "News is a Conversation," n.d., http://www.spokesmanreview.com/blogs/conversation/ (accessed August 27, 2007).

21. Haas, *The Pursuit of Public Journalism*, 5.

22. Ibid., 6.

23. Tom Goldstein, "Good Question," *New York Times*, November 14, 1999, http://www.nytimes.com/books/99/11/14/reviews/991114.14goldstt.html http://www.nytimes.com/books/99/11/14/reviews/991114.14goldstt.html (accessed August 27, 2007).

24. Haas, *The Pursuit of Public Journalism*, 50.

25. Ibid., 51.

26. Jay Rosen, interview by Richard Poynder, "Open Source Journalism," March 28, 2006, http://ia310134.us.archive.org/1/items/The_Basement_Interviews/Jay_Rosen _Interview.pdf (accessed August 27, 2007).

27. Lewis A. Friedland and Sandy Nichols, "Measuring Civic Journalism's Progress: A Report Across a Decade of Activity," Pew Center for Civic Journalism, 2002, http:// www.pewcenter.org/doingcj/research/r_measuringcj.html (accessed August 27, 2007).

28. Goldstein, "Good Question."

29. Friedland and Nichols, "Measuring Civic Journalism's Progress."

30. Ibid.

31. Ibid.

32. Marilyn Greenwald, "Considering 10 Years of Public Journalism," June 12, 2002, http://www.asne.org/index.cfm?id=3603 (accessed August 28, 2007).

33. Brent Cunningham, "A Publisher's Life: Reid Ashe of the *Tampa Tribune*," *Columbia Journalism Review*, May/June 2000, http://backissues.cjrarchives.org/year/00/2/ cunningham.asp (accessed August 28, 2007).

34. Rosen, *What are Journalists For?*, 213.

35. William Glaberson, "The Media Business: Press; Fairness, Bias and Judgment: Grappling with the Knotty Issue of Objectivity in Journalism," *New York Times*, December 12, 1994, 7.

36. W. Joseph Campbell, *The Year That Defined American Journalism: 1897 and the Clash of Paradigms*, (New York & London, Routledge, 2006), 198.

37. Jay Rosen, *Pressthink: Ghost of Democracy in the Media Machine*, http:// journalism.nyu.edu/pubzone/weblogs/pressthink/ (accessed August 28, 2007).

38. Jay Rosen, *The Huffington Post*, http://www.huffingtonpost.com/jay-rosen# (accessed August 28, 2007).

39. Haas, *The Pursuit of Public Journalism*, 117–135.

40. Ibid., 18–19.

41. Search of Communication & Mass Media Complete database via EBSCO Host, http://web.ebscohost.com/ehost/search?vid=2&hid=22&sid=2cb22bb2-7d52-4aa2-8d0e -446ff59b10d9%40SRCSM1 (accessed August 28, 2007).

42. David Sheeden, "Public Journalism Bibliography," March 15, 2007, http://www.poynter.org/content/content_view.asp?id=1223 (accessed August 28, 2007).

43. Associated Press Managing Editors, "National Credibility Roundtables," http:// www.apme-credibility.org/index.php (August 27, 2007); Carol Nunnelley, *Building Trust in the News* (New York: Associated Press Managing Editors, 2006), http://www.apme -credibility.org/Building_Trust_2006_Chapter_One_Mission_Accepted.pdf (accessed August 29, 2007).

44. Nunnelley, *Building Trust in the News*, 12.

45. Ibid., 13.

46. Ibid., 49.

47. "The Transparent Newsroom," *Spokesman-Review*.

48. Jay Rosen, "The People Formerly Known as the Audience," June 27, 2006, http:// journalism.nyu.edu/pubzone/weblogs/pressthink/2006/06/27/ppl_frmr.html (accessed August 28, 2007).

49. Joyce Nip, "Exploring the Second Phase of Public Journalism," *Journalism Studies* 7 (2006): 212–236.

50. Mark Glaser, "Your Guide to Citizen Journalism," *MediaShift*, September 27, 2006, http://www.pbs.org/mediashift/2006/09/digging_deeperyour_guide_to_ci.html (accessed August 29, 2007).

51. Jan Schaffer, *Citizen Media: Fad or the Future of News* (College Park, MD: J-Lab: The Institute for Interactive Journalism, 2007), 6.

52. Journalism That Matters Roster, August 7–8, 2007, http://www.mediagiraffe.org/wiki/index.php/Jtm-dc-roster (accessed August 28, 2007).

53. Journalism that Matters—The DC Sessions: What Will Happen When Only the Journalism Is Left? August 2, 2007, http://www.mediagiraffe.org/wiki/index.php/Jtm-dc -links (accessed August 29, 2007).

54. Victo S. Yarros, "A Neglected Opportunity and Duty in Journalism," *The American Journal of Sociology* 22 (September 1916): 203–211.

55. Haas, *The Pursuit of Public Journalism*, 146.

56. Ibid., 148.

57. Tim O'Reilly, comment on "What Is Web 2.0," the O'Reilly Blog, comment posted September 30, 2005, http://www.oreillynet.com/pub/a/oreilly/tim/news/2005/09/30/what-is-web-20.html (accessed August 31, 2007).

58. Haas, *The Pursuit of Public Journalism*, 13–17.

59. Steve Smith, e-mail message to author, August 29, 2007.

CHAPTER 9

1. Hans Christian Andersen, *Tales*, XVII, Part 3. *The Harvard Classics*. (New York: P.F. Collier & Son, 1909–14), http://www.bartleby.com/17/3/3.html (accessed June 7, 2007).

2. Jon Stewart, interview by Paul Begala and Tucker Carlson, "Jon Stewart's America," *Crossfire*, October 15, 2004, http://transcripts.cnn.com/TRANSCRIPTS/0410/15/cf.01.html (accessed February 25, 2007); see also Robert Mancini, "Jon Stewart Bitchslaps CNN's 'Crossfire' Show," October 15, 2004, http://www.mtv.com/chooseorlose/headlines/news.jhtml?id=1492305 (accessed February 25, 2007).

3. Stewart, interview by Paul Begala and Tucker Carlson.

4. Jon Stewart, Ben Karlin, and David Javerbaum. *America (The Book): A Citizen's Guide to Democracy Inaction* (New York and Boston: Warner Books, 2006), 131.

5. Ibid.

6. Ibid., 133.

7. Ibid.

8. Gilbert Highet, *The Anatomy of Satire* (Princeton, NJ: Princeton University Press, 1962), 231.

9. Stewart, interview by Paul Begala and Tucker Carlson.

10. Michael Citrome, "Stewart's Jab at *Crossfire* Host a Hot Commodity Online," *The Gazette*, November 4. 2004, D2. Available from Lexis-Nexis Group, Dayton, Ohio.

11. Fareed Zakaria, "TV, Money and *Crossfire* Politics," *Newsweek*, November 1, 2004, http://www.fareedzakaria.com/ARTICLES/newsweek/110104.html (accessed June 15, 2007).

12. Business Editors, "Jon Stewart's 'Crossfire' Transcript Most Blogged News Item of 2004, Intelliseek Finds; Yahoo! News the Top News Source, Boing Boing the Top Blog, Says BlogPulse.Com Year-End Review," *Business Wire*, December 15, 2004, http://findarticles.com/p/articles/mi_m0EIN/is_2004_Dec_15/ai_n8571777 (accessed June 25, 2007).

13. The Abstract Factory, "Tomorrow, I Will Go Back to Being Funny, and Your Show Will Still Blow," October 23, 2004, http://abstractfactory.blogspot.com/2004/10/tomorrow-i-will-go-back-to-being-funny.html (accessed June 25, 2007).

14. Bill Carter, "CNN Will Cancel *Crossfire* and Cut Ties to Commentator," *New York Times*, January 5, 2005, http://www.nytimes.com/2005/01/06/business/media/06crossfire.html?ex=1262754000&en=0f719be53ea0367c&ei=5090 (accessed June 15, 2007).

15. Business Editors, "Viacom Completes Acquisition of AOL Time Warner's 50% Interest in Comedy Central," *Business Wire*, May 22, 2003, http://findarticles.com/p/articles/mi_m0EIN/is_2003_May_22/ai_102161708 (accessed March 17, 2008).

16. Comedy Central.com, "About the Show," *The Daily Show with Jon Stewart*, http://www.comedycentral.com/shows/the_daily_show/about_the_show.jhtml (accessed June 15, 2007).

17. Pew Research Center for the People and the Press, "Today's Journalists Less Prominent," March 8, 2007, http://people-press.org/reports/display.php3?ReportID=309 (accessed June 25, 2007).

18. Alison Romano, "Record Ratings for Daily Show," *Broadcasting & Cable*, October 1, 2004, http://www.broadcastingcable.com/article/CA458060.html?display=Breaking+News&referral=supp (accessed June 15, 2007).

19. Tim Goodman, "Stewart Puts Smackdown on *Crossfire*," *San Francisco Chronicle*, October 20, 2004, E1. Available from Lexis-Nexis Group, Dayton, Ohio.

20. Tim Goodman, "Taking a Comic Seriously, CNN Opts to Focus on What It Does Best: News," *San Francisco Chronicle*, January 10, 2005, C1. Available from Lexis-Nexis Group, Dayton, Ohio.

21. James B. Lemert, "Throughout media history, it has been far easier to find critical statements than critical analysis concerning the news media. Critical analysis is characterized by appeals to standards and values that can be understood and shared by everyone and uses methods that are at least revealed to everyone. Further, whatever criticism or praise results from this analysis also is freely shared with journalists, other critics, and the public." *Criticizing the Media: Empirical Approaches* (Newbury Park, CA: Sage Publications, 1989), 19.

22. Lee Brown, *The Reluctant Reformation: On Criticizing the Press in America* (New York: David McKay Co., 1974), 13–14.

23. Eric Deegans. "Jon Stewart Is for Real," *St. Petersburg Times*, January 18, 2007, http://www.sptimes.com/2007/01/18/Floridian/Jon_Stewart_is_for_re.shtml (accessed June 15, 2007).

24. CNN Reliable Sources, "Big-Name Anchors Report from Tsunami-Ravaged Asia; *CROSSFIRE* Goes Off Air," January 9, 2005, http://transcripts.cnn.com/TRANSCRIPTS/0501/09/rs.01.html (accessed June 15, 2007).

25. See Robert W. Snyder, Jennifer Kelley, and Dirk Smillie, "Critics with Clout—Nine Who Matter," in Everette Dennis, *Media Studies Journal: Media Critics 2* (Spring 1995): 12–14.

26. Bill Kovach and Tom Rosenstiel, *The Elements of Journalism* (New York: Three Rivers Press, 2001), 17.

27. Robert Griffith, *The Politics of Fear: Joseph R. McCarthy and the Senate* (Amherst: University of Massachusetts Press, 1970), 259.

28. David Bauder, "CNN Lets *Crossfire* Host Carlson Go," *Associated Press Online*, January 6, 2005. Available from Lexis-Nexis Group, Dayton, Ohio.

29. Antonia Zerbisias, "It Took Jon Stewart to Gun Down *Crossfire*," *Toronto Star*, October 19, 2004, C05. Available from Lexis-Nexis Group, Dayton, Ohio.

30. Ibid.

31. Paul Kedrosky, "Downloading the Good Bits," *National Post's Financial Post & FP Investing (Canada)*, November 6, 2004, FP11. Available from Lexis-Nexis Group, Dayton, Ohio.

32. Noam Cohen, "That After-Dinner Speech Remains a Favorite Dish," *New York Times*, May 22, 2006, 5.

33. Gilbert Highet, *The Anatomy of Satire* (Princeton, NJ: Princeton University Press, 1962), 26.

34. George A. Test, *Satire: Spirit and Art* (Tampa: University of South Florida Press, 1991), 10.

35. Ibid., 10–11.

36. George L. Roth, "American Theory of Satire, 1790–1820," *American Literature*, 4 (January 1958): 407.

37. Ben Jonson, *The Staple of News*, ed. Devra Rowland Kifer (Lincoln: University of Nebraska Press, 1975), 10.

38. Mitchell Stephens, *A History of News* (New York: Penguin Books, 1988), 157.

39. Marcus Nevitt, "Ben Jonson and the Serial Publication of News," *Media History*, 11, April–August, 2005): 53–68: 55.

40. Jonson, *The Staple of News*, xi.

41. Ibid.

42. Mark Z. Muggli, "Ben Jonson and the Business of News," *Studies in English Literature, 1500–1900* 2 (Spring 1992): 335.

43. Jonson, *The Staple of News*, 85.

44. Ibid., 14.

45. Nevitt, "Ben Jonson and the Serial Publication of News," 54.

46. Rachel Smolkin, "What Mainstream Media Can Learn from Jon Stewart," June/July 2007, *American Journalism Review*. http://www.ajr.org/Article.asp?id=4329 (accessed June 10, 2007).

47. See Edward C. Wilson, "Egregious Lies from Idle Brains: Critical Views of Early Journalism," *Journalism Quarterly* 2 (Summer 1982): 260–264.

48. See Humphrey Carpenter, *That Was Satire That Was: The Satire Boom of the 1960s* (London: Victor Gollancz, 2000).

49. James Poniewozik, Hillary's SNL Startegy," *Time*, February 29, 2008, http://www.time.com/time/magazine/article/0,9171,1718548,00.html (accessed March 19, 2008).

50. Mark Jurkowitz, "Combative Clinton Gets Media to Cover Itself," March 4, 2008, http://pewresearch.org/pubs/752/obama-media-coverage-vetting (accessed March 19, 2008).

51. See Kathryn S. Wenner, "Peeling the Onion," *American Journalism Review*, September 2002, http://www.ajr.org/Article.asp?id=2618 (accessed June 19, 2007).

52. "A Conversation with Comedian Stephen Colbert," *Charlie Rose*, December 8, 2006, http://www.charlierose.com/shows/2006/12/08/2/a-conversation-with-comedian-stephen-colbert (accessed June 19, 2007).

53. Comedy Central Videos, "Paris Hilton Gets in a Car," June 11, 2007, http://www.comedycentral.com/motherload/player.jhtml?ml_video=88430&ml_collection=

&ml_gateway=&ml_gateway_id=&ml_comedian=&ml_runtime=&ml_context=show
&ml_origin_url=%2Fshows%2Fthe_daily_show%2Fvideos%2Fmost_recent%2Findex
.jhtml%3Fstart%3D16&ml_playlist=&lnk=&is_large=true (accessed June 20,
2007).

54. Ibid.

55. Ibid.

56. Ibid.

57. Ibid.

58. *The American Heritage College Dictionary* (Boston: Houghton Mifflin Company,
2002).

59. Frederick, "Re-Improved Colbert Transcript," April 30, 2006. http://www.daily
kos.com/storyonly/2006/4/30/1441/59811 (accessed June 21, 2007).

60. Ibid.

61. The Radio-Television News Directors Association (RTNDA), "Code of
Ethics and Professional Conduct," September 14, 2000, http://www.rtnda.org/pages/
media_items/code-of-ethics-and-professional-conduct48.php (accessed June 21,
2007).

62. Society of Professional Journalists, "Code of Ethics," 1996–2007, http://
www.spj.org/ethicscode.asp (accessed June 21, 2007).

63. Jake Tapper, "Guess Who's Not Coming to Dinner," April 23, 1999. *Salon. com,*
http://www.salon.com/news/feature/1999/04/24/press_corps/index.html (accessed
June 21, 2007).

64. Rem Rieder, "The Party's Over," *American Journalism Review,* April/May 2006,
http://ajr.org/Article.asp?id=4110 (accessed June 21, 2007).

65. Commission on Freedom of the Press. *A Free and Responsible Press: A General
Report on Mass Communication: Newspapers, Radio, Motion Pictures, Magazines, and Books*
(Chicago: The University of Chicago Press), 20–21.

66. Kovach and Rosenstiel, *The Elements of Journalism,* 134.

67. Ibid., 135–136.

68. Stewart, interview by Paul Begala and Tucker Carlson.

69. Ibid.

70. Kovach and Rosenstiel, *Elements of Journalism,* 140.

71. Paul Begala, "Mitt Steps in Shit; Media Says It Smells Like Roses," *The Huffington
Post.com.* June 6, 2007. http://www.huffingtonpost.com/paul-begala/mitt-steps-in-shit
-media_b_51019.html (accessed June 22, 2007).

72. Smolkin, "What Mainstream Media Can Learn from Jon Stewart."

73. Ibid.

74. Howard Kurtz, "Media Backtalk, *Washington Post,* October 10, 2005, http://www
.washingtonpost.com/wp-dyn/content/discussion/2005/10/03/DI2005100300794.html
(accessed June 22, 2007).

75. Smolkin, "What Mainstream Media Can Learn from Jon Stewart."

76. Ibid.

77. Ibid.

78. Ibid.

79. Michael Piafsky, "An Interview with Writers of *America,*" *Missouri Review* 28
(Spring/Summer 2005): 94–118.

CHAPTER 10

1. See Hazel Dicken-Garzia, *Journalistic Standards in Nineteenth-Century America* (Madison: The University of Wisconsin Press); Marion Tuttle Marzolf, *Civilizing Voices: American Press Criticism 1880–1950* (New York & London: Longman, 1990).

2. Bill Carter, "CNN Will Cancel 'Crossfire' and Cut Ties to Commentator," *New York Times,* January 5, 2005. Available from Lexis-Nexis Group, Dayton, Ohio.

3. Howard Kurtz, "CNN's Jordan Resigns over Iraq Remarks," *Washington Post,* February 12, 2005, A01, http://www.washingtonpost.com/wp-dyn/articles/A17462-2005Feb11.html (accessed July 16, 2007).

4. Richard Chiachiere, comment on "Imus Called Women's Basketball Team 'Nappy-Headed Hos,'" Media Matters for America, comment posted April 4, 2007, http://mediamatters.org/items/200704040011 (accessed July 9, 2007).

5. Dennis Murphy, "The Inside Story: The Decisions and Discussion inside NBC News during the Imus Firestorm," April 15, 2007, http://www.msnbc.msn.com/id/18126093/ (accessed July 10, 2007).

6. "Don Imus," *Time,* April 21, 1997, 44. Available from ProQuest LLC, Ann Arbor, Michigan; see also http://www.time.com/time/covers/0,16641,1101970421,00.html (accessed July 6, 2007).

7. Murphy, "The Inside Story."

8. Fairness & Accuracy in Reporting, "Why Does Tim Russert Associate With Don Imus' Bigotry?" March 1, 2000, http://www.fair.org/index.php?page=1751 (accessed July 6, 2007).

9. Philip Nobile, "Philip Nobile to Imus Show Guests: You Want to Appear on This Show???" May 16, 2000, http://www.tompaine.com/Archive/scontent/3082.html (accessed July 9, 2007).

10. Eric Burns, interview by Scott Simon, "Watchdog Group Monitored Imus for Show Content," *National Public Radio, Weekend,* Weekend Edition, April 14, 2007, http://www.npr.org/templates/story/story.php?storyId=9585218 (accessed July 9, 2007).

11. WCBSTV.com, "Rutgers Protesters Denounce Imus's Comments," http://wcbstv.com/topstories/local_story_101145016.html (accessed July 9, 2007).

12. See James Bohman, *Public Deliberation: Pluralism, Complexity, and Democracy* (Cambridge, MA: The MIT Press, 1996), 4–21.

13. Brooks Barnes, Emily Steel, and Sarah McBride, "Behind the Fall of Imus, A Digital Brush Fire," *Wall Street Journal,* April 13, 2007, A1. Available from ProQuest LLC, Ann Arbor, Michigan.

14. Filip Bondy, "Time to Put a Stop to Don Imus," *New York Daily News,* April 6, 2007. Available from ProQuest LLC, Ann Arbor, Michigan.

15. Murphy, "The Inside Story."

16. MSNBC Staff and News Service Reports, "MSNBC Drops Simulcast of Don Imus Show," April 13, 2007, http://www.msnbc.msn.com/id/17999196/ (accessed July 11, 2007).

17. John S. Brady, "Incorrigible Beliefs and Democratic Deliberation: A Critique of Stanley Fish," *Constellations* 3 (2006): 374–393.

18. Shawn W. Rosenberg, "Types of Democratic Deliberation: The Limits and Potential of Citizen Participation, " Center for the Study of Democracy, November 2, 2006, Paper 06-12, http://repositories.cdlib.org/csd/06-12 (accessed July 16, 2007).

19. Pew Research Center for the People & the Press, "Whites Say Imus Story Has Been Overcovered, Blacks Disagree; Most Say Imus's Punishment Was Appropriate," April 18, 2007, http://people-press.org/reports/pdf/320.pdf (accessed July 11, 2007).

20. See Open Project Directory, "News: Media: Watchdogs," Netscape 1998–2007, http://dmoz.org/News/Media/Watchdogs/ (accessed July 16, 2007).

21. Jon Meacham, "Top of the Week: The Editor's Desk," *Newsweek*, April 23, 2007, 2.

22. Media Matters for America, "Who We Are," 2007, http://mediamatters.org/about_us/ (accessed July 9, 2007).

23. *Mother Jones*, "RADIO: Bio of Media Matters President David Brock," January 8, 2006, http://www.motherjones.com/radio/2006/01/brock_bio.html (accessed July 9, 2007).

24. Media Matters for America, "Staff/Advisors," 2007, http://mediamatters.org/about_us/staff_advisors (accessed July 15, 2007).

25. Eric Burns, interview by Scott Simon.

26. Media Matters for America, "Radio/TV Shows," 2007, http://mediamatters.org/issues_topics/shows_publications (accessed July 9, 2007).

27. "Staff/Advisors," http://mediamatters.org/about_us/staff_advisors.

28. Abigail Tucker, "Media Watchdogs a Tipping Point for Imus' Downfall," *Baltimore Sun*, April 9, 2007, 1E.

29. Eric Burns, interview by Scott Simon.

30. Chiachiere, "Imus Called Women's Basketball 'Nappy-Headed Hos.'"

31. *School Daze* (1988) is the correct title of the Spike Lee move.

32. Ibid.

33. Joseph Brown, "*NY Times* Public Editor Calame: '[C]heapened' Feedback from *Media Matters* Readers Goes 'Straight into a Folder,'" June 12, 2006, http://media matters.org/items/200606120008 (accessed July 9, 2007).

34. Pithaughn, comment on "Imus Called Women's Basketball 'Nappy-Headed Hos,'" Media Matters for America, comment posted April 4, 2007, http://mediamatters.org/items/200704040011?offset=0&show=1#comments (accessed July 13, 2007).

35. Ibid., comment posted by Cartoon Messiah.

36. Ibid., comment posted by MGHAMMA, http://mediamatters.org/items/200704040011?offset=20&show=1#comments (accessed July 13, 2007).

37. Tim Curprisin, "Inside TV & Radio: Plagued by Soft Ratings, O'Briens Ousted as CNN Morning Anchors," *Milwaukee Journal Sentinel*, April 5, 2007, B news, 6. http://www.redorbit.com/news/entertainment/894119/inside_tv__radio_plagued_by_soft_ratings_obriens_ousted/index.html (accessed July 10, 2007).

38. *WNBC.com/News*, "Imus Apologizes for Controversial Comments about Rutgers Players," April 4, 2007, http://www.wnbc.com/news/11537229/detail.html (accessed July 10, 2007).

39. Murphy, "The Inside Story."

40. Lestarr21, April 6, 2007, http://www.youtube.com/watch?v=ui1jPNDWArM&mode=related&search=MMA's (accessed July 10, 2007).

41. Aclusux, April 7, 2007, "Don Imus and Nappy Headed Hos," http://www.youtube.com/watch?v=RF9BjB7Bzr0&mode=related&search=MMA%27s (accessed July 10, 2007).

42. Barnes, Steel, and McBride, "Behind the Fall of Imus."

43. Murphy, "The Inside Story."

44. Barnes, Steel, and McBride, "Behind the Fall of Imus."

45. Ibid.

46. Ibid.

47. Wayne Dawkins, "Why Imus Fell: He Crossed a Line of Decency Even Shock Jocks Must Recognize," *Black Alumni Network* no. 5 (May 2007), http://www.trottergroup.org/don_imus.htm (accessed July 16, 2007).

48. Bondy, "Time to Put a Stop to Don Imus."

49. Andrew Hampp, "Imus Mess Makes Arbiters of Advertisers; Proliferation of Options Allows Marketers to Bail Out Fast from Controversy," *Advertising Age,* April 16, 2007, 43. Available from Lexis-Nexis Group, Dayton, Ohio.

50. Ibid.

51. Ibid.

52. Ibid.

53. Ibid.

54. Media Matters for America, "Timeline: A Week in the Life of *Imus in the Morning,*" http://mediamatters.org/items/printable/200704120001 (accessed July 3, 2007).

55. David Hinckley, "Black Radio Fired Up Over Imus 'Ho' Remark," *New York Daily News,* April 9, 2007, 88, http://www.nydailynews.com/entertainment/tv/2007/04/09/2007-04-09_black_radio_fired_up_over_imus_ho_remark.html (accessed July 11, 2007).

56. *USA Today,* "What Readers Are Talking about at Usatoday.com," April 9, 2007, 3C. Available from ProQuest LLC, Ann Arbor, Michigan.

57. Murphy, "The Inside Story."

58. Ibid.

59. Brian Montopoli, "Imus in the Morning," *CBS News's Public Eye,* April 12, 2007, http://www.cbsnews.com/blogs/2007/04/12/publiceye/entry2678036.shtml (accessed July 12, 2007).

60. Pew Research Center for the People & the Press, "Whites Say Imus Story Has Been Overcovered, Blacks Disagree.

61. Murphy, "The Inside Story."

62. *Columbia Broadcasting System v. Democratic National Committee,* 412 U.S. 94, 118 (1973).

63. Earl Ofari Hutchinson, "Anticipation Builds for Don Imus' Return to Radio—But Who Says He Ever Left?" July 6, 2007, http://www.blackamericaweb.com/site.aspx/bawnews/stateof/hutchinsonreport706 (accessed July 12, 2007).

64. Jessica Heslam, "Don Imus Returns," December 3, 2007, http://www.bostonherald.com/business/media/view.bg?articleid=1048482 (accessed March 17, 2008).

65. CNN.com, "Transcripts: *American Morning,* Cruise Ship Sinking: Passengers to Lifeboats in Alaska; Can Buyout Firm Fix Chrysler? Florida Wildfires," May 14, 2007, http://transcripts.cnn.com/TRANSCRIPTS/0705/14/bn.01.html (accessed July 12, 2007).

66. Radio-Television News Directors Association & Foundation, "Code of Ethics and Professional Conduct," 1997–2007, http://www.rtnda.org/pages/media_items/code-of-ethics-and-professional-conduct48.php (accessed July 12, 2007).

67. In re Request of Infinity Broadcasting Operations, Inc. for a Declaratory Ruling, 18 FCC Rcd. 18603 (2003).

68. Ralph Barney, "The Imus Affair: Lessons in Media Power, Herd Instinct, and Greed," *Media Ethics,* 18, no. 2 (Spring 2007): 4. http://media.www.mediaethics

magazine.com/media/storage/paper655/news/2007/07/01/AnalysesCommentary/The-Imus
.Affair.Lessons.In.Media.Power.Herd.Instinct.And.Greed-2923342.shtml (accessed
July 16, 2007).

69. Ibid.

70. Jeffrey Dvokin, "The Curious Allure of Don Imus," Committee of Concerned Journalists, April 13, 2007, http://concernedjournalists.org/node/732 (accessed July 17, 2007).

71. Murphy, "The Inside Story."

CHAPTER 11

1. Marion Tuttle Marzolf, *Civilizing Voices: American Press Criticism 1880–1950* (New
York: Longman, 1991), 12.

2. James B. Lemert, *Criticizing the Media: Empirical Approaches* (Newbury Park, CA:
Sage Publications, 1989), 19.

3. Marzolf, *Civilizing Voices*, 30.

4. Commission on Freedom of the Press, *A Free and Responsible Press: A General Report
on Mass Communication: Newspapers, Radio, Motion Pictures, Magazine, and Books*
(Chicago: University of Chicago Press, 1947).

5. Margaret A. Blanchard, *The Hutchins Commission, The Press and the Responsibility
Concept* (Lexington, KY: Association for Education in Journalism, 1977).

6. Ibid., 43.

7. Commission on Freedom of the Press, *A Free and Responsible Press*, v.

8. Stephen Bates, "Realigning Journalism with Democracy: The Hutchins Commission, Its Times, and Ours," The Annenberg Washington Program in Communications
Policy Studies of Northwestern University, 1995, http://www.annenberg.north
western.edu/pubs/hutchins/hutch14.htm (accessed October 11, 2007).

9. Katharine Q. Seelye, "2 Editors Resign at Web Site Linked to Journalism Review,"
August 11, 2006, http://www.nytimes.com/2006/08/11/business/media/11mag.html
(accessed October 10, 2007).

10. Ibid.

11. Fox News Watch, "Should Press Protect Privacy of Duke Lacrosse Players Accused
of Rape?" April 24, 2006, http://www.foxnews.com/story/0,2933,192835,00.html
(accessed October 9, 2007).

12. Stephen Frantzich and John Sullivan, *The C-SPAN Revolution* (Norman: University of Oklahoma Press, 1996), 152–153.

13. Steven Brill, "Holding Media Accountable in the Age of Osama, Kobe, and
Arnold," October 3, 2003, http://journalism.wlu.edu/knight/Institute/brill.html (accessed
September 24, 2007).

14. Robert C. Post, *Constitutional Domains: Democracy, Community, Management*
(Cambridge, MA: Harvard University Press, 1995), 134.

Bibliography

BOOKS

The American Heritage College Dictionary. Boston: Houghton Mifflin Company, 2002.

Andersen, Hans Christian. *Tales*, XVII, Part 3. *The Harvard Classics*. New York: P.F. Collier & Son, 1909–1914. http://www.bartleby.com/17/3/3.html (accessed June 7, 2007).

Andersen, Robin. *A Century of Media, A Century of War*. New York: Peter Lang, 2006.

Bachrach, Peter. *The Theory of Democratic Elitism: A Critique*. Boston, Little Brown, 1967.

Bagdikian, Ben H., *Bagdikian on Political Reporting Newspaper and Economics Law and Ethics*.
(Fort Worth: The Texas Christian University Press, 1977.

———. *Double Vision: Reflection on My Heritage, Life, and Profession*. Boston: Beacon Press, 1995.

———. *The Effete Conspiracy and Other Crimes of the Press*. New York: Harper & Row, 1972.

———. *The Information Machines: Their Impact on Men and the Media*. New York: Harper & Row, 1971.

Bagdikian, Ben H., and Leon Dash. *The Shame of Prisons*. New York: Pocket Books, 1972.

Baker, C. Edwin. *Human Liberty and Freedom of Speech*. New York: Oxford University Press, 1989.

———. *Media Concentration and Democracy*. Boston: Cambridge University Press, 2007.

Bertrand, Claude-Jean. "Press Councils." In *An Arsenal for Democracy: Media Accountability Systems*. Edited by Claude-Jean Bertrand. Cresskill, NJ: Hampton Press, Inc., 2003.

Blanchard, Margaret A. *The Hutchins Commission: The Press and the Responsibility Concept*. Lexington, KY: Association for Education in Journalism, 1977. In endnote 7, Chap. 11.

Bohman, James F. *Public Deliberation: Pluralism, Complexity, and Democracy*. Cambridge, MA: The MIT Press, 1996.

Boylan, James. "Gnats Chasing an Elephant." In *What's Next?* Edited by Robert Giles and Robert W. Snyder. New Brunswick, NJ: Transaction Publishers, 2001.

Brignolo, Donald, E. "How Community Press Councils Work." In *Readings in Mass Communication*. Edited by Michael E. Emery and Ted Curtis Smythe. Dubuque, IA: William. C. Brown Co., 1972.

Brown, Lee. *The Reluctant Reformation: On Criticizing the Press in America*. New York: David McKay Co., 1974.

Brown, Les, and Savannanh Waring Walker. *Fast Forward: The New Television and American Society: Essays from Channels of Communications*. Kansas City and New York: Andrews and McMeel, 1983.

Campbell, W. Joseph. *The Year That Defined American Journalism: 1987 and the Clash of Paradigms*. New York and London, 2006.

Carpenter, Humphrey. *That Was Satire That Was: The Satire Boom of the 1960s*. London: Victor Gollancz, 2000.

Cohen, Jeff. *Cable News Confidential: My Misadventures in Corporate Media*. Sausalito, CA: PoliPointPress, 2006.

The Commission on Freedom of the Press. *A Free and Responsible Press: A General Report on Mass Communications—Newspapers, Radio, Motion Pictures, Magazine, and Books*. Chicago: University of Chicago Press, 1947.

Cooper, Stephen D. *Watching the Watchdog: Bloggers as the Fifth Estate*. Spokane, WA: Marquette Books, 2006.

Cowan, Brian. *The Social Life of Coffee: The Emergence of the British Coffeehouse*. New Haven, CT: Yale University Press, 2005.

Crawford, Nelson Antrim. *The Ethics of Journalism*. New York: Greenwood Press, 1969.

Crossley, Nick, and Michael John Roberts. *After Habermas: New Perspectives on the Public Sphere*. Oxford, UK: Blackwell Publishing, 2004.

Croteau, David, and William Hoynes. *Media/Society: Industries, Images, and Audiences*. Thousand Oaks, CA: Pine Forge Press, 2000.

Cumings, Bruce. *War and Television*. London and New York: Verso, 1992.

Dahlrgen, Peter. *Communication and Citizenship: Journalism and the Public Sphere in the New Media Age*. New York: Routledge, 1991.

Day, James. *The Vanishing Vision: The Inside Story of Public Television*. Berkeley, CA: University of California Press.

Dicken-Garzia, Hazel. *Journalistic Standards in Nineteenth-Century America*. Madison: The University of Wisconsin Press.

Eberly, Rosa A. *Citizen Critics: Literary Public Spheres*. Urbana and Chicago: University of Illinois Press, 2000.

Frantzich, Stephen, and John Sullivan. *The C-SPAN Revolution*. Norman: University of Oklahoma Press, 1996.

Griffith, Robert. *The Politics of Fear: Joseph R. McCarthy and the Senate*. Amherst: University of Massachusetts Press, 1970.

Haas, Tanni. *The Pursuit of Public Journalism*. New York and London: Routledge, 2007.

Habermas, Jürgen, *The Theory of Communicative Action, Vol. 1: Reason and The Rationalization of Society*. Beacon Press, Boston, 1985.

Halberstam, David. *The Powers That Be*. New York: Knopf, 1979.

Highet, Gilbert. *The Anatomy of Satire*. Princeton, NJ: Princeton University Press, 1962.

Irwin, Will. *The American Newspaper*. Ames: Iowa State University Press, 1969. Reprinted from *Collier's* (January–July 1911).

Isaacs, Norman E. *Untended Gates: The Mismanagement of the Press*. New York: Columbia University Press, 1986.

Jarvik, Laurence. *PBS: Behind the Screen*. Rocklin, CA: Prima Publishing, 1997.

Jonson, Ben. *The Staple of News*. Edited by Devra Rowland Kifer. Lincoln: University of Nebraska Press, 1975.

Kovach, Bill, and Tom Rosenstiel. *The Elements of Journalism: What Newspeople Should Know and the Public Should Expect*. New York: Crown Publishers, 2001.

Labunski, Richard. *Libel and the First Amendment: Legal History and Practice in Print and Broadcasting*. New Brunswick, NJ: Transaction Publishers, 1989.

Lemert, James B. *Criticizing the Media: Empirical Approaches*. Newbury Park, CA: Sage Publications, 1989.

Lumsden, Linda J. "Press Criticism." In *American Journalism: History, Principles, Practices*. Edited by W. David Sloan and Lisa Mullikin Parcell, 55–65. Jefferson, NC: McFarland & Co., Inc., 2002.

Mapes, Mary. *Truth and Duty: The Press, the President and the Privilege of Power*. New York: St. Martin's Press, 2005.

Marzolf, Marion Tuttle. *Civilizing Voices: American Press Criticism, 1800–1950*. New York: Longman, 1991.

Meisler, Stanley. "Teaching Notes: The Massacre in El Mozote." In *Thinking Clearly: Cases in Journalistic Decision-Making*. Edited by Tom Rosenstiel and Amy S. Mitchell. New York: Columbia University Press, 2003. http://www.concernedjournalists.org/node/435 (accessed September 10, 2007).

Nemeth, Neil. *News Ombudsmen in North America: Assessing an Experiment in Social Responsibility*. Westport, CT, & London: Praeger, 2003.

The *New York Times, Ethical Journalism: A Handbook of Values and Practices for the News and Editorial Departments*. September 2004, 19–22. http://www.nytco.com/pdf/NYT _Ethical_Journalism_0904.pdf (accessed October 9, 2007).

Nunnelley, Carol. *Building Trust in the News*. New York: Associated Press Managing Editors, 2006. http://www.apme-credibility.org/Building_Trust_2006_Chapter_One _Mission_Accepted.pdf (accessed August 29, 2007).

Pollack, Richard. *Stop the Presses, I Want to Get Off*. New York: Random House, 1978.

Post, Robert C. *Constitutional Domains: Democracy, Community, Management*. Cambridge, MA: Harvard University Press, 1995.

Pratte, Paul Alfred. *Gods within the Machine: A History of the American Society of Newspaper Editors, 1923–1993*. Westport, CT: Praeger Publishers, 1995.

Rivers, William L., et al., *BackTalk: Press Councils in America*. San Francisco: Canfield Press, 1972.

Rosen, Jay. *What Is Journalism For?* New Haven and London: Yale University Press, 1999.

Schaffer, Jan. *Citizen Media: Fad or the Future of News*. College Park, MD: J-Lab: The Institute for Interactive Journalism, 2007.

Snow, Nancy. *The Arrogance of American Power*. Lanham, MD: Rowman & Littlefield, 2006.

Stephens, Mitchell. *A History of News*. New York: Penguin Books, 1988.

Stewart, Jon, Ben Karlin, and David Javerbaum. *America (The Book): A Citizen's Guide to Democracy Inaction*. New York and Boston: Warner Books, 2006.

Test, George A. *Satire: Spirit and Art*. Tampa: University of South Florida Press, 1991.

Theobald, John. "The Intellectual Tradition of Radical Mass Media Criticism: A Framework." In *Radical Mass Media Criticism: A Cultural Geneology*. Edited by David Berry and John Theobald. Montreal: Black Rose Books, 2006.

Urban, Christine D. *Examining Our Credibility: Perspectives of the Public and the Press*. Reston, VA: American Society of Newspaper Editors, 1999. http://www.asne.org/kiosk/reports/99reports/1999examiningourcredibility/ (accessed September 7, 2007).

Ward, Stephen J. A. *The Invention of Journalism Ethics: The Path to Objectivity and Beyond*. Montreal & Kingston: McGill-Queen's University Press, 2006.

Wyatt, Wendy N. *Critical Conversations: A Theory of Press Criticism*. Cresskill, NJ: Hampton Press, 2007.
Young, Iris Marion. *Inclusion and Democracy*. Oxford, UK: Oxford University Press, 2000.

ARTICLES AND PAMPHLETS

"ASJA Honors Ben Bagdikian as Journalism's 'Most Perceptive Critic.'" *Journalism Educator* 33 (October 1978): 6–39.
Bagdikian, Ben. "Conglomeration, Concentration, and the Media." *The Journal of Communication* 39 (1980) 59–64.
Bates, Stephen. "Realigning Journalism with Democracy: The Hutchins Commission, Its Times, and Ours." The Annenberg Washington Program in Communications Policy Studies of Northwestern University (1995). http://www.annenberg.northwestern.edu/pubs/hutchins/hutch14.htm (accessed October 11, 2007).
Brady, John S. "Incorrigible Beliefs and Democratic Deliberation: A Critique of Stanley Fish." *Constellations* 3 (2006): 374–393.
Carey, James. "Journalism and Criticism: The Case of an Undeveloped Professional." *The Review of Politics* 36 (1974): 227–249.
Dennis, Everette E., and David L. Stebenne. "Requiem for a Think Tank: The Life and Death of the Gannett Center at Columbia, 1984–1996." *Harvard International Journal of Press/Politics*. 8 (Spring 2003): 11–35.
Fengler, Suzanne. "Holding the News Media Accountable: A Study of Media Reporters and Media Critics in the United States." *Journalism & Mass Communication Quarterly* 80 (Winter 2003): 818–832.
Ferree, Myra Marx, William A. Gamson, Jurgen Gerhards, and Dieter Rucht. "Four Models of the Public Sphere in Modern Democracies." *Theory and Society* 31 (June 2002): 289–324.
Furlong, Patrick J. Untitled. Review of *Vietnam: A Television History* by Richard Ellison. *The Public Historian* (Summer 1984): 121–122.
Heim, Shannon M. "The Role of Extra-Judicial Bodies in Vindicating Reputational Harm." *CommLaw Conspectus* 15 (2007). http://commlaw.cua.edu/articles/v15/15_2/Heim.pdf.
Krasnow, Erwin G. "The 'Public Interest' Standard: The Elusive Search for the Holy Grail." Briefing paper prepared for the Advisory Committee on Public Interest Obligations of Digital Television Broadcasters, October 22, 1997. http://www.ntia.doc.gov/pubintadvcom/octmtg/krasnow.htm (accessed October 10, 2007).
Maier, Scott. "Getting It Right? Not in 59 Percent of Stories." *Newspaper Research Journal* 23 (Winter 2002): 10–24.
Marzolf, Marion Tuttle. "Honor without Influence." *Media Studies Journal* 9 (Spring 1995): 47–57.
McChesney, Robert W. "The Problem of Journalism: A Political Economic Contribution to an Explanation of the Crisis in Contemporary US Journalism." *Journalism Studies* 4 (2003): 299–329.
Michelman, Frank I. "Review: Must Constitutional Democracy Be 'Responsive'?" *Ethics* 107 (July 1997): 706–723.
Muggli, Mark Z. "Ben Jonson and the Business of News." *Studies in English Literature, 1500–1900* 2 (Spring 1992): 323–340.
Murphy, James, Stephen A. J. Ward, and Aine Donovan. "Ethical Ideas in Journalism: Ethical Uplift or Telling the Truth?" *Journal of Media Ethics* 21 (2006): 322–337.

Nemeth, Neil, and Craig Sanders. "Meaningful Discussion of Performance Missing." *Newspaper Research Journal* 22 (Winter 2001): 52–64.

Nevitt, Marcus. "Ben Jonson and the Serial Publication of News." *Media History* 11 (April–August 2005): 53–68.

Olien, Clarence N., George A. Donohue, and Phillip, J. Tichenor. "A Guard Dog Perspective on the Role of the Media." *Journal of Communication* 45 (Spring 1995): 115–132.

Parker, Edwin B. Untitled. Review of *The Information Machines: Their Impact on Men and the Media* by Ben H. Bagdikian. *The Public Opinion Quarterly* 35, no. 3 (Autumn 1971): 504–505.

Piafsky, Michael. "An Interview with Writers of *America*." *The Missouri Review* 28 (Spring/Summer 2005): 94–118.

Post, Robert C. "The Constitutional Concept of Public Discourse: Outrageous Opinion, Democratic Deliberation, and *Hustler Magazine v Falwell*." *Harvard Law Review* 103 (January 1990): 601–686.

Pritchard, David. "The Impact of Newspaper Ombudsmen on Journalists' Attitudes." *Journalism Quarterly* 70 (Spring 1993): 77–86.

Rivers, William L. "More Thoughts on Chilton Bush: He Cut His Own Path." *Journalism Educator* 31 (October 1976): 22.

Rosenberg, Shawn W. "Types of Democratic Deliberation: The Limits and Potential of Citizen Participation." *Center for the Study of Democracy* (November 2, 2006), Paper 06-12. http://repositories.cdlib.org/csd/06-12 (accessed July 16, 2007).

Roth, George L. "American Theory of Satire, 1790–1820." *American Literature* 4 (January 1958): 407.

Snyder, Robert W., Jennifer Kelley, and Dirk Smiller. "Critics with Clout—Nine Who Matter." *Media Studies Journal* 9 (Spring 1995): 1–18.

Starck, Kenneth, and Julie Eisele. "Newspaper Ombudsmanship as Viewed by Ombudsmen and Their Editors." *Newspaper Research Journal* 20 (Fall 1999): 37–49.

Sterling, Christopher H. "Seeking Influence: The Dozen Most Important Electronic Media Books since 1956." *Journal of Broadcasting & Electronic Media* 40 (Fall 1996): 597–600.

Wilson, Edward C. "Egregious Lies from Idle Brains: Critical Views of Early Journalism." *Journalism Quarterly* 2 (Summer 1982): 260–264.

Yarros, Victo S. "A Neglected Opportunity and Duty in Journalism." *The American Journal of Sociology* 22 (September 1916): 203–211.

LEGAL CASES

Associated Press v. United States, 326 U.S. 1, 20 (1945).

Boos v. Barry, 485 U.S. 312, 322 (1988).

Brandenburg v. Ohio, 395 U.S. 444 (1969).

Columbia Broadcasting System v. Democratic National Committee, 412 U.S. 94, 118 (1973).

Hustler Magazine, Inc. v. Falwell, 485 U.S. 46, 53 (1998).

McIntyre v. Ohio Elections Commission, 514 U.S. 334 (1995).

NAACP v. Claiborne Hardware, 458 U.S. 886 (1982).

Nelson v. McClatchy Newspapers, Inc., 931 P.2d 870 (Wash. Feb. 20, 1997).

New York Times v. Sullivan, 376 U.S. 254 (1964).

Watts v. United States, 394 U.S. 705, 706 (1969).

Whitney v. California, 274 U.S. 357 (1927).

Index

ABOUT THE AUTHOR

ARTHUR S. HAYES is Associate Professor of Communications and Media Studies at Fordham University. He is former director of the graduate journalism program at Quinnipiac University, from which he took a JD. A journalist for 24 years, he worked for the *Wall Street Journal*, *American Lawyer*, and the *National Law Journal*.